CW01084243

Democracy Lives in Darkness

JOURNALISM AND POLITICAL COMMUNICATION UNBOUND

Series editors: Daniel Kreiss, University of North Carolina at Chapel Hill, and Nikki Usher, The University of Illinois at Urbana-Champaign

Journalism and Political Communication Unbound seeks to be a high-profile book series that reaches far beyond the academy to an interested public of policymakers, journalists, public intellectuals, and citizens eager to make sense of contemporary politics and media. "Unbound" in the series title has multiple meanings: It refers to the unbinding of borders between the fields of communication, political communication, and journalism, as well as related disciplines such as political science, sociology, and science and technology studies; it highlights the ways traditional frameworks for scholarship have disintegrated in the wake of changing digital technologies and new social, political, economic, and cultural dynamics; and it reflects the unbinding of media in a hybrid world of flows across mediums.

Other books in the series:

Journalism Research That Matters
Valérie Bélair-Gagnon and Nikki Usher

Reckoning: Journalism's Limits and Possibilities
Candis Callison and Mary Lynn Young

Imagined Audiences: How Journalists Perceive and Pursue the Public
Jacob L. Nelson

Democracy Lives in Darkness

How and Why People Keep Their Politics a Secret

EMILY VAN DUYN

OXFORD

UNIVERSITY PRESS

OXFORD
UNIVERSITY PRESS

Oxford University Press is a department of the University of Oxford. It furthers
the University's objective of excellence in research, scholarship, and education
by publishing worldwide. Oxford is a registered trade mark of Oxford University
Press in the UK and certain other countries.

Published in the United States of America by Oxford University Press
198 Madison Avenue, New York, NY 10016, United States of America.

Library of Congress Cataloging-in-Publication Data
Names: Duyn, Emily Van, author.
Title: Democracy lives in darkness : how and why people keep their politics a secret /
Emily Van Duyn.
Description: New York, NY : Oxford University Press, [2021] |
Includes bibliographical references and index.
Identifiers: LCCN 2021029375 (print) | LCCN 2021029376 (ebook) |
ISBN 9780197557013 (hardcover) | ISBN 9780197557020 (paperback) |
ISBN 9780197557044 (epub)
Subjects: LCSH: Political sociology—United States. | Mass media—
Political aspects—United States. | Secret societies—Political aspect—
United States. | Party affiliation—United States. |
United States—Politics and government.
Classification: LCC JA76 .D92 2021 (print) |
LCC JA76 (ebook) | DDC 306.20973—dc23
LC record available at https://lccn.loc.gov/2021029375
LC ebook record available at https://lccn.loc.gov/2021029376

DOI: 10.1093/oso/9780197557013.001.0001

Hardback printed by Bridgeport National Bindery, Inc., United States of America

For my parents

Contents

Acknowledgments

The road from research project to dissertation to book is a long and arduous one, so it's only fitting that this book begins with a thank you to many of the people who helped make it happen. First, I am grateful to the women of CWG, who invited me into their lives, who entertained my relentless questions and my frantic typing in the back of the room. Telling and learning from your story has been one of the greatest honors of my life.

Thank you to my advisor and mentor Talia Stroud. It was her brilliance and enthusiasm that first pulled me into research, and it was her who brought me back to it. She continues to inspire me every day, with her care and tenacity, and with her vision for scholarship that is connected and accountable to democracy. Thank you for bringing me into your world and for your tireless service to society.

Thank you to the other members of my dissertation committee, who were essential to the development of this book. To Rod Hart, who was an early champion of this work and is my writing inspiration, thank you for opening my eyes to a new kind of research and for inspiring me to see the bigger picture. Thank you to Sharon Jarvis, who is one of the greatest teachers I have ever had and whose strategic and thoughtful approach to research and writing has touched many parts of my academic journey and this book. Thank you to Wenhong Chen, whose fresh and bright orientation to social network research greatly improved the contribution of this work.

I would also like to recognize several outstanding people who have offered valuable feedback and help along the way, including Shannon McGregor, Millie Harrison, Dave Karpf, Ashley Muddiman, Cynthia Peacock, Josh Scacco, Alex Curry, Jessica Collier, Kyser Lough, Ori Tenenboim, Martin Riedl, Gina Masullo, Marc Ziegele, Regina Lawrence, Danna Young, Katherine Haenschen, German Alvarez, Elliott Morris, Katie Searles, Antonis Kalogeropoulos, Ben Toff, Nate Persily, Rob Reich, Alessandro Vecchiato, Megan Metzger, Kirsten Pool, Shaimaa Khanam, and John Murphy.

I conducted most of this research while at the University of Texas at Austin, where I was supported and encouraged by the Department of Communication and Center for Media Engagement. I am also indebted to

UT's Annette Strauss Institute for Civic Life, which allowed me to use survey data from the Texas Media and Society Survey, and to Patricia Witherspoon, whose award helped support my research and (many) travels to and from rural Texas.

Thank you to my colleagues in the Department of Communication at the University of Illinois at Urbana-Champaign, especially the members of my virtual writing group, who helped see me to the completion of this book, and during a global pandemic, no less. I am also grateful to the Program on Democracy and the Internet and the Center on Philanthropy and Civil Society at Stanford University, which offered support and feedback as this book developed during my postdoctoral fellowship.

Thank you to Oxford University Press and my series editors, Daniel Kreiss and Nikki Usher, who advocated for this work and helped shape its contribution. Thank you also to Amanda Aronczyk and WNYC for helping me tell part of CWG's story to a wider audience before this book was possible.

I relied on the work of many tremendous scholars who I admire greatly. To Susan Herbst, Kristin Luker, Kathy Cramer, Lilliana Mason, and Nina Eliasoph, who wrote important books that challenged how we think about the social world, thank you for blazing the trail.

To my family—Mom, Deb, and Kat—thank you for loving and encouraging me, and to my dogs—Roosevelt and Annie—for being the best.

Finally, thank you to my husband, Jay. I love you.

1

Democracy in Darkness

On the morning of January 21, 2017, around four million people across the globe gathered to protest the inauguration of Donald Trump. Following the 2016 election, Teresa Shook, a retired lawyer from Hawaii, posted in her secret Facebook group of Clinton supporters a call to march on Washington. After sensing support from her fellow members, Shook created a public Facebook event called the "Women's March," which provided public details for the event and allowed anyone on Facebook to "RSVP." Then she went to bed. When she woke, 10,000 others had RSVP'd to the event[1] and a month later, 300,000 had RSVP'd.[2] The march's original focus and mission, as listed on the event page, focused on threats to gender equality and social justice that were expected under Trump's forthcoming presidency. After its inception, the mission expanded to include a variety of progressive platforms, including climate justice, reproductive justice, and healthcare reform. So too did its reach expand. "Sister marches" across the country, and then across the world, popped up on Facebook.

One of these sister marches happened in Austin, Texas, where, at the time, I was working on my PhD. My actual sister, a friend from graduate school, and I decided to attend together. The march was expected to be huge, so we walked to our closest bus stop to catch a ride downtown. On our walk we watched our neighbors spill out of their dated apartment complexes or their outrageously priced bungalows, carrying signs and wearing pink hats with ears on them. "This pussy grabs back," read one of the signs, in reference to the *Access Hollywood* tape, in which Trump claimed he could do "anything" to women—even "grab them by the pussy."

When we arrived at the bus stop, we quickly discovered that getting on the bus at all would be impossible. We watched one bus roll past after another, each a blurry amalgamation of signs and humans, and each with an apologetic bus driver whose typical Saturday route had taken a noticeable turn. We had nearly resorted to walking the four miles downtown when a man at the bus stop offered to give us and two other women at the stop a ride.

Democracy Lives in Darkness. Emily Van Duyn, Oxford University Press. © Oxford University Press 2022.
DOI: 10.1093/oso/9780197557013.003.0001

My sister and I exchanged glances with the other women, scanned the man's appearance, and shrugged our shoulders. Looking back, on any other day piling into a strange man's 1998 Toyota Camry would (accurately or not) feel like a death sentence—something young girls had been warned against since elementary school. But this was not any other day.

Our driver, who turned out to be a very safe and kind professor at the University of Texas, dropped us off on the edge of downtown and we made our way through a sea of people on foot. The march itself was an out-of-body experience, as if we were all in a perfectly constructed sociological experiment testing the behavior of crowds or the effects of collective action.

Part of the march was about Trump. The crowd was angry about his electoral victory and his inauguration—this was made obvious by the hundreds of signs referencing his name, as well as the effigies of him floating on broomsticks through the crowd. But it was about something else, too. It was about identity. For every sign that was about Trump, there was another referencing thought leaders and pioneers of social justice—Audre Lorde, Martin Luther King Jr., Gloria Steinem. When it was all over, no one wanted to leave. Everyone was unified in their anger and that made them feel less alone.

That day, many of the attendees wore shirts that the march organization had created and sold in advance online. In a bold font it featured a quote from Dinos Christianopoulos, a Greek poet who was ostracized from the literary community because he was gay. "They tried to bury us," the shirts read, "but they didn't know we were seeds."

The day after the march, journalists tried to make sense of what happened, while President Trump tried to belittle it. Headlines ranged from "What Democracy Looks Like: Women's March on Washington"[3] to "The Somehow Controversial Women's March on Washington,"[4] highlighting the problematic divisions between factions of the women's movement writ large. Scholars would go on to question the value of this demonstration, which has since been called the largest in history[5]—whether it was simply a moment of catharsis or the spark point for a growing movement.[6] I had a sense that what I saw that day was not just a passing moment of sadness and solidarity. Three months later, I received a call from an acquaintance, and then I knew it was not. As it turns out, there were many more buried seeds who had yet to find the surface.

The Buried Seeds

I grew up in Texas and lived across several different areas, which meant I had accumulated a number of connections across the state. Shortly after the Women's March, I got a call from a friend who told me she thought I would like to know she had joined a group of progressive women in her part of rural Texas. The group had formed after the 2016 election, starting out as a therapy session for affected Clinton voters in their small county, but over the past several months it had become an actual political organization. The catch was that it is a *secret* organization—a secret organization of more than 130 women. Its members, a mixture of real estate agents, schoolteachers, business owners, and retired grandmothers, all meet in secret to protect themselves from social, economic, and even physical retaliation issued by their conservative neighbors, friends, and family. With some help and convincing on the part of my confidant, I started interviewing members. Within four months of those interviews, I started attending the group's meetings.

My first meeting was in August at one of the group's rotating locations, an effort to draw little attention to their gatherings. It was an unbearably hot day, as it always is in August in Texas, and when I came into the room I was met by the draft of heavy air-conditioning and the strong scent of Chardonnay. Scattered across the room for their pre-meeting social hour were a group of 25 or so women who all fired skeptical stares in my direction until my confidant quickly introduced me. After I had been vetted, their glances softened, and I shook the hands of people I had previously spoken with over the phone and was meeting for the first time in person. Every woman in the room was White. It took very little time for me to blend in.

After the introduction and a few plates of cheese and crackers, the women gathered in a semicircle and started their meeting. The blinds were closed on the windows surrounding them, and the women looked uneasy when the door opened and a few latecomers grabbed seats in the back. After all, everyone in the room had voted for Hillary Clinton, and nearly everyone outside had voted for Donald Trump.

The women started with the pledge of allegiance, directing their gaze to a small American flag poking out of an easel with a tattered piece of poster paper. The paper displayed the group's confidentiality agreement: "No publishing anything referring to this group without explicit permission from members, no speaking explicitly about any member in reference to this group, identity should be protected outside of this group, and recruit women individually that you know well."

The meeting continued with updates on old business. At some point during these announcements, the easel at the front began to buckle, sending the poster paper and the American flag flying. A number of audible gasps echoed through the room while several women ran from the back to ensure the flag did not touch the ground. After their efforts, the facilitator repositioned the flag back into the easel and the women resumed the meeting. I sat in the middle in awe, noticing a strange feeling among these nervous women. It was the coexistence of dissent and patriotism. It was the coexistence of conviction and fear.[7]

Democracy Lives in Darkness is about this group—the unforeseen seeds of democracy—and their context, their choices, and, ultimately, their incubation. But it is also about what buried them—the political prejudice and hostility that marginalizes and makes people afraid, and the growing political, social, and geographic cleavages that now make even mainstream dissent challenging and risky. This book will focus on how we got here and what this means for how we move forward. It will ask why mainstream partisans—average Democrats or Republicans—feel the need to hide their political beliefs from others, why they feel afraid of those from the opposite political side, how they stay engaged in secret, and how this can transform them and their communities. This book is concerned with not only how the great experiment of democracy may die—that is, how our democracy is currently failing us—but also where it *lives*—how people keep democracy going not just despite of darkness, but through it.

My goal in this book is to show you that these women are not an anomaly, but a growing necessity—an example of just how far political polarization can push people underground. This book asks questions of all of us. Why, nearly 100 years after they gained the right to vote, did a group of white grandmothers feel the need to create a secret political organization? How is it that in the age of social and digital media, an era where most everyone can have a voice, some people try to keep their voices hidden?

To answer these questions, it is necessary to first consider the context in which this group was formed—to understand these women's experiences not in isolation from their surroundings but alongside them. To echo the work of scholars of communication before me, this means understanding people's relationship with political values and power,[8] their "social context and the dialogues of communities,"[9] and their "identities rooted in [geographic] place."[10] In turn, I focus here on these three contexts—the political, the social, and the geographic—that drove an experience of political isolation and spurred political secrecy among the women in Texas.

Political Context

In the years leading up to the women's meeting, both Texas and the United States had undergone dramatic political transformations. The presidency had swung from a two-term Christian conservative, to a two-term Democratic Black man, to a loudmouth Republican television mogul. The United States had been through a major economic recession and a populist movement for income equality in Occupy Wall Street. Video footage of police brutality against Black Americans had sparked a national movement in Black Lives Matter to stop Black deaths at the hands of police. Nationally, the country was wrestling with calls for reform and social justice on the left, and nationalism and freedom from government on the right.

The politics of Texas reflected a starker and longer lasting change. While the presidential race in Texas had slowly shifted toward Republicans since Reagan in 1980, the number of Democrats in statewide office started to decline with the 1994 gubernatorial election. This decline was steepened in 2000 after redistricting resulted in a district map that favored Republicans, which was ultimately reviewed and reified by a Republican-led Legislative Redistricting Board. As a result, after electing a Democratic governor in 1990—a woman, no less—the state switched to solid Republican dominance and has not elected a Democrat to the governor's office since then. Such a strong Republican hold resulted in weak Democratic infrastructure across the state, particularly in rural areas where Democrats started performing poorly for many elections in a row. A state-level Democrat, for example, had not visited the county where the women's group was founded in over 20 years.

Although the Republican and Democratic Parties had oscillated at the national and state levels, there was also growing divisiveness within the parties themselves. Trump's nomination had sent the Republican Party into a tailspin. On the one hand, the "Never Trump" faction of the party held strong to the idea that Trump's nomination would deteriorate the party's values, with some, like Senator Mitt Romney and former Ohio governor John Kasich continuing this rhetoric even after Trump's nomination, and some, like Senator Lindsey Graham, switching sides entirely. On the other hand, many Republicans rallied around Trump's nomination, compartmentalizing the man's Twitter persona and party priorities into distinct mental camps.

The Democratic Party faced different fissures in 2016. Hillary Clinton, a longtime Democrat and wife of a former Democratic president, was an establishment candidate who proposed calculated policy reforms. In turn, Bernie Sanders was a progressive Independent who called for institutional revolution. These two sides faced their own tensions during the 2016 primary, when Sanders won 23 states to Clinton's 34.

Toward the end of the primary and his loss, the Sanders campaign yielded many complaints about how the nomination process had played out. For one, they were disgruntled with what they called the "Bernie Blackout," a term for the media's poor pre-primary coverage of Sanders. They were not incorrect. The Bernie Blackout was partially supported by later research showing that Clinton did receive more coverage than Sanders, although that coverage was more negative than the coverage Sanders received.[11]

Then the Sanders campaign issued accusations of primary "rigging" when superdelegates, typically elite party loyalists, announced ahead of the convention that they would support Clinton in the primary. After this criticism, the Sanders campaign was again successful in influencing party structure by having the superdelegate policy, which had been in place since 1982, overturned in 2018 to make the process more (small d) democratic.

There was also the behavior of a subset of White and male Bernie supporters, pejoratively termed "Bernie Bros." Since the term was coined in October 2015,[12] the Bernie Bros have been defined in various ways, ranging from clinical terms—"a specific subset of Sanders supporters who are particularly active on social media (especially Twitter) and can be particularly aggressive in defending their candidate"[13]—to more irreverent terms—"the Bernie Bro is now what happens when Reddit eats a fairly liberal, if irritatingly opinionated White guy, and spits him out."[14] The Bernie Bro contingency was associated with online harassment and bullying of Clinton supporters and Sanders critics. After the primary began in 2015, Bernie Bros were accused of mailing threatening letters and death threats to suspected Bernie critics, harassing female reporters, and directing online attacks toward women and the Black community.

The relationship between a portion of Bernie supporters and Clinton supporters remained tense after the primary was over, particularly when it was clear that a substantial number (around 12%) of Bernie supporters had not turned out for Clinton in the general election but had instead voted for Donald Trump.[15] On her part, Clinton launched her own criticisms of Sanders, in particular his "unrealistic proposals," or his inability to get things done, which only made the divide between these factions worse.

Beyond intra- and interparty turmoil, there was also very simply Donald Trump, who had run a notoriously divisive campaign in 2016 and won. Trump's campaign had uniquely played to anger and anxiety around race and class. In their post-election audits, media pundits and scholars went on to argue that Trump had won precisely because he stoked economic anxieties among the White working class—specifically, that these voting blocs felt economically "left behind" by progressive policies.[16]

Still, others argued that Trump's stronghold with the White middle and working class was evidence not of economic anxiety, but of racial resentment[17] and "perceived status threat"[18] among those from historically dominant groups in the United States (e.g. Whites, men, and Christians). These theories explained Trump's election as a last-ditch cling to power as those who had been historically at the top of the social and economic hierarchy lost control amid changes in technology, immigration, demographics, and civil rights.

Tensions along lines of race and class were also rampant in the political rhetoric of the campaign. Trump was vocal about his goal to build a wall between the United States and Mexico, calling Mexican immigrants "criminals," "drug dealers," and "rapists." He called for a ban on Muslims entering the country (which he eventually enacted through executive order during his presidency), equated Black Americans to poverty and unemployment, and retweeted messages from blatant White supremacists. Increasingly, his rhetoric pitted racial and ethnic identities against one another and made his trademark slogan, "Make America Great Again," a reference to a time when racism and prejudice in America were more normalized, and not just a time when America was economically robust.

Beyond conflicts between identities, the 2016 election was also notable for its disinformation campaigns and foreign influence.[19] The prominence of misinformation about both candidates was proliferated through social media that had few, if any, protective measures to limit the spread of false statements, fabricated information posing as actual news, or doctored images and videos. The emergence and weaponization of the term "fake news" was also consequential for how the public saw the information environment before and after the election.[20] Both the spread of "fake news" and discussion of it hurt trust in democratic institutions like the news media[21] and the electoral process altogether.[22] This was also true for trust in election polling and predictions, which many felt had failed to accurately inform them or predict the election outcome in 2016.[23]

Most obviously, the 2016 campaign had laid bare the stark reality that Republicans and Democrats are increasingly different from and dislike one another. From the standpoint of presidential and down-ballot voting, the election had been the most polarized in history. For example, despite an unusual and anti-establishment Republican candidate, the 2016 election featured a record rate of straight-ticket voting and was the first time in history that all states who elected a Republican senator in 2016 also voted for a Republican president.[24]

From the perspective of the American public, social and ideological distance between the two parties was substantial and growing. In fact, research has shown that, over time, Democrats and Republicans increasingly love their own party and hate the other party more. In 2010, when asked how they would feel if their child married a member of the other party, 49% of Republicans and 33% of Democrats said they would be upset. This is compared to 27% of Republicans and 20% of Democrats just two years before, and a measly 5% of Republicans and 4% of Democrats 50 years before.

In addition, partisans are now more likely to award and choose members of their own party to work or cooperate with than members of the opposite party.[25] Not only is political polarization on the rise, but so is *perceived* polarization,[26] that is, how much people *think* Republicans and Democrats are politically or socially at odds, as well as the media coverage of polarization, which showcases the differences between parties at a broader scale. Altogether, not only do Republicans and Democrats feel increasingly distant from one another, but this is also how they think those from the other party feel about *them*.

All of this tension—the growing animosity between and within parties, the uncertainty about truth, the growing intersectional animosity around ideology, race, class, and gender, made for a political context that was not only unpleasant but *risky*. It was in this political context that a group of Texas women found themselves afraid to share their opinions with their neighbors, husbands, friends, and family.

Social Context

The women in the group also existed in a broader social context that informed if and how they talked about politics with those around them. By "social context" I mean the people who inhabited their interpersonal networks and informed their thoughts, attitudes, and choices.

Just as political context has changed over the past several decades, so too has the entire fabric of social life. Individuals are no longer limited just to their local community, but now have diverse social networks that span multiple communities unlimited by space and time.[27] Where once people were members of a local neighborhood that also comprised their friends, family, and patrons, people are now part of multiple communities and multiple social circles that span different places, different interests, and different beliefs.

Alongside and in response to this change in social network structure was a change in the available tools for social network formation. The rise of digital and social media facilitated social connection that was not limited to a specific area or a specific time.[28] People in Singapore could connect to people in Kansas, just as people in Alabama could connect with others in New York City. As technology further developed, the visibility of those connections could change as well. Now individuals can connect and communicate covertly through social tools that allow the creation of private or hidden communities online, like secret Facebook or WhatsApp groups—the very same kind that Teresa Shook used to devise and organize the Women's March on Washington in 2016.

Over time, people's social experiences have also become increasingly related to their political context. One of the ways this happens is through a process that scholars call "social sorting." Research on social sorting has found that over the past two decades the American public is sorting itself into groups with similar political and social identities. For instance, Republicans are more likely to be evangelical Christians, while Democrats are more likely to be secular.[29] This is also true of race, gender, and education. Black and Hispanic Americans are more likely to be Democrats than Republicans.[30] On the other hand, men are more likely than women to be Republicans, and this is especially true when comparing college-educated men and women.[31]

This is not to say that we have all become predictable boxes of political partisanship. Despite the intensification of social sorting, there are still many people in social circles or in relationships in which they experience political disagreement. Anecdotally, many of us know someone we deem to be an anomaly—a friend whose family is all conservative but who consistently votes liberal, or vice versa. But there is also a strong line of empirical evidence to back up the existence of these "anomalies." For example, the number of Democrats who report being evangelical Christians is not infinitesimal—in 2014, 28% of evangelical Christians reported that they were also Democrats. At an even smaller level—the political affiliation of one's spouse—there are still a good number (30%) of Democrats and Republicans married to someone from the other political side.[32] To put that in proportion, this is greater than the number of people across the entire country who voted in the Republican primary in 2016.[33]

The women in Texas experienced this disagreement—in relationships with others with whom they politically disagreed, in families whose members voted differently from them, in churches where most members had voted for the other political side. They had to balance these relationships; that is, they had to balance their social identities with their political one.

But there was also a more blatant threat to the women's identity. Trump had run a campaign that upset a number of different groups across the country and across the globe. This was especially true for many women, who felt first attacked by his rhetoric and personal history of subjugation and violence against women, and then dismissed and enraged by his electoral victory over a female candidate.[34] Trump had made claims of sexual violence that many Republicans dismissed as "locker room talk" and many Democrats highlighted as misogyny. He referred to Hillary Clinton as a "nasty woman" in the third presidential debate, interrupting her during an explanation of her proposed tax policy. These offenses reminded women across the country of men who had harassed, provoked, or interrupted them. And, as research on social identity and politics suggests, as Trump increasingly threatened women's identity, that identity became increasingly important in their evaluations of him.[35] With each offense, gender became more central to the campaign and more influential for women voters, including the women in the room I found myself in in August 2017.

Geographic Context

It is important to consider not just how the women's political and social identities intersected, but also how these identities were connected to "place," as the political scientist Kathy Cramer (2016) puts it. Over the past few decades, the boundaries of geographic place—the experience of urban, suburban, or rural—have become starker. For instance, both urban landscapes and population across the country have expanded, while rural populations have largely declined.[36] In 2018, 84% of the U.S. population resided in urban areas, compared to just 64% in 1950.[37]

The state of Texas had seen similar shifts in its social and political landscape. Like the rest of the country, rural counties in Texas have mostly declined. The rural share of the population dropped from 19.7% in 1990 to 15.3% in 2010, with most rural counties experiencing population decline. Urban areas in Texas, on the other hand, have seen great booms in total population—gaining 3.55 million people between 2010 and 2018, largely in metropolitan counties.[38]

In addition to changes in the density and growth of geographic areas, there are also changes in their political composition. Just as people are socially sorting, they are also sorting geographically. Republicans are more likely to live in rural areas, while Democrats are more likely to live in urban ones. When looking at the county level, the number of counties in which a presidential candidate had a victory margin of 20% or more has increased over time. It is also true that people are now likely to move to a place with more residents of their own partisanship than they were several decades ago.[39]

To be sure, there are exceptions to these arguments. Although individuals may be sorting into geographic communities based on their partisanship, those who differ politically from the majority of their community still exist. Take Texas, for example, where Hillary Clinton won mostly urban and border areas while Donald Trump won in rural ones. Clinton's urban victories, while clearly islands of blue in a sea of red, were not landslides, just as the counties that went decidedly for Trump were not devoid of Clinton voters. For instance, in Harris County, including inner-city Houston, Clinton won 54.2% of the vote while Trump received 41.8%. In Montgomery County, the closest county immediately north of Houston, Trump won 74.2% of the vote while Clinton received 22.5%. What these numbers suggest is that people are sorting into physical communities that tend to share their political beliefs, but the American public is not *perfectly* sorted.

Since the 2016 election, a lot of media and scholarly attention has been paid to rural communities across the United States. This makes sense, considering some of the biggest surprises and upsets on election night in 2016 came from "middle America," where much of the rural population in the United States remains. Journalists surged on this explanation for Trump's upset. "Rural Voters Played a Big Part in Helping Trump Defeat Clinton"[40] and "Revenge of the Rural Voter"[41] were some of the many headlines that used rural-urban divisions as a way to summarize Trump's unexpected victory. Broadcast journalists hopped on tour buses and sought reparations with rural America for not adequately covering that part of the country. In the weeks following the 2016 election, American audiences watched Lester Holt and David Muir meet with disgruntled farmers and factory workers with expressions of concern tainted with a tinge of repulsion.

To the journalists' credit, they *had* done a bad job at covering rural areas, but often with strapped and continually declining staff and resources.[42] And the rural-urban divide was not just a red herring, as there was actual evidence that this geographic divide was at play in the election's outcome. For example, sociological research shows that rural Americans increasingly feel ignored by democratic institutions and threatened by geographic, racial, and political outsiders.[43] Research from political science also paints a picture of complex identity and political preferences. For instance, Kathy Cramer's (2016) groundbreaking book on rural Wisconsin finds that this us-and-them distinction has led to a unique resentment among rural residents toward urban residents, and toward traditional politicians and political parties. In turn, rural communities have formed political attitudes that are driven by their feelings of exclusion from government spending and elite priorities. The growing urban-rural divide in this evidence, then, has helped scholars and journalists understand how Trump performed so favorably in rural areas and so unfavorably in urban ones.

But there are many other reasons that rural communities are politically and socially different from more urban areas. For one, rural communities are home to distinct social networks. Because of the size of rural areas, residents have less choice in who from their local community is a part of their personal network, particularly those residents for whom a neighbor is the closest access to support for many miles. For instance, rural fire departments and emergency medical services (EMS) often cover large geographic jurisdictions, meaning that response time can sometimes be much longer than the typical response time in dense urban or suburban areas.[44] As a result, neighbors sometimes rely on one another as first responders to mitigate the spread of fire or assist in time-sensitive cases.

Rural residents also rely on each other for economic livelihood and social support. Owning a local restaurant in a rural area means that you depend on local residents to visit your restaurant, unlike in urban areas where support from those physically surrounding the restaurant is less paramount. And, given the smaller number of potential social contacts in rural communities, organizing institutions like the local high school, church, or civic groups, like the Lion's or Rotary Club, often serve as associational cornerstones that bring people together and form communal identity.[45] In turn, rural communities often build identity around larger organizing boundaries, like towns or counties, rather than neighborhoods or subdivisions.

Despite this range of unique experiences, research on politics and communication has typically focused on the differences in self-reported networks like friend or discussion groups between neighborhoods at the county level, without a distinction between urban and rural, or communities entirely at the city level.[46] Because being similar to one's neighbor is both expected and important for building and establishing resources and support, rural communities like the community in which the group in Texas was formed offer one context where being the political minority, alongside other identities, is especially consequential to whether or how you express your political beliefs.

Networked Silence

The women in Texas were living with and engaging in politics in the contexts discussed in the previous sections. The county in which the group was formed reflected the same political and demographic shifts that the state had seen over the past two decades—a switch from Democratic to Republican dominance, a decline in rural population, and an increase in immigration. The group developed in reaction to Trump's upsetting victory over Clinton. The women were in a heavily Republican rural community where they depended on their neighbors for patronage and support. What is more, many of the women were in churches or social groups, from families or in marriages, in which they were in political opposition. As their state and country changed, as they watched the first female presidential nominee lose to Donald Trump, and as violating the majority political identity increasingly meant violating their other identities, the more they hid their beliefs.

This book tells their story. It asks a number of questions: Why did *mainstream* Democrats feel the need to form a secret political organization? How did these women come to double-check that the blinds were shut during meetings and flinch whenever the door was opened? Why would they stay politically active in an environment like this? How did they do it? And what happened as a result? In other words, this book is interested in the kind of opposition people face in the current political (and social and geographic) climate and how they respond to that opposition.

From this story I make the case for studying politics and people in context. In this book, I argue that the changes in the political, social, and geographic contexts have led to changes in *if* and *how* people express their political beliefs. I highlight three specific phenomena that have had this influence: (1) the amalgamation of political identity with other identities, (2) intensifying political prejudice that has raised the stakes for expressing dissent, and (3) the ability to hide one's political identity from one part of one's network. I argue that these changes have given people both a reason to hide their beliefs from some and the ability to hide them.

Together, these phenomena mean that whether someone is silent or expressive about their political beliefs depends on where you look. To say that the women in Texas were silent in the face of opposition would be incorrect. They were expressive and engaged, but on their own terms, in their own way, and in their own self-constructed community. I call this difference "networked silence."

I use the term "networked silence" to allude to two areas of research in sociology and communication. The first is "networked individualism,"[47] which says that the rise of digital technology created more opportunity for people to become social free agents. This line of work argues that through globalization and the expansion of communication technology, like cell phones and social media, individuals can now join, create, or be a part of multiple networks of people rather than just one.

The second area of research is from the "spiral of silence,"[48] which says that when people believe they are in the political minority, they do not express their beliefs out of fear of social isolation from that environment. In turn, the perceived minority opinion is phased out of public discourse altogether. When separate, these two areas of research say that people have only one outcome from their experience—to express themselves or not. In tandem, these two traditions say that people can now express themselves with greater ease when, where, and to whomever they choose.[49]

The phenomenon I call networked silence has three main components: (1) that people experience political opposition in one part of their social network, (2) that people intentionally conceal their political beliefs from that part of their network, and (3) that they express their political beliefs away from that part of their network. Networked silence means that people can appear silent in one context—the women in Texas who withhold their beliefs from their neighbors—and expressive in another—the same women who robustly discuss, debate, and engage with political topics together behind closed doors. I find that the choice to express your beliefs in one context can in turn make you more willing to express them in another. Over time, the women in Texas did not all keep their politics a secret, some "came out" as Democrats to their local community.

This is not how research on politics and communication has typically thought about political expression. For one, this line of work tends to focus on counting—how many people in X area believe Y, how many people in Y area engage in X—and what these numbers can tell us about trends in Z. This area of research has also privileged *active* and *public* expression in the analysis of political discourse. For instance, surveying individuals about their discussion networks, while useful for understanding the social composition of political communication, generates only information about the people with whom we discuss politics, not those with whom we look to avoid the topic. Likewise, scraping Twitter or other social media yields content and conversations only from accounts that are public. Networked silence—and this book—will say that merely counting and scraping will tell you little about the complexity and context surrounding people's choices to express themselves or not, because they tell you little about how people experience, process, and respond to political opposition.

I am by no means the first to think about how people traverse contexts when deciding if and how to express their political beliefs. There is a long history of research on the "public sphere," for instance, which examines how and why people express their beliefs in some cases and not in others. In fact, historically marginalized groups along racial/ethnic or gender/sexuality lines have used what scholars call "counterpublic" spheres to communicate and discuss political issues for decades and even centuries.[50] I will address this line of work in greater depth in a later chapter, but I will echo here the foundation of their work and mine, which is this: if we want to understand how people talk about and engage with politics—to know the core of how they navigate democracy in all its imperfections—we should look at the people for whom that engagement is risky, both hard and fleeting, but who do it *anyway*. It is not enough to know about how much people do express or engage, we have to know all the gritty details of why they do and do not.

The novel part of this argument is that networked silence is no longer reserved for those from marginal social identities or political identities, but from mainstream ones as well. This book is not about members of the far right or far left who are afraid to express their beliefs to others in their community. It is not about the social and political marginalization of Black Americans or immigrant communities. This book is about a group of mostly White, privileged women who are afraid of expressing their moderately progressive views to their conservative neighbors, friends, and family. The difference between the far right or far left and a group of moderate progressives in rural Texas is that the far right or far left, at this point, rarely receive a majority of votes in a national election, while moderates regularly do. The difference between racial/ethnic communities and the women's group in this book is that the latter faces far fewer structural and institutional biases. My point in these comparisons is that, like expression, marginality depends on context.

This book and the idea of networked silence will also challenge a bigger assumption of contemporary research and practice. That people who hold mainstream political views, like the women in Texas, feel they need to hide those beliefs presents an uncomfortable challenge to the idea of liberal democracy in the United States. It asks us all to consider whether American democracy is a place where ideas can be freely and openly expressed, and whether our society can and does live up to that ideal. I believe good research asks more questions than it can answer. And, in that spirit, I do not have an answer to this question. My point in this book is that this question is worth asking.

A New Schema

In the late 1990s, psychologists at Harvard showed participants in an experiment a video in which several basketball players passed a ball and back and forth.[51] The participants were asked to keep track of the number of times the ball was passed. During the video, as the ball was shuffled between players, a man in a gorilla suit walked through the middle of the court. After the experiment, when the psychologists asked the participants if they noticed the gorilla, only half said they had. The researchers attributed this to the participants' "cognitive blindness" and the prominence of their "activated schema." In other words, the researchers said the participants had missed the gorilla because they were too focused on the basketball. They had not expected a gorilla.[52]

The point of this story is not that between the basketball and the gorilla, one is more important than the other. The point is that when you are focused only on one phenomenon you often overlook another. Like the basketball study (or the gorilla study), the goal of this book is not to comment on which processes of politics and communication are more important than others. The goal is to show that by looking only at one thing—the thing we have been trained or primed to see—we may miss the thing that is lurking behind or beneath us—the thing that we are not expecting to see. The goal of this book is to pose a new schema for those interested in politics, people, and communication—to look for the new, unseen, and perhaps hidden parts of democracy that are happening in between passes.

And because this work involves looking for something for which we have little schema, this requires the robust and iterative work of inductive inquiry. It requires listening, questioning, and theorizing about what is happening without the complete constraints of what we already know. I draw from the pioneers who came before me—the people who found value in studying conversation, marginality, and sense-making[53] to build a new framework of communication in an era of polarized politics.

I do this through three approaches. First, I focus on the group of women in Texas, whom I followed for four years. During this time, I conducted a series of in-depth interviews with 40 of their members, interviewing most twice, and a few several times.[54] Second, I engaged in participant-observation of their meetings and events over four years, relying on group recorded minutes to supplement my analysis when I was not present.[55] The data I collected in my study of this group is particularly good at telling us about the women's context and how it influenced their communication and lack thereof. It is not as useful in telling us the scope of this phenomenon, about how many people feel afraid to express their beliefs and how many engage in networked silence as a result. Therefore, I also include evidence from a nationally representative and Texas-representative survey in which I asked people about the extent to which they feel the need to hide their political beliefs and whether or not they've talked about politics in secret.[56]

This question of scope is the most common question I receive when I tell the women's group's story—at academic conferences, on Twitter, and even at family dinners. How much of this secrecy, people ask, is actually happening? This is a question I will address in later chapters, but it is also a question I think is worth previewing here. Of the national sample of U.S. residents, 22.3% said they feel the need to hide their political conversations from others. A similar 22.6% of Texas residents said the same thing.[57] When I asked U.S. and Texas residents if they had joined a private group to secretly discuss politics in person or online, 9.4% of both samples said they had done so in the past two years.

To put these numbers in context, 22% of the U.S. population is more than the percentage of registered voters who voted in the midterm primary in 2018. Likewise, 9% is more than the number of 18–29-year-olds who voted Republican in the 2018 midterms. While these numbers are not enormous, they are meaningful. My answer when people ask me how much political secrecy really happens, then, is that it is happening more than you might think.

Both my data from CWG and my data from the survey let me study networked silence in diverse ways. I can assess the depth of the women's experiences while getting a picture of the breadth of this phenomenon. This data is less good, however, at telling me the order or influence of things. I cannot, for example, know whether this group caused the women to make their beliefs public to their community or whether they would have done this on their own accord without the group's existence.

It is also worth pointing out that this book includes a case study of a group of progressive women in a conservative rural area. I do this because (1) this was the case that was accessible to me, and (2) because Texas is a worthy context for exploring political communication. Importantly, my focus on this group does not mean that networked silence happens only to or among progressives, women, or those in Texas. In fact, the survey data offers some evidence that both Democrats and Republicans may be similarly likely to hide their political conversations or secretly express their beliefs offline or online.[58] It is likely that there are many other ideologies and contexts in which people hide their political opinions. Conservatives, for instance, may feel the need to hide their beliefs from their coworkers but not from their family. On these various contexts and conditions, it is an understatement to say that more research is needed.

People who are counting the basketball are likely to see things in this book that I did not, and that is okay. In fact, it is necessary. I imagine if you asked the study participants to look for a man in a gorilla suit, they would have had a hard time keeping up with the ball. There are many important components in this story, and important questions that this story cannot answer. I offer this book as a tool for future work, not as the end of inquiry.

Plan of the Book

This book started with an explanation of the contexts in which this research came to be. The rest of the book will be focused on what happened as a result of these political, social, and geographic divides—how the women in Texas came to form their secret organization, why they did it, and how it affected them and their community. From this story, I consider what this means for the study and practice of democracy.

In the next chapter, I describe my methodology, which focuses on the individual in context: her perceptions and experiences, as well her interactions with others. I provide details about how I found the group at the core of this book, how I gained access to individual members and their meetings, and how I built relationships with members and earned their trust. I lay out my own positionality within the group, which of my traits afforded me their trust, and how, over time, I sought to maintain the group's confidentiality in my own work.

Chapter 3 addresses the group's development and its contours. First, I attend to how digital media was at the heart of the group's formation, allowing members to coordinate away from disagreeable spouses and neighbors and to discuss, engage, and grapple with politics in a protected space both online and offline. In this chapter, I also focus on the members' characteristics and habits, including their past experiences with politics and media, particularly the role of the local newspaper in constructing perceptions of disagreement within their community.

Chapter 4 turns to the reasons why the women hide their beliefs from their community. Unlike existing theories of silence, which focus on a psychological fear of social isolation, this chapter depicts the sociological components of fear—including power and social and economic interdependence—which were at play in the women's decision to keep their politics a secret. I outline three types of fear in response to partisan hostility: social, economic, and physical. I recount the women's stories of actual retaliation within these categories, as well as the role of narrative in fueling fear and building camaraderie.

Chapter 5 emphasizes the group's internal fissures and identity negotiations, including their decision to remain only women, as well as their choices to align themselves with the Democratic Party, avoid discussions with conservatives, and maintain their confidentiality. This chapter highlights the unique characteristics and decisions of secret organizations and networks whose private nature can create turmoil and insulate members. This chapter also highlights the confluence of gender and political identity that further mitigated the women's social power and their willingness to publicly dissent.

Where Chapter 5 focuses on members' insulation, Chapter 6 addresses the group's incubation. Specifically, I explore the members' willingness to "come out" as local Democrats, a link between this story and those of earlier LGBT movements, and an example of how political marginalization now mirrors the language of other marginalized identities. In this chapter, I also recount the ways in which the group covertly supported and revitalized the local Democratic Party by helping to coordinate events and stepping into leadership roles.

While Chapters 3 through 6 use data collected from 2017 to 2018, Chapter 7 looks at the buildup and reaction to the 2020 election. In this chapter, I include my observations of the group prior to and after the election, as well as interviews with several group members prior to the election results. I consider how 2020 reflects the same realities as the years before it, and, given the uniqueness of the year and the changes it presents, how this raises new questions about if and how people express their political beliefs.

Finally, in Chapter 8 I showcase the broader findings of this work and their theoretical and practical implications. I urge readers of this book to think about how people intentionally conceal their political beliefs by engaging in networked silence and why they may do this. I will argue that the fear laid bare in the women's experiences are evidence that liberal democratic norms are under attack. But I will also argue that mainstream partisans can and are forming congenial communities to build intra- and interpersonal power, and that they can use these communities to overcome threatening conditions.

This book is called *Democracy Lives in Darkness* because I believe that these are dark times for democracy. But I also want to redefine what darkness can mean. For many, it conveys subversive or clandestine behavior—the hooded robes of the Ku Klux Klan or trolls using anonymity online to issue death threats. But darkness can also be useful for people who hold normal and valuable perspectives but who are isolated, intimidated, or threatened. In contrast to the *Washington Post*'s famous slogan "Democracy Dies in Darkness," this book suggests that democracy in the United States already exists in darkness, but also, more optimistically, that despite this darkness, it keeps going. This book will take you into the dark parts of democratic life, into the lives of a group of women, their challenges and fears, their failures and their victories, what led them to close the doors in the first place, and how to open them again.

2

Studying Political Secrecy

I drove a white Honda Accord during the time I conducted the research in this book. On the bottom right of the bumper was a sticker that says, "Don't Mess with Texas Women." The sticker, a reference to the 1985 "Don't Mess with Texas" anti-littering campaign, never garnered much attention in the various majority liberal or conservative areas in which I lived. I figured that Democrats must perceive it as a symbol of my stance on gender equality and Republicans must perceive it as a symbol of ruggedness or support for the Second Amendment.

When many scholars of politics and communication talk about "methodology," or the way they approach their study of some political phenomenon, they do not begin with a story of the bumper sticker on their car. That is because cars are not often relevant to politics. It is also because some social scientific methods, and many in my field of choice, are about the impartiality of the researcher—how to limit the researcher's influence on the study's outcome as much as possible. This approach includes surveys, experiments, and large-scale content analysis of data scraped from across the Web. This is so that findings can be replicated, a continuous process of rejecting null hypotheses or offering support for hypotheses across different contexts, samples, and time. The idea is that from the ability to replicate, certainty can emerge.

This is an important way of studying the social world, because in many cases having certainty is important. In fact, this is the way that I came to study politics and communication—to identify an independent and dependent variable and to empirically assess the scope, size, and order of their relationship. But this is not how I choose to study politics and communication in this book, at least not the only way I choose to study this topic. On the contrary, I choose two approaches. One approach lacks both the ability to replicate and the influence of the researcher (me). The second supplements the first with replicable data from survey research. Together these approaches tackle two different questions: (1) How and why do people intentionally hide their political beliefs from others? (2) How much of this is really happening?

Democracy Lives in Darkness. Emily Van Duyn, Oxford University Press. © Oxford University Press 2022.
DOI: 10.1093/oso/9780197557013.003.0002

I mentioned my bumper sticker at the beginning of this chapter because it tells you something about me and my connection with the state of Texas and with my gender. These are two things that very much relate to the topic of this book. I am a proud native Texan. I received all of my college degrees from universities in the state. I was also raised in a house full of women. I take pride that I know both the urban and rural experience of my home state, and I take pride that I am a woman with expertise and ambition. It is these perspectives and experiences that colored my view of Texas and led me to hold connections across different areas and regions of the state.

The very fact that I am a progressive Texan and, at the time of the 2016 election, was living in the state capitol meant that I had my ear to the ground more in Texas than anywhere else. I was part of groups on Facebook for Texas progressives. I went to local events for the county and state Democratic Party. Following the 2016 election, I spoke to a number of people I had known in other areas of the state who were horrified at Trump's election. It was in this emotional postmortem that I received the phone call from my acquaintance in rural Texas who told me about the group I call Community Women's Group, or CWG for short.

In this chapter, I'll tell you about my methods and my data. First, I focus on how I found CWG, how I studied them, and the composition of their group and broader community. Second, I focus on how I assess the prominence of their experiences—of the likelihood of hiding one's political beliefs in one context and strategically expressing them in another—among the broader U.S. and Texas populations. Throughout this chapter and throughout the entire book, I use pseudonyms for the women of CWG to protect their identity.

Studying Networked Silence in CWG

Despite my familiarity with Texas and its politics, during and after the 2016 election, I was very much in a liberal bubble. When I walked around my neighborhood in Austin, I saw yard signs that broadcasted my neighbor's intolerance of "hate"—a not-so-subtle reference to Trump's rhetoric and impending policies. When I drove through town, I saw bumper stickers that boasted of their "resistance" to Trump's presidency; and when I commiserated with my graduate school friends, it was always about Trump's unfathomable win and not about how Trump would make America "great again."

To be sure, I had Facebook friends and relatives who had supported Trump in the 2016 election, but they were a blip in a long feed of anti-Trump diatribes, images, and videos. After the election, I spoke with my uncle, a strong evangelical supporter of Trump, which gave me a taste of the elation that much of the country was feeling. But my uncle lived in Georgia, which was far enough away that I connected very little with what he said about his community and his view of the world. I loved him, but I did not understand him.

When I got the call from my acquaintance—the member of CWG—I was struck by how much my immediate surroundings had insulated me. I was reminded that those who supported Trump were not just my uncle and his friends in Georgia, but many others nearby. In our first conversation, my confidant told me about the tenor of the 2016 election and the women's absolute shock that others in their community were just as upset at the election results as they were. She told me how thrilled she had been after going to these meetings. They had given her life, a feeling of purpose.

I asked her if she could put me in touch with the membership. It would be interesting to hear what they have to say, I told her, given that my PhD research is concerned with why people do not express their political beliefs to those around them. She told me it would be unlikely, not because the members would not want to talk to me, but because the group itself was confidential. She had already broken their rule by telling me about the group, she said, and was uncertain that anyone would be willing to be identified.

It took me a second to grasp exactly what my confidant was describing. Was this not just a group of women drinking wine and wallowing in their pain over Clinton's loss or Trump's victory? And just how "confidential" were they? Surely these women were not abiding by Chatham House Rule and banging a gavel to establish order. It was hard to reconcile my immediate thought of a *confidential* group—the Ku Klux Klan, Anonymous, Skull and Bones, to name a few—and the kind of people that were in this confidential group—middle- to old-aged moderately progressive mothers and grandmothers.

My confidant then told me about the group's leaders, committees, and monthly meetings with old and new business. She told me about their rotating meeting locations to avoid unwanted attention and suspicion and about their secret Facebook group and private email listserv through which members coordinated, shared information, and kept in touch with one another between meetings. She told me about their newly crafted mission statement and the confidentiality agreement that all members were required to sign. The agreement specified that members would not publish anything about the group without explicit permission, would not speak of the group or anyone in the group without permission from members, and would personally recruit only like-minded women they knew well. This was not Chatham House Rule, these were the rules of Fight Club.

Because I had learned about social science in the replicable and impartial approach I spoke about in the beginning of this chapter, my first inclination was to survey the group of 136 women. This would allow their responses to be anonymous, I thought, and to quantify their experiences into neat boxes. I put together an online survey with 15 questions that asked the women about their comfort with expressing their beliefs to their community, their psychological predisposition to fear social isolation, and their perception of their community's political beliefs, all on a 5- or 7-point Likert-type scale. I added a few open-ended questions about their "personal experience" with politics at the end for good measure, and that was that.

I shared my survey idea with a mentor of mine at the University of Texas, Dr. Rod Hart. Rod is very good at seeing things in a unique light, which makes him a fantastic scholar and an even better mentor. On this day, I sat in his office beaming naively about the survey idea I had come up with. He sat across from me wearing a smirk that originally looked like good-natured humor but quickly revealed itself as utter disbelief. Upon mention of my open-ended questions about the women's experience with politics, he shook his head. "You have to *talk* to them," he said, and that was that.

So, for the next several years I talked to the women of CWG. It took a few weeks after that first phone call before I got word that the leaders had agreed I could speak to a few members confidentially. I asked if my confidant could circulate a survey (old habits die hard), so that the women could select a time for our interview and so that I could securely gather contact information by which to reach them. The leaders agreed, and in mid-April I went through a review process with the university's Institutional Review Board (IRB), which is required of any university researcher looking to conduct human subjects research.[1] After I received IRB approval, I circulated my survey link to the group's leadership committee—what they called their "focus group." Although I had wanted to do video interviews, my confidant told me that the Internet connection in rural Texas was weak, which would make video interviews a hard if not impossible medium. And because I could not afford to travel to and from rural Texas for every interview in person,

I decided phone interviews would work for now. By late April, I had five phone interviews scheduled.

Those first five interviews were very important. I went into them with a semi-structured interview guide that I put together (Appendices D–F), drawing from some of the only other interview guides that were available in the field of political ethnography.[2] Very quickly I learned that these interviews would be more unstructured than structured. These were women who had a lot to say about politics and no one to say it to for many years, some even for decades. Although I had imagined that most interviews would last less than 45 minutes, most went on for well over an hour. Some of these women spoke to me in their car, some of them spoke to me at home. One of them took our call while making a poster for an upcoming "March for Science." I spoke to them about the group, about their personal histories with politics, and about their feelings and fears regarding their community. I asked about their families. I never told them my exact beliefs—whom I had voted for, what I felt about abortion or universal healthcare—I did not have to. They assumed I shared their beliefs and I never confirmed. In fact, looking back on those first five transcripts, I said very little. Most of our conversations involved the women talking—with anger and emotion and purpose and fear—and me listening.

Some would call this study of CWG a "*method* of listening,"[3] some would call it "soaking and poking,"[4] but both would regard this approach as ethnographic research. In my case, my study required a notable step beyond just listening. It required trusting. This was, after all, a secret group, and my presence was a threat not only to their anonymity but also to their sense of safety. My being a woman with progressive ideals who knew someone in the group got me a phone call. My being trusted among the majority of group members got me into the room.

After the first five interviews, I asked if my confidant could circulate the sign-up survey to the larger group. The group's leaders agreed. They had spoken to me, I had listened. I had not recorded and distributed our conversations. I had not relayed their identities and beliefs to the broader community.[5] I was safe. I was one of them.

After my confidant circulated my survey to the broader group, I spoke to 11 more members. Each interview was different but very much the same. The women wanted to talk about the election and the group. They wanted to talk about their shock at the first CWG meeting they attended. But they also wanted to talk about the difficulty of being where they were—of how they could never put yard signs in their yard, could never talk about politics with their friends, families, or spouse, or even how they felt uncomfortable voting in the primary. I listened to their concerns. I shared their discomfort at hearing of people being fired for their political opinions or of friends being run off the road because of a political bumper sticker.

By mid-July, one of the women I had interviewed suggested I come to a meeting. I asked the group's leaders and my confidant if it would be alright, and they agreed. It would be my first time meeting the women face to face, and the leaders thought that would help engage more members who had initially balked at the idea of being interviewed. My first meeting in August quickly turned into many meetings after that. On occasions that I was not able to make the CWG monthly meeting, I used the minutes taken by the group's secretary, whose job it was to record important details from each meeting and distribute the minutes through the group's listserv.

What was striking about these meetings was their simultaneous formality and informality. Each meeting included an agenda, which was prepared by the focus group ahead of time. If you had something to pitch, share, or raise to the group, it had to be sent to the focus group ahead of time in order to appear as a formal agenda item. If you did not submit your announcement ahead of time, you could share it during open discussion at the end of the meeting.

During the old business section of the meeting, each chair of the various committees, which were dedicated to different issues (e.g., environment, immigration), was expected to report on the committee's current projects. There was a facilitator who led each meeting, a job that rotated each week, and a timekeeper who helped keep the meeting on schedule. Despite their best intentions, however, the meetings could quickly get out of hand. With so many people wanting to talk about what was happening in the country, and many with nowhere else to talk about it, it was common for the women to talk over one another, or for the "discussion" period of each agenda item to extend well beyond its allotted time. Every meeting felt like I was both at a raucous meeting of the British Parliament and at a regimented meeting of the Junior League.

At these meetings, I sat in the back with my laptop. I started taking notes after I greeted everyone and hunkered down to observe the social hour, which happened during the first 30 minutes of the meeting. As the women circulated the room with their beverage of choice and a plate full of home-baked items, I watched and listened to conversations about their past few weeks. Some of the time these conversations were about the weather, shared friends, or news from the county. Most of the time they were about what was going on in their state and country at large. Everyone wore name tags at the meetings, including me, although they were rarely needed. It was the same 30–50 people who circulated in and out each month.

Although I wore a name tag like everyone else, the women desperately wanted me to sign in to the meetings; to be counted as a member. I resisted this, not because putting my name on their member sheet could make me impartial in my study of the group, but because it could make the group expect something else from me other than what I was there to accomplish. The women knew that, at the end of my interviews and observations, I would no longer be engaged in their activities. I was not a member, but I did become a fixture of their meetings, a receptacle for their excitement, confusion, anger, and worry.

The difference between my age at the time I started my interviews (26) and the median age of the group (62) was stark. This meant their dynamic with me often felt like a grandmother-granddaughter interaction. For example, across my years of phone calls and meetings with the women, I was sometimes lectured, albeit in a caring way, about the importance of young people voting and women running for office. Sometimes I was updated about children and grandchildren, and one time they tried to send me home from a meeting with leftover snacks.

The older age of the group was also evident in how the meetings proceeded or, on the contrary, were interrupted. A cell phone policy had to be instated because at every meeting I attended in 2017, cell phones would go off at random intervals. The members would forget to turn them off at the beginning. The women were older and had time to give to the group. And, in some ways, they were precisely the demographic in their community who wanted to meet at nighttime and drink white wine, pledge allegiance to a flag, recount what they saw as the horrors of the current political situation, and do what they could to stop it.

Beyond my early blunders in surveying when I should have been listening, I had also made hasty assumptions about what it is I was studying altogether. I had entered the study of this group wanting to know about the women's silence—why it was that they *did not* express their political beliefs altogether. I approached my study this way because this is what was available to me. This is what I had read in my graduate courses and heard presented at conferences. But I was watching the basketball and not looking for a gorilla.

What I came to see was that silence was only half of the story. I found that the women of CWG *were* expressing their beliefs, just in a place that could not be seen from the surface.

CWG and Community Composition

CWG exists within its own context outside of their meetings. To give you a picture of what CWG's community is like without giving away their location, I will provide loose descriptions rather than exact ones. In the rural Texas county where CWG formed, the general population is largely White and skews older. Like more recent sociological and demographic research on shrinking rural communities,[6] an aging county makes sense in the context of broader U.S. trends. There has been a steady exit of a younger rural generation who previously might have stayed to work on family farms or run family businesses. Now, this younger generation has turned to urban metropolises to attend college or find work as the small-town industries they leave behind become more obsolete.[7]

This is not to say that the insular economy of small towns has not persisted across rural communities, including the county in which CWG was formed. Although expanding infrastructure and ease of transportation might mean that shopping in a neighboring town is now more possible, the role of local business remains important to the daily functioning of rural communities and the people who live within them. Small-town businesses are cornerstones of their communities, often containing the town's name within the business name itself[8] and contributing to and funding town-sanctioned events. This holds true in CWG's county.

In terms of race and ethnicity, the county is less diverse than the state as a whole. According to Census population estimates from 2018, well over two-thirds of the county was White/non-Hispanic/Latino, which is significantly more than the 42% of the state identifying as White/non-Hispanic/Latino. In the county, less than a third identified as Hispanic/Latino, compared to the nearly 40% estimated to be Hispanic/Latino in the state. The county also slightly underrepresents Blacks/African Americans as compared to the state. When comparing the county with other similar rural counties from the area, the numbers were similar.

Like other rural areas, race relations in the county are strained.[9] To say that racism is entrenched and persistent across not just rural communities, but urban ones as well, would be an understatement. There is some evidence that race relations in rural areas, particularly in the South,[10] are especially tense given there is little overlap between White, Black, and Hispanic communities, and because there is hostility in the working class across racial/ethnic backgrounds.[11]

CWG itself mirrored, if not exaggerated, the older population and the lack of racial and ethnic diversity in its surrounding community. More specifically, the median age of CWG is around 62 and almost entirely White. When I asked members about the demographic composition of the group, they all recognized that it was not diverse in terms of either age or race. A member, whom I'll call Joyce, told me about the group's homogeneity in near statistical terms.

> Well, mostly the group is very educated White women. We would love to have some Black women as members, but we only have one, well we've had two attend, but we've only had one that's kind of active. And so we don't have a cross-section. (Joyce, 2017)

Some recognized this homogeneity as a larger problem for the group's longevity than did others. Alice, who is in her 40s, saw the older membership as a problem for keeping the group going, but it was also the product of available time—the older women simply had more time to give to CWG and political activism in general.

> A: I'm also disappointed in the demographics of the group, and I don't know. . . I think that's the biggest for any group, I think it's probably the biggest challenge is to be a diverse group. I haven't seen one yet, but I think it's important.
> E: What do you think is the general demographic right now?
> A: Old ladies? [laughs] Is that fair?
> E: That's fair.
> A: I mean I don't think we have anybody . . . if we've got anybody in their 30s I'd be surprised, maybe one or two. But, certainly heavily into 50s, 60s, 70s. And a lot of it has to do with time. (Alice, 2017)

In 2017, when I first spoke to one of the cofounders of the group, whom I will call Deborah, she brought up the age of the membership as a concern for whether it could continue over time.

Many of us complain about being worn out, of being tired of all the hard work. I just have no idea. We'll see. You know, you see the ages of the women in this group and we've already got one in the hospital with a brain tumor and then Roberta had broken her ankle after that last meeting. We're not spry, we're—most of us are over 60. So, in order for it to survive, we'll have to get younger blood. And I think all volunteer groups say the same thing. (Deborah, 2017)

Alice and Deborah are right, the women of CWG are older. Roberta in fact *had* broken her ankle leaving a meeting I attended in August 2017—my first meeting, no less. In response, the women had to quite literally lift and carry Roberta off the ground and into an ambulance, all while worrying about whether the local EMS would wonder why they were gathered there in the first place.

The women of CWG are not just old, but, in general, they have a higher median income than the general population of their county. Most of the women live in nice homes and went to college, which, compared to the socioeconomic background of their surrounding county, is quite a contrast. In 2017 I spoke with Paula, who recognized the difference in the group's average income compared to the county. "I think most people, of the women in this group, they have above average income in this county," she said, "and that's gotta affect your outlook, right?"

All of these facets of demographic uniformity were exacerbated by the group's confidentiality statement, which required that recruitment was limited to only those who members knew and knew well. This often resulted in recruitment that was covert, elaborate, or both. Ann told me the story of her own recruitment, which happened after the group's formation, and involved a very covert exchange at a community event.

We were at a [event] here in town just down the road at [a local establishment]. I was talking—I didn't actually know a lot of people there, it was the first time I had actually been to one of their events—so I struck up a conversation with one of the women, and we talked about how she played piano in church and maybe had played at the Jewish temple and talking about how they didn't have a large congregation—just something about church and religion. And then somehow, we got on the Muslim faith and I just said something like, "Well, you know in the Muslim faith they revere Mary and Jesus, it's actually part of the Quran" and they just kind of . . . I could tell

I had gone a bit far. I could tell that the conversation had probably gone as far as it should so that this woman didn't somehow declare, "Oh my god, we have a Muslim lover here." And so, I think [a woman in the group] had come up and said, "I see you were talking to [a woman at the event]" and just kind of where the conversation had gone. And she mentioned there was this group. . . . One of the other women who was instrumental in getting it started was also there, so she introduced me to her with a little bit of a wink and saying, "this is so and so" and she put me on the list. (Ann, 2017)

This insular recruitment, like that of hidden and "core-stigmatized" organizations of various stripes,[12] also meant that efforts to bring in more diverse members were often unsuccessful, because the women either did not know women of color or working-class women, or were too afraid to broach politics with them. Paula recognized this, too. After we got off the phone, she sent me an email to express a concern about the group's membership that she had not been able to verbalize on the phone earlier.

I have heard members express frustration about the difficulties of reaching out to women who may not exactly fit the makeup of the group—Black, Latino, younger (in addition to discussions about how to speak to Trump voters.) Right now, unless we come up with a strategy and some kind of campaign that would draw people in, I think we've nearly reached our maximum membership, all coming from friends of members. (Paula, 2017)

Although CWG itself is almost entirely White "old ladies," there is one Black woman, as Joyce mentioned, who attends meetings on occasion. I was present at the group's meeting in November 2017 when the women brought up how to deal with issues of race within and outside of the group. Robin, the only woman of color present at the meeting, originally stood up during discussion to consider the use of the word "liberal." After some talk among the group, she turned the discussion to race by saying, "I know I'm the token Black person."

The other (White) women were immediately outraged. "No!" cried four or five women at once. From the front where she was facilitating, Deborah called, "You're the only Black woman who's ever come!" Eventually the women let Robin explain. "The things I hear you say are not the things I experience," she told them. "I hear from my White side that families are being broke up [by Trump], but from my colored side, it's not like that."

Robin went on to tell the women that they have been isolated from reality. That they do not understand the experiences of other people in their community, in particular people of color. After a brief discussion, Robin asked to stand and say something to the group. She opened her statement with "My sisters," and eyes filled with tears around the room. She thanked the women for listening and said she was grateful to be a part of the group.

I recount this particular event from November 2017 because it is reflective of the group in several ways. These are, for the most part, privileged White women. Many had not only avoided politics but avoided or overlooked, perhaps unintentionally, the experiences and suffering of others in their community because they were not their own experiences. In many ways, this moment made the women confront the fact that while they suffered judgment and fear based on their politics, there were many with much more stacked against them, people who have experienced fear and persecution for a very long time. The women of CWG are not racists, but some were unknowingly complicit in overlooking the experiences of people of color in their community. This complicity is nothing new to the dominant race and generation of CWG. White women have a sordid history and contemporary practice of overlooking or blissfully ignoring the unique experiences of women of color,[13] and CWG is not immune from those trappings.

Although explicit racism was not generally evident in the women's comments, stigmatized rhetoric around race sometimes appeared in how the women spoke about immigrants. After all, although the women identified as progressives, most had grown up in conservative households and conservative areas all their life. For instance, Barbara, a woman whose husband had voted for Trump and with whom she could not discuss politics, spoke freely about the need to educate "illegals."

> And I'm more sympathetic to any illegal that's trying to make a living here. You know, they pay taxes indirectly, never fear. If they rent and don't own property their rent pays the property taxes. So, there's different ways of skinning a cat, and people don't know that. . . . The reason I brought up education is because we have to educate the illegals. And we can do it and they will become strong. They want to work. They will become a strong backbone for our community if we just let them. (Barbara, 2017)

It was not that Barbara wanted to exclude the Hispanic community when she used the word "illegals," it was that her language had not caught up with her politics. In fact, the desire to find a "new word" for "illegals" was discussed at a meeting I attended in February 2018. After the women vented about "horrifying moments" from a local state representative candidate's forum, Cynthia mentioned she thought the group should come up with a different word for "illegal immigrants," because it made them sound "bad." That many of the women were unfamiliar with the word "undocumented," which is the adjective of choice in most progressive literature, reflects either just how disconnected they had been to progressive political activism, or just how entrenched they were in the rhetoric and language of their surrounding community, where the word "illegals" was common.

Although the women of CWG, in many ways, reflected their community demographically and sometimes linguistically, they were also very different from it. Not only were they more educated with higher incomes than their surrounding neighbors, but they were also generally newer to the county itself. The median number of years the women of CWG had lived in the county was 16, and this number had a substantial range between two and 40 years. Some of these women had moved from neighboring cities to retire, some of them moved back to the area after having grown up in the county as a child, and some moved to be with their husband's side of the family.

Certainly, a shorter tenure in the county could make dissenting from it easier. It means relationships are less solidified and one's identity and connection to the community is not as strong. But it could also make any form of engagement less likely. Research shows that those who feel closer to their community are also more likely to engage in it,[14] meaning a shorter tenure may mean less connection and less engagement. Research on rural communities also suggests that although rural residents rely uniquely on one another in economic and social ways, they are also particularly likely to be critical and skeptical of newly arrived "outsiders."[15] This makes those who are dependent on the local community for social and economic support especially susceptible to maintaining the status quo or wary of defying the majority. In other words, the women, whether newly arrived or old-timers, had plenty of reasons not to speak out.

Naturally, because CWG remains a secret group, my discussion of their community in the following chapters—their interactions, their media, their events—will all be kept vague. It is also important to note that, in order to maintain the group's confidentiality, I do not speak with their families or spouses, I do not speak to members of the women's community, and I do not include examples of op-eds from their local paper.

Omitting any discussion with community members could be seen as a limitation in that my perspective comes from only those in CWG. In another light, talking with the broader community may actually be unnecessary to understand how and why people keep their politics a secret. After all, whether or not it was warranted, the women of CWG were afraid.

Studying Networked Silence in Texas and the United States

Although the study of CWG helps to establish how and why networked silence may happen, it is possible that this group is an exception to the rule. Even in the case of their exceptionalism, CWG offers an important perspective on how contemporary politics has changed the game for communicating about politics—prompting people to keep their politics a secret in some contexts and not in others. Still, while CWG can help us understand the depth of networked silence, understanding the scope will require data that can be counted.

In this book, I use survey data to approximate how much networked silence is happening. I use both nationally representative survey data (n = 1,062) as well as Texas-representative survey data (n = 1,004) that asks two important questions related to networked silence: (1) How often do people feel the need to hide their political conversations? (2) Have they joined a private group in person or online to secretly discuss politics? These two questions tell us at least something about the respondent's intentions for secrecy: "feeling the need to hide" their political conversations and joining a private group for political discussion.[16]

Anyone who has run or analyzed surveys knows that two questions do not yield a lot of data. They offer no reliable assessment of latent constructs. They offer no sense of how different people interpret these questions differently. What these two questions can offer us is a start. A start at understanding not only how much political secrecy exists, at least in a generalizable sense across a population, but also how to measure political secrecy. This may not be the optimal measure for networked silence, but it is a springboard.

Throughout the following chapters, I lean on this survey data not as a way to explain networked silence, but as a way to contextualize its reach. Throughout my discussion of CWG, for instance, I may reference this data to emphasize how many others outside of CWG share their sentiments. I also use this information to address the skeptical readers, readers who see this story, and perhaps this entire book, as a throwaway case. It is my job to convince you not only that CWG's story is important, but that it is not an anomaly.

Analyzing the Data

The next few chapters of this book include my observations of and interviews with CWG members. These chapters are also peppered with descriptive analyses of both the national and Texas survey data. While my main goal of this book is to show you how both politics and communication are changing each other, my ulterior goal is to show you how our methods should change with them, to offer an example of how qualitative studies with depth can be combined with quantitative studies of scope to tell a cohesive story and build a cohesive theory.

This is easier said than done. Collecting data about CWG between 2017 and 2018 took nearly two years of observations and interviews and a lot of transcribing. By the time I was done collecting data in 2018, I had interviewed 23 members, 18 of them twice, for a total of 40 interviews (see Appendix B). I had 25 meeting observations, 10 of them my direct observations and 15 of them detailed minutes taken by CWG's secretary.

Then came the real work—I had to make sense of this information. As with any method, there are a number of ways to cut the data. In qualitative inquiry, that number can be astronomical. This is because qualitative analysis is inductive—what communication methodologists Lindlof and Taylor (2011) refer to as the process of inferring "a principle from many particulars of discourse and action" (p. 243), where the particulars are not clean numbers but messy people. This is also because qualitative inquiry relies on theoretical traditions to drive coding and categorization schemes. Someone studying how medical residents communicate diagnoses, for instance, will likely use a different frame for analysis than I will use in this book.

Because there are so many ways to interpret the data, it is helpful to have a systematic way to do what qualitative researchers call "data reduction." Unlike studies where statistics or numerical comparisons are used to make sense of the data and data reduction and analysis are two separate processes, in qualitative research data reduction and analysis are the *same* process. It is then useful to have some systematic way to reduce the data—to take the masses of observations, interviews, and artifacts and cut them into meaningful categories for interpretation.

Two common approaches to data reduction in the world of ethnography—the "method of listening" or "soaking and poking" that I referred to earlier in the chapter—are *grounded theory* and *extended case method*. Grounded theory is interested in how people make sense of and experience their surroundings, but not necessarily how these experiences extend to or inform our understanding of the larger social order. Extended case method is interested in the emergent social order from people's experiences—how people's experiences reflect power structures at a larger scale. Both methods involve drawing from existing schema for understanding each case, each unit of data, and both methods happen continuously and iteratively, with analysis commencing the moment the researcher enters the field. Both methods have their strengths and their limitations. Grounded theory is good at telling us about the micro but not the macro, while extended case method is good at telling us about the macro but not the micro.

To analyze the qualitative data in this book, I used sociologist Kristin Luker's (2009) inductive method, her "logic of discovery" which combines the two methods just described. The logic of discovery is about using the micro to speak about the macro. To Luker, the point of qualitative inquiry is to build theory—that qualitative research can generalize "logically" about what is going on in the world even if it cannot generalize "statistically." In turn, it is up to quantitative research to test our theories, establish their boundaries across a population, and do the work of "verification."

I will spare you the messy details of my data reduction process, which on a graduate school budget involved a lot of post-its, occupied floor space, and time. I will tell you that I went into my analysis with an eye to what we already know about political discussion, about silence, and about political organizing (the basketball). I also went into my analysis looking for surprises—things that were contrary to what we already know (the gorilla). I identified themes that drew from existing theories and added to them—units of data that reflect existing schemas, units of data that reflect the distinctiveness of the women's experiences, and units of data that reflect the exceptionality of the current time. In the following chapters, you will see a lot of reference to the work that came before me—what we already know about these topics—but you will also see a lot of additions to that knowledge. This is the contribution of qualitative data—the assumptions are only as constrained as the researcher.

Conclusion

The goal of this chapter was to provide a sense of how I conducted the research in this book. It was to provide you with background on the group and the women that will occupy the next few chapters. It was also to propel my case for a multimethodological study of politics and communication and the value of qualitative inquiry for theory-building.

I conducted this research at a time when the method in many studies of politics and communication was computational—a focus on how "big data" could shed new light on phenomena. And, in many cases, big data has provided new insight into the social world that has long been untestable or unobservable. In other cases, the methodological prowess of "big data" has grown independent from the value of its answers. The unofficial motto in many social scientific fields has become "the bigger the data, the better the data."

That motto is true depending on how you define "better." In this book, I define better as not just a contribution of novelty but a contribution of nuance. Our society and the contexts in which we find ourselves—online or offline—are changing rapidly. This means we need a way of looking at the world with the guidance, but not restraint, of what we already know. We do not just need to count people, we need to understand people.

Data has become the currency of our social world. The sociologist Pauline Bart once said, "Data, data everywhere and not a thought to think."[17] Her point, and my point, is that sometimes bigger data is not better data. *Democracy Lives in Darkness* offers a small but valuable slice of the data in our world. My hope is that the following chapters can interpret the data in ways that are not paralyzing but provocative; personal not perfunctory.

3

Forming a Secret Group

In March 2018, about two weeks before the midterm primary in Texas, CWG met for the first time on a Sunday afternoon instead of their usual Tuesday evening. A month prior, the women had voted to change the meeting time after several members cited child-care requirements and difficulty driving at night as reasons for their previous absence. Looking around the room, their strategy did not seem to have been effective: the same 25 people huddled around a table with snacks and a tray of printer cartridges labeled "free ink."

As the meeting got started, the first item of new business was the group's "Calling Project," a phone campaign to inform 65+ voters in their county of the option to vote by mail. At the previous meeting, the group had organized a small contingency of women to make calls and to update the Voter Activation Network (VAN)—the Democratic Party's voter file—where information was missing or inaccurate. At this meeting, one of the leaders of the project, whom I will call Theresa, asked for more volunteers as another member circulated thank-you gifts in the form of Easter candy to members who already made calls.

As Theresa waited for reluctant volunteers, I overheard two women to my right discussing their aversion to phone banking. "Well, *I* can't," said one, "[Her husband] is at home with me and could overhear." The woman next to her nodded furiously in sympathetic understanding. In the past, CWG had organized what they referred to as "calling parties" precisely for this reason: phone calls at home were not private.

I tell this particular story because it shows just how important the *mode* of communication matters to the *substance* of that communication; how publicly engaging in politics can be a privilege, not an absolute. When we think about political expression and political activism, we do not always think about these calculations. We assume that in a liberal democracy, being political can happen anywhere, with anyone, through any means. In CWG, phone calls in which politics was the topic of conversation were off limits for some members because they shared a house with someone who would disapprove. In-person discussion, while safer for some, was also a more challenging

Democracy Lives in Darkness. Emily Van Duyn, Oxford University Press. © Oxford University Press 2022.
DOI: 10.1093/oso/9780197557013.003.0003

commitment for others. The common denominator for the group was digital communication—the path through which members could control who saw their political beliefs. It was through digital media that CWG was able to bring in people for whom engaging in politics had previously been only a liability.

In this chapter I describe the group's (and its members') development. Secrecy was key to the women at a personal level. They hid their beliefs from family, friends, and neighbors. It was also key to the women at the organizational level. They hid their organization from others in their community so that they could openly express their beliefs there.

The novelty of CWG is not that they formed a secret organization to express their beliefs privately. Oppressed groups along lines of race/ethnicity and gender/sexuality have been forced to organize in secret for decades,[1] just as extremist groups have used secret groups to propagate hate speech and even subversive doctrine for just as long.[2] The novelty of CWG is who was sitting in the room.

In this chapter, I will also detail another interesting quality of the group—the simultaneous influence of digital and traditional media for the group's development and for its continuation. Members rely on digital media—their email and secret Facebook group—to help coordinate and communicate, but also on the local newspaper to help construct and interpret views of their community. They use online tools to grow and connect with their group but meet in person offline. CWG reflects what media scholars would call the "hybrid media system,"[3] and what scholars of political organizing would see as the changing platform for where activism and expression take place.[4] CWG is further evidence that it is nearly impossible to sort political groups into offline or online categories.[5]

As I outline their development, it is important to note that CWG has continued since I started researching them in 2017. In fact, at the time I write this book, they are still secretive and still only women. Members have come and gone, and leadership has fluctuated, but they remain an important lifeline for progressives in their community.

Group Development

"I had you pegged for a liberal."

When I began to interview the women of CWG in April 2017, I heard various versions of their origin story. After getting through my first few questions that were meant to warm up our conversation—what they do/did for a living, how long they had lived in their county—it was my questions regarding how they heard about the group and what it was like when they joined that brought the women alive. Their individual recounting of the creation and development of their group told me a lot about their situation—how they compartmentalized politics and community, and why they established a secret organization in a community where there existed few secrets. It seems only fitting, then, that I start with the group's origin.

In November 2016, after Donald Trump won the presidential election, the two founders of CWG—whom I will call Joyce and Deborah—drove around their small town while crying. The women were reeling from Trump's victory and the place they felt the safest was in one of their cars with each other.

Over the next two years, I came to know these two women very well. Both women are in their 60s. Joyce has a raspy voice, a big bright smile, and a tone that makes you think you are in trouble. Deborah, on the other hand, is more reserved with an equally dry and warm disposition. Over the years, I came to notice that Deborah loves to whisper. Often when I saw her at meetings, she greeted me with a piece of information on the sly.

Joyce and Deborah had seen a lot of political change and upheaval over the past decades, but 2016 hit differently. Joyce had gone to bed right before the result was announced and awoke to her husband telling her the news, certain that he was playing a practical joke.

> He's really a jokester and he woke me up and he told me Trump had won and I really thought he was kidding me . . . he kept saying, "I'm not joking, I'm not joking," and I went into a complete tailspin, I was devastated. (Joyce, 2017)

Deborah reached out to Joyce in an effort to get support after hearing the devastating news. They had been friends since they separately moved to the county many years ago, and Joyce was one of the only people Deborah new who shared her beliefs. Deborah had previously been a grief counselor, which helped her recognize she needed help processing the election outcome.

> I was a therapist, and my specialty was grief counseling, so I think that's why I really recognized that I was grieving after the election. And I knew what I needed to do—I needed to get support. (Deborah, 2017)

Unbeknownst to them, at least 136 other women across their small county, around the same place where they drove their cars and cried, were feeling exactly the same thing. People—women especially—were angry they had watched the first female presidential candidate from a major political party lose to someone they deemed a misogynist. Some of this anger was directed at Trump, but some of it was directed at Americans writ large. Another member of CWG, upon hearing the results of the election, said she actually felt betrayed by her country.

> It was one of the most dreadful, heartbreaking, scary times I can actually re-member in my life and I'm 75.... You have the feeling of betrayal. You have the feeling of dear God in heaven, what is going to happen to my country? This man is crazy, and he's horrible about women—horrible... I cried for at least two days. (Roberta, 2017)

Another woman who would later join CWG said she watched the election returns alone that night simply because she had no one else with whom to watch them.

> I can best describe my personal experience as isolation. All of our social friends for the most part, I would say I have one friend who is the exception, but everybody else gathered together to celebrate what they saw as Trump's sure victory. So, I chose my conversations carefully and watched privately. (Alice, 2017)

As Joyce and Deborah drove around their little town and grieved what they considered to be the loss of their country to a "crazy man," they knew they needed more support. So, on November 13, 2016, Deborah sent the following email to eight people:

Box 3.1 Original Email From CWG Founder

Dear Friends—This has been such a shocking and tough week on all of us. The only way I have been able to cope is by reading everything I can find on "Coping with Election Results 2016." There are many many good things to glean from these articles, but two seem to stand out: Get together for sup-port, and Act. I would like to suggest that we get together for support and see where that takes us. For now, it may be as simple as grieving together.

> Let me know if you would like to do this and also if there are any women
> I have left out in the "TO" section. I would like to contact [another woman]
> in [town in the county] but don't have her e-mail address yet. [Woman in
> thread], if you know anyone in [town in the county], please forward this.
>   Deborah

This was a hard ask for the founders. For one, Deborah and Joyce had made distinct efforts *not* to be political during the campaign. Joyce self-described as "politically inactive," largely because she felt outnumbered by everyone around her, especially her family.

> I was not active. I had never been to a Democratic Party meeting. I had never done anything. My theory was my vote counts. I tried to talk to my family, who, my mother died, and she was a Democrat, but my sister's a wacko Republican. She's one of the conservative Christian far-right, I guess. She and I had many upsetting discussions and the rest of my family too, who told me that they were all going to vote for Trump and they didn't care if he's a bad person because they wanted *Roe v. Wade* overturned. (Joyce, 2017)

Joyce had experienced political disagreement, particularly with her family, and withdrawn from politics, outside of voting. Likewise, Deborah told me that she "avoided politics like the plague," because she felt it was too contentious, especially where she lived. Sending that email, she told me, was out of character for her.

> But when I sat there [after the election]—I mean this was really a moment for me—when I sat at that computer and thought, "I need to find some support to help grieve this." And I thought, "Am I going to do this? I just have to. Because if people like me don't stand up and speak that's why this happened." I have on the front of my CWG notebook, "The only thing necessary for the triumph of evil is for good people to do nothing," and I thought "okay, that's it, I'm doing it," and I sent the email. (Deborah, 2017)

That original email to eight got forwarded to many other women, almost all within the five- to 10-mile radius where Joyce and Deborah had driven the day after the election. While the email had been meant for eight, on the night of the convening, around 50 women showed up.[6] They followed a dark road to a barn and discovered a room full of women, many of whom they had no idea felt the way they did.

Every time I heard this story, the women described the scene with awe. Alice, who previously felt in complete "isolation," mentioned she felt the need to do a secret handshake upon arriving at the first meeting by nightfall.

> Just the day of driving in, in the middle of nowhere in the country and seeing taillights and taillights and taillights behind you. . . . I think I was the first one to pull in, and then every car after that—people getting out. It was truly the feeling of, like, we should do a secret handshake and look around us in the bushes. It was a very surreal kind of feeling. But knowing there were that many, and then seeing who they were and not having had a clue before that those people felt the same way as I did. I don't know, it was a very unique experience. (Alice, 2017)

Even though Deborah sent the original email outing her feelings about the election result, many women at that first meeting, although knowing Deborah previously, discovered her political leanings for the first time.

> Some of the women were shocked to see some of the other women walk in there. And they'd say "You? I didn't know!" And someone said to me, "Ah, I had you pegged for a liberal." (Deborah, 2017)

One of the people at this first meeting was Roberta, who had spent the days after the election pent up inside, crying about the result. Hearing about the meeting had revived her, so she recruited four more Democrats and went.

> I couldn't stop crying. And then somebody sent out the email that was forwarded by somebody else, to somebody else, and it ended up being forwarded to me, and I said, "Hell yes, I'm going." You know it was, if you're as devastated about the outcome of this election as I am, we're gonna get together and talk about it at this point, at this time, and this place. And so, I called another couple of friends and we ended up, four of us, ended up going. (Roberta, 2017)

Others described this first meeting not only as a surprise, but a sense of relief. Kathleen, another woman within Joyce and Deborah's county, walked into the room full of women she had previously just "assumed were Republican." "It was such a relief in some way," she told me. "It's like 'yes, we are out here, thank goodness, I didn't know.' It was a real feeling of joy and connectedness."

Another member, whom I'll call Melanie, was struck by how so many in such close proximity to her felt the same way she did. Decades of Republican dominance in their county, narratives of political homogeneity across rural Texas,[7] and an inactive local Democratic Party had convinced the women who showed up that night they were mostly alone in their beliefs.

> I just couldn't believe this group existed. That we were all from this area. It was quite a surprise to see that there were this many people that felt the same way I did and lived within 10–15 miles of me after feeling like I was the only blue dot in a sea of red dots. So, I was very happy—just felt very lucky. (Melanie, 2017)

This political connection to a physical place—that one's politics is closely related to or informed by one's geography—is a growing trend in people's political experience in the United States.[8] People live in neighborhoods, cities, and even counties that are increasingly politically like-minded. Whether their politics are shaped by their neighborhood or whether they choose their neighborhood based on their politics is not entirely clear.[9] What is clear is that people have political expectations about where they live—what their neighbors believe and how they should participate in politics.[10] In other words, politics and geography are uniquely informed by one another.

This is especially true in rural areas, where a sense of geographic identity is practically baked into the social fabric. People in rural areas go to schools with the town or county in the school's name, the local high school logo becomes the town emblem, and town rituals reflect the heritage and history of residents.[11] Consequently, rural residents can have an exceptionalism about their community—a sense of "us" versus "them"—more so than urban communities.[12]

The connection between place and politics is also one of the unique features of political organizing that, by the nature of federalism and political jurisdiction, often means focusing on distinct districts or precincts.[13] This is as true online as it is offline. Political organizations that often form as dispersed entities eventually form offshoots that are connected to in-person meetups or activism specific to local efforts.[14] Any of these connections between place and politics are perhaps why Melanie felt so "lucky" when she walked into that meeting. She could reconcile her local connection—her identity with her rural county—with her political beliefs and her desire to affect political change.

Many of the women who showed up that night were not part of the initial eight who received Deborah's email. The message had been dispersed through their individual networks, which allowed a greater reach than each member's network in isolation. This is one of the contributions of digital media to social movements and political organizing that sociologists and communication scholars have documented over the past decade.[15] But it was also especially helpful for covert recruitment,[16] a topic I return to in Chapter 5. The transmission of their message to others through email was also crucial. The women did not have to call other women to recruit them and risk relatives or spouses overhearing the conversation. All they had to do was click forward.

While the women's digital networks were useful for recruitment, they also presented challenges. Because the invitation to this original meeting had come through email, and sometimes by forwarding that was delayed, several of the women received notice only moments before the event even happened. Cynthia, for instance, was only aware of the invitation shortly before the meeting commenced, and she still managed to get there.

> I learned about it about 45 minutes before it was to take place. I just happened to check my email that evening, and then I called a friend and got a ride out there. And it was way out there, out in the country at a farm. . . . And we just went around that night and told about our feelings and some women cried. It was just an opening up of our hearts about what had happened. (Cynthia, 2017)

What had happened was that the women in that room had an awakening. They had realized their feelings of isolation were no longer in isolation, that they could be political in their community—perhaps not with it, but *within* it. Those women who had once thought that they would meet for "wine and solidarity" were now faced with the choice to retreat back into political dormancy or to keep it going. They decided on the latter.

Group Structure

"Some of the husbands don't know where these women are going."

After the first meeting, the women unanimously agreed that they should meet again. One of the original attendees, Roberta, volunteered to have the second meeting at her place as Deborah scrambled to manage the growing number of emails from people saying they wanted to come. She figured they would need some sort of political organization. The problem was, she did not know how to start one.

> I had never started anything like this—I had no clue what to do. So, I went online and I Googled "starting a political group." You're going to love this—the only website that addressed it was an anarchist website [laughs], nobody else talked about it. So, I copied it and I followed what it said. It said you should have a broad political goal, to give everybody a job, for nobody to be in charge, and we've honored this—that you rotate leadership—and to have fun. (Deborah, 2017)

This development was also the case for many other bourgeoning political activists across the country, for whom digital media also played an important role. Activist groups popped up across Facebook, many as closed or "secret" groups and many of which were run by suburban housewives or people who had previously been politically disengaged.[17] Groups like "Pantsuit Nation" and "Indivisible" gained millions of followers across the country, all filled with the same energy as CWG at these early meetings:, and with the need to do something and the uncertainty of where to start.

At CWG's next meeting, on November 26, 2016, Deborah mentioned her research on how to form a political organization, and the women broke into small groups to discuss what their name and goals should be. The women decided to take minutes at this meeting, which could later be emailed to everyone on the original list. This meant that even those who were not in attendance could stay in touch with the group as it developed. In the minutes from that second meeting, the group "decided to shelve the name choice, and wait until we have solidified our goals." They then formed a "focus group," whose job it would be to "discuss the ideas suggested and narrow them down succinctly." Deborah, who was not part of the early focus group, recognized that two other subgroups coexisted: those who were looking to act immediately, and those who were interested more in the longevity of the group.

> A lot of people were impatient with us taking time to delineate our goals and objectives—they just wanted to jump in and start working. But those of us who had been involved in something like this knew we just couldn't do that, we had to build our foundation. (Deborah, 2017)

It was at the third meeting, on January 3, 2017, that they named their group and that the focus group, having met and discussed ideas generated at the second meeting, unveiled a working mission statement and goals. Even though they had grown from digital means, the group had much of the formality and structure of offline political organizations of decades past.[18] The first statement of their goals read in the minutes as follows:

Box 3.2 CWG Goals

We, a diverse group of Texas, District [# of their county], women, are concerned about how recent electoral results affect the present and future of our country, and we believe that grass roots action is required.

- We will SUPPORT and ADVOCATE for each other and other at risk and marginalized people
- We will EDUCATE ourselves and others on issues and legislative actions, and ADOVCATE for our beliefs
- We will TAKE ACTION together and independently for what we believe is crucial for our country

---

The group's goals were intended to be hierarchical. To get to resistance, particularly for a group who had avoided politics, the women had to first find social support for their views and get educated about what politics entailed and what was on the agenda. Joyce described the goals as building up to resistance.

> I happen to believe that support and education is fine in order to get to the resistance. I think the resistance is the most important part because if we

just remain as we are, we're going up the creek. I mean our democracy is actually in danger of collapsing is how I feel. (Joyce, 2017)

Such a hierarchy offered flexibility to members who were perhaps less willing to engage in the full fire hose of activism of which other members were more eager to be a part. This variety in activity and the associated "transaction costs,"[19] or resources required to partake in those activities, meant members could give whatever they had to give. A member I'll call Connie, for instance, knew she was unwilling to go to protests, but felt she could still be a part of the group because she could do more behind the scenes work, and the group did not demand more.

> I was able to see what was going on and to see what I could do in my comfort zone 'cause some of the women, you know, they go to Austin, and they bring letters to congressmen, that sort of thing. And you know, that's not anything that I would really be interested in doing, but you know, just by going, and by reading the minutes they send out, you can kind of pick and choose what you'd like to do. (Connie, 2017)

That the group's mission ranged along a degree of publicness reflects the diversity of its members. Yet that diversity of experience and intention was not always an easy mixture when members felt a sense of urgency to do something rather than sit back and build support or get "educated." Paula, a member I spoke to several months after the group was formally established, expressed frustration with the amalgamation of willing and motivated activists with those who, as they saw it, just wanted a "support group."

> So, I have felt as an individual, trying to see what I can do but I don't really want to spend time trying to drum up support amongst a group that I perceive as sort of on the fence still. You know, sort of mulling over their own personal comfort levels with activism. (Paula, 2017)

Still, others who were previously more politically active felt they were doing something good by engaging those who were new to politics and being respectful of their apprehension. A woman I'll call Nancy has been a lifelong activist in the Democratic Party. Helping many of the women new to political activism learn the ropes was one part of the group she found most important.

And it's empowering to have other people thinking and doing things along with you. I have to say that I feel like we are helping a group of women who've never done anything like this before. And so now, I feel some obligation to do that and be there and help everybody come to places where they can, you know, be positive and feel that we are doing something. (Nancy, 2017)

To meet the diversity of goals, interests, and "comfort levels," the group developed a committee structure that allowed members to focus on issues to which they were the most committed and to do as much or as little as they were comfortable doing. Members started or joined committees focusing on healthcare and the Affordable Care Act, public education, women's issues, gun control, voting, the National Endowment for the Arts, the environment, immigration, science, and marginalized and LGBTQ rights. According to the minutes from the fourth meeting, on March 7, 2017, the time at which these committees were established, each committee and its respective chair were asked to "research and educate us about what Congress is doing, and what we need to be aware of for actions in response to both Federal and State threats to our democracy." This was the urgency and sincerity with which the members of CWG approached their work.

As time went on, the committees became less and less a cornerstone of the group's structure. At the fifth meeting, on April 4, 2017, nearly half of the committee chairs were "not present and no report was given." In later meetings, several committees continued, including the immigration and healthcare committees, but the rest fell by the wayside. By the tenth meeting, in September 2017, no committees were even mentioned.

It is possible that the failure of the committee structure was in part due to members' earlier concerns that the group was more a self-help sanctuary and not one oriented around activism. That almost all committee chairs, except for Alice, continued coming to the meetings and participating in the group's activities suggests otherwise. Instead, it is likely the committee structure failed to continue because what the women truly wanted was a place to be together—to feel the sheer volume of each other's presence after feeling alone for so long. Perhaps the committee structure demanded too much from many women for whom politics had long been a place of conflict and risk, of avoidance and suppression, and they needed to practice politics before jumping in headfirst.

Regardless, what is striking about the existence of the committees at all is that, despite the changing political tides and the rising number of new political activists, committees felt like the *old* way of organizing. This was the approach taken decades before—before political organizing became more about expressing oneself than following procedures[20]—and before the age of "slacktivism" and online petitions.[21] Yet this was how CWG members approached their new organization, because it was how many of them had last organized many years earlier.

In addition to committees, at the seventh meeting the women agreed they would need a plan to run meetings efficiently. Efficiency was often a critique from those who had attempted to join the local Democratic Party—pointing to the party's "inefficiency" and "monotonous meetings" as evidence for the party's dismal performance since the 1990s. One of the ways the women gave structure to their meetings was through ritual. In May 2017, the minutes reflect that they initiated a practice of starting meetings with the pledge of allegiance, and this continued until the last meeting I attended in November 2018. Only once did the facilitator forget the flag, and the women had to pledge to a flag on a toothpick in their apple slices.

Beyond meeting rituals, the women agreed they should have rules dictating when, how, and who gets to speak. At their meeting in September 2017, they implemented four rules:

Box 3.3 CWG Meeting Rules

1. **One person** will speak at a time
2. Members will **actively listen** to the speaker rather than anxiously waiting to express a point of view
3. The **facilitator** recognizes each person to speak
4. Each facilitator **reviews these points of order** with the next

---

With the rules came a timekeeper who would help the facilitator stick to a strict schedule. In the meeting minutes from that September, the group decided that these rules would be good practice for talking with the "other side," (i.e., Republicans), stating that they "will assist us as we work on talking with and understanding people with political views that differ from ours." Although these rules were originally developed as a proactive measure against the Democratic Party's dysfunction, one of the active Democrats in CWG ended up taking these practices to the party itself.

It was at the third meeting that the women decided they would have a confidentiality agreement. This struck me as coming late in their development, since, after all, the first time they had met had already felt like an underground society. A few members, but not the founders, were the first to bring up the confidentiality agreement to the group. Some had said they thought it was implied, while others thought it was a problematic idea. Eventually they came to the decision that they would have a formal confidentiality statement to which every member would have to agree. In the minutes, the confidentiality statement was featured as a bulleted list:

Box 3.4 CWG Confidentiality Agreement

---

1. **Confidentiality**: After discussion, the group decided that:
   - No one would speak for the group and
   - We will not speak for each other unless previously discussed and agreed upon
   - Our identities would be protected and not revealed outside the group
   - Email addresses will only be shared personally if desired; the group list of emails will not be shared, even within the group, until ballots are in and counted
   - No references will be made by any individual group member or "the group" in any publications
   - Recruiting of new members is up to each individual, with those you know well
   - No mass public recruiting at this point

In later reflections on that decision, the women had mixed feelings. Some wanted exactly what the agreement outlined—a group identity and membership that were both hidden. Others wanted the group to be public, but the membership to be hidden. CWG followed the same struggle over visibility that other social movements and political organizations have followed. The publicness of a movement or organization can vary drastically—from completely covert to open secrets.[22] This is a hard decision when members disagree about how open and visible they want to be.[23] A CWG member present at the meeting, whom I will call Dawn, felt those who were comfortable being public should be able to make statements on behalf of the group without revealing who is in it.

> Nothing can be said publicly in the name of the group because of the secrecy. And I think . . . I think we should not be secret. But I think that the women's identities, and that group who want to be secret, should be protected. (Dawn, 2017)

Others indicated that although they thought the secrecy was important, it might be impermanent. Kathleen, also at the third meeting, said that while she was not sure how long the group would or should be secret, at the time she thought secrecy was important for her personally and for the comfort of other members.

> At this time, I agree with that. Again, because it [being a progressive] is a minority. Several of the women that I did not know were Democrats are actually shop owners in [a small town in the county] and they feel like it would hurt their business if people knew that and I agree with them. I think it would. So, you know, I just like everybody to feel okay with things and if it's not okay with them, I want to respect that. For me personally, I don't feel like I'm ready to have my picture in the paper, or have my name in a newspaper article, so no, no I wouldn't feel comfortable with that. (Kathleen, 2017)

This concern with being publicly "outed" as a Democrat was one of the cornerstones for the petition for secrecy, and one that is both conceptually and linguistically similar to secret organizations from other eras or social groups. It is an understatement to say there is a long history of people organizing in secret along lines of race/ethnicity or gender/sexuality. The Underground Railroad, for instance, might be the most accessible (if not obtuse) example.[24] But there were also smaller movements that used secrecy to organize for action or solidarity, like local slave communities organizing for micro-resistance in the antebellum South,[25] or the suffragette movements in the United States and the United Kindgom.[26]—and these are only the examples that can be largely seen as *pro*-democratic.[27]

In contemporary contexts, many people of color or those from marginalized social identities still create separate or hidden spaces to build networks of solidarity,[28] to exchange resources like information or connections,[29] or to avert state-sanctioned persecution.[30] Even in terms of phrasing, the notion of "outing" comes directly from the gay community and was made especially popular during the gay liberation movement. Many members of the LGBTQ community had to (and have to) keep their sexuality and/or sexual and gender identity hidden less they risk ostracism, retaliation, persecution, or even violence.[31] In fact, the notion of being "outed" versus "coming out" is an important distinction for the LGBTQ community, as it is for CWG. When someone is "outed," their sexuality and/or gender identity is revealed outside of their control or without their permission—either executed or influenced by a third party[32]—whereas "coming out" entails a decision to reveal this information by the individual's own design or on their own terms.[33] In a similar way, members of CWG faced the fear of being "outed" as Democrats, either by another member mentioning their name or through their public affiliation with the group. This concern would also shape the membership of the group to come, a point I address in greater detail in Chapters 4 and 6.

In the end, the women agreed on confidentiality, which took different language over time (see Figure 3.1), some begrudgingly and some with a sense of relief. That they had each member agree to the confidentiality statement shows just how much they relied on collective complicity—if one member messed up, it could mean another was outed. I sensed that most women respected that, even if it meant their personal vision for the group was not possible.

As might be expected, communicating while remaining secret proved challenging. At first, the group relied heavily on email. This allowed the women to communicate easily from one to many, but it also had its limitations. Women in the group who wanted to share information with all of the other members had to go through the email administrator (Joyce), who then had to send the information out to the entire group. Yet with an overwhelming amount of content, she was simply unable to quickly and efficiently compile and forward all the information to members of the group. "I will acknowledge receipt of your email," she wrote to members, "unless, however, it is extremely time-sensitive, and until we solidify our group goals, I will hold the links in a file and then send the file to the group with all the links in one email between now and the next meeting in January. I am not in a position to do this more frequently."

Just as in other covert networks, email meant communication among CWG members during this developmental phase was highly centralized. Without knowing it, the women had actually chosen the mathematically *best*

Figure 3.1 Confidentiality Statement at CWG Meeting, November 2017.

route—according to social network research—for secret organizations to communicate during their initial development.[34] Keeping the communication centralized through the email listserv—and through Joyce—allowed the women more control over what was said and to whom it was said, but it also decreased the probability of exposure of the entire group, while increasing the risk of exposure for Joyce.

Although email helped them centralize information and limited members' risk of exposure, it was less helpful in allowing the women to communicate interpersonally or for members to share information directly with one another. At the third meeting, on January 3, 2017, the members discussed whether they could rely on a Facebook group as a tool for communication between members directly. In the minutes from that meeting, it was clear the women were uncertain about Facebook as an accessible tool for all members. "Some members do not use Facebook," the minutes read, "others do not text, and some do not email. Most used cell phones on some level."

As a result, they decided to stick with the inefficient email system for a little longer. Joyce asked that they be patient and allow her a 10-day turnaround time, and they agreed. To see if their email system could be less centralized, the women brought up the idea of sharing email addresses for individual members so they could contact each member directly. Several members were uncomfortable with this, expressing concern that their contact information would be shared with members outside of the group without their knowing. This was, after all, only the third meeting, and the women were still uneasy that they could be "outed." To assuage this concern, the group established an opt-in system whereby members could share contact information at their own discretion.

By the fourth meeting, on February 7, 2017, the women were ready for something new. Email had been clunky—sending messages to four or five people at once meant threads were long and there was still uneasiness about whether messages could be forwarded to email addresses outside of the group. In response, at this meeting the women agreed to establish a secret Facebook group for "dispensing information among the members." Paula was put in charge of building and managing the new Facebook group, while Alice was put in charge of teaching people exactly how to use Facebook through a "hands-on Facebook lesson." Several members did not know how to join or use a group on Facebook.

Given the confidentiality agreement and self-admitted technical challenges of many of the members, the creation of the secret Facebook group was not without confusion or conflict. One member I spoke with several months after the group was created mentioned that she was still unsure about how the Facebook group was able to remain secret. "We're on a Facebook page, that's totally, I don't know how they do that, but it doesn't go to anybody but the members." Confusion around the group's visibility is reasonable given that it is often unclear who exactly sees what on one's social media page, something scholars would call the "imagined audience" of social networking sites.[35]

Another member, whom I'll call Gail, spoke about the secret group almost as if it was supernatural. Although she used Facebook frequently to connect with old friends and family members, she was uncertain about the visibility of her posts and her membership. In fact, even though Gail had already joined the Facebook group, she asked me for assurance that her friends outside of the group would not see her posts within the secret group. What was striking was that despite seeing the Facebook group as a black box—to the point that she verified with me that her posts were secure—Gail told me she could "trust it."

> For me it's really kind of crazy—and you may know better about this, I'm very technically challenged—but what gets posted on the private Facebook group shows up in my regular Facebook page, but supposedly nobody else can read it on my Facebook page? It doesn't go to all my Facebook friends, but it goes to me in both places? I don't know how that works, but I trust it. (Gail, 2017)

One of the concerns with the creation of the secret Facebook group for CWG was upholding the confidentiality agreement online. It was easy to gain compliance in person—the women just had each prospective member physically sign an agreement. Online, this compliance was a different story. To assure that the same confidentiality was upheld online as it was offline, the group required those joining the online group to first agree to the confidentiality statement before being admitted. Anyone invited by an existing member to join the Facebook group was first required to agree to the confidentiality statement and send a statement expressing their agreement to the group's administrator, Paula.

For the most part, incoming members who were added to the Facebook group obliged. On one occasion, someone who had been invited to join their group by another member had been unwilling to agree to the confidentiality agreement and was prohibited from joining.

Although the confidentiality continued, over the two years that I followed CWG, the Facebook group became more and more an ancillary resource. In the beginning, it was explicitly used to post calls to action "in the order of effectiveness." In other words, those actions that the women believed could make the most difference were posted first, including visiting a representative at a town hall or in person, sending postcards to voters on special elections, or sending letters directly to representatives' offices. Unlike other types of political "calls to action" that have erupted since political organizations have transitioned to online,[36] these calls to action were not shareable beyond the group—only the women of CWG saw them and only they could respond.

Beyond that, the women used the Facebook group primarily as a tool between meetings where they could communicate with one another. Over time, however, this became less and less the case. The group had fewer posts and received fewer interactions from members. The email listserv once again became the primary way that the women stayed in contact. This seemed partly because the woman who had run the Facebook group, Paula, quit the group and moved out of the state, and partly because the women were more familiar with using email as an organizing tool. They knew how to attach documents, include links, and send replies through email. While not everyone in the group used Facebook, everyone seemed to use email. It also seemed like the members who had been previously reticent about providing their email address for interpersonal contact were now more comfortable sharing that information with others in the group.

Such forms of private communication were especially important given that other mediums were unreliable for some members. For instance, many women in the group had husbands who supported Trump, who did not know the group existed, or who did not know exactly where their wives went when going to meetings. This meant phone calls, letters, or other more obvious and even physical forms of connection would alienate those members who were keeping secrets even in their own home.

The political disagreement between these romantic partners could range from open conflict to complete avoidance. For some it was debilitating, for others it was something they learned to live with. Linda, for example, leaned heavily on friends to talk politics because she disagreed with her husband too much to have political conversations together. "Before this last election there was so much bitterness, including with my own husband who was supporting Trump," she told me, "we just couldn't even discuss it."

Beyond talking about politics, Linda felt her husband would not understand or appreciate her participation in CWG. In fact, she did not tell her husband she was in the group or where she was going when she left for meetings.

E: So, does he know you're in the group?

L: No, he doesn't really know anything about it. . . . I just—I don't discuss it. I don't even think he knows about the group. He knows I go someplace but he doesn't know the nature of what it's about. (Linda, 2017)

Others disagreed with their husbands, but still talked about it. One member, Barbara, said that she and her husband would have heated conversations about the election to the point where it became hard "to even have a conversation" with her husband about politics.

My particular situation was a little bit difficult because my husband did vote for Trump and we had terrible discussions. He couldn't pick Hillary, and felt she was concealing and broke the law, and could not forgive that part of her, if forgiving needed to be. And, of course, Bernie Sanders was way out there for him. He wanted a change in the tax code, he wants more money in his pocket. He falls into a tax bracket where we are paying quite a few taxes and that bothers [him]. (Barbara, 2017)

Oftentimes, this disconnect meant that the women did not tell their husbands about the group or lied about where they went when going to meetings. Ann told me about her husband, who supported Trump in the general election. The political distance between her and her husband, and even between her and her community, was painful and scary for Ann as she tried to reconcile caring for someone who supports a candidate she was not only against, but feared and resented.

I mean my husband was not a Trump supporter from the very beginning but certainly when he seemed to be beginning to emerge as the front runner, got on board with that I think pretty quickly. . . . Those are the things that are scary—we talked about fear—scary that even good people like my husband, like a lot of other people in the community who are doing a lot of good things—the people at the food pantry, at the whatever—can be triggered like that and/or be taken in by someone like Donald Trump. And I would never speak this in terms of expressing it—to me, it's like Hitler, who could persuade, who could convince people it was somebody else who was causing these problems. (Ann, 2017)

That distance and the group's confidentiality also kept Ann from telling her husband about CWG, choosing instead to use another group of which she was a part as her cover.

E: Does your husband know that you're in the group?

A: He actually does not per se. I have told him that—when I've gone to the group—that I'm going to meet with some women about issues about [another nonprofit group]. But yes, he doesn't know that there's really this group, or how many, or that it's more than just an opportunity to talk about things from the [other nonprofit group's] perspective. (Ann, 2017)

These mismatched partnerships sit in contrast to a growing trend in the United States. Compared to any time before, people are now more likely to already have a spouse who shares their political partisanship, or at least are more likely to select a romantic partner from the same political party.[37] Yet, like the members of CWG, there are still a good number of people— Republicans and Democrats—married to someone from the other side.[38] CWG offers evidence that cross-cutting romantic partnerships have consequences for political behavior and where people go to engage in or discuss politics.

Unsuspecting husbands were not exclusive to those in partnerships where there was a political mismatch, however. Nancy, whose partner knew she went to meetings, said he seemed supportive and unconcerned, almost playful, after she told him. Although she did not share the name of the group or who was in it, Nancy and her partner came up with their own pseudonym so they could talk about it while upholding, at least somewhat, the group's confidentiality.

N: I go home, I have a boyfriend, so I go home, and he knows. I'm not telling people . . . I'm sticking to that "say nobody's name," but I think—I mean he thinks sometimes I overdo, I get involved in too much. But in this one, he's been really supportive, and I think he sees it too that, you know, it's a good thing. So, he's kinda proud of me doing it.

E: He doesn't know the name, but he knows it exists?

N: No, he still calls us . . . he goes, "What do you call yourself?" I said, "I'm going for WWW—Worried Women Warriors." It was just being silly, you know, and I held up the three fingers, you know, a secret sign. So he still calls us the WW—the Worried Women— and I don't think he has any idea what Senate district we're in or who's coming. (Nancy, 2017)

For others, despite shared political beliefs, the risk of letting a partner know about the group overwhelmed their desire to share that part of themselves. When I first spoke to Connie in 2017, she told me her husband "pretty much feels the same way" as her about politics, but she felt for the women in the group who could not express their political opinions to their husbands and who had not told their husbands about the group's existence.

The other ones are unfortunate enough to be married to somebody who is for Trump, and I guess they're not even comfortable, you know, coming out in front of their own spouse, in front of their husband. And you know, some of the husbands don't know where these women are going. It's crazy. (Connie, 2017)

When I spoke to Connie again in 2018, she mentioned to me that in fact *her* husband did not know she was in the group or where she was going when she went to meetings; she worried that if she told him he would, accidentally, out the group to others in the community.

C: I haven't told my husband, no one really knows . . .
E: You haven't told him about the group?
C: You know, I don't remember if I mentioned it to him . . . it's been so long that he's kind of off in his own world anyway. But I'm afraid that he would slip up. (Connie, 2018)

There were other ways, outside of staying tight-lipped at home, that CWG has kept a less conspicuous profile from others in the community. The group established early on that they would meet at night and rotate the location of the meeting—a tactic common to other secret societies of notably different purpose.[39] But this was not always the case.

For their second meeting, the group met at a more noticeable location closer to town and received what Nancy called a "trickle back" from the community about concerns that women had been conspicuously meeting at night.

We have one of our members, her husband—and once again I'm going, "Really?"—he's running for a Republican commissioner's position, I think.

And so, he was at one of the—the Republican women have a club here and meet and have talks, lectures, and coffee and stuff—and he said it had come up that "oh, yeah, there were these liberal women meeting," which I think is kind of good because they're scared. And the funny part is that they were saying hundreds, there were *hundreds!* [laughs] Okay, let them think that there are hundreds of us organizing! (Nancy, 2017)

After this speculation, the women never met in that space again. The group continued rotating meeting locations until April 2018, when they settled on a permanent space on Roberta's property. The new meeting space was big with lots of seating, and you had to take two different gravel roads to get there.

The founding of a secret organization of grandmothers might sound improbable. Just as I had been skeptical of their existence at the beginning of my research, there might be many readers of this book who think of CWG's story as an abnormality. Although I cannot speak to the exact generalizability of the conditions in which CWG formed, I can say that their existence is not in isolation.

The survey data offers some evidence that this is true. For instance, from the U.S. sample, around 9% (100 respondents) said they had met in private to secretly discuss politics with others either online or in person over the past two years. This was true in the Texas sample as well. Nine percent of respondents (94 people) said they had done this over the past two years. CWG Is not a wild card.

Personal Development

"She says, 'I don't even know a Democrat,' and I said, 'Hello?'"

Over the time I got to know the members of CWG, I came to see that the women's individual origin stories—their personal development—was just as important to understanding why they kept their politics a secret. For instance, many of the women in CWG were completely new to political activism, some were flexing atrophied political muscles, and a few were lifelong political activists. Shirley, a longtime resident of the county, had previously been involved in politics, but had switched parties frequently.

E: Were you or are you active in the Democratic Party in [the county]?

S: No, no, I'm not. I've never really been in any political party. I used to run campaigns many years ago, and I never worried, my husband called me a political whore because I didn't care what party they were. If I liked the candidate, I would handle their campaign. And the candidates I worked with, some were Republican, some were Democrats, some were Independents, some were who knows. It was never important to me. And when I met my husband he was very Republican and he didn't quite get it—why I could do both. (Shirley, 2017)

Many of the women stopped being political when they moved to the county and saw how conservative it was. Linda stopped talking about politics to others in the community or doing public political activities when she moved to the county about 30 years ago. Previously, however, she had been a very active Democrat in the state.

And during that time—that was when the women's movement was very very strong. It was the early days of the women's movement and I was very much involved in that and I actually was one of the people who signed the petition in *Roe v. Wade*. The actual petition to legislate abortion, which led to *Roe v. Wade*. And I worked in Sissy Farenthold's campaign. . . . And I would canvass the neighborhood and take leaflets and pamphlets door-to-door and try to talk to people, and my kids were little then, so I had them with me carrying shopping bags filled with political literature and that sort of thing. . . . So yeah, at that time I was very politically active. And then I didn't continue, you know, doing things like that, but I always was very interested in what was going on in terms of policy and legal things and human rights, all different kinds of civil rights and human rights and women's rights and that sort of thing. (Linda, 2017)

Before she moved to the county in which CWG was formed, Roberta had run for office in her small town outside of the major metropolis where she lived. When I asked her whether she had continued that activism in her current county, she said she had not.

I was not active in the party here in [CWG county], but I had been active in the party in [her former county]. And I had actually run for [office] in my little town. . . . So I was somewhat, not very politically active, but somewhat politically active. I was there when we formed, way back in the 70s, when we formed the [local] women's political caucus, and I was very active at that point. (Roberta, 2017)

Beyond their past experience with political activism, the women also had poignant experiences with politics with regard to their families. There was, among the women of CWG, a common negative socialization around politics that led them to be wary of political conflict. This was especially true for the women who had grown up in the South with politically and socially conservative families. Scholars know a lot about the effects of "political socialization" in families for information-seeking, preference formation, and voting,[40] but know very little about how political socialization in families specifically affects political expression.

For example, I sometimes heard stories from the women recounting memories of conflicts they had about politics as children, or what it was like when they first challenged the prevailing politics of their families. One story was especially horrifying. When I spoke with Virginia in 2018, she told me the story of her "first political argument" when she was eight years old, which she had with her father, a "Reconstruction Democrat." She recalled driving with her father to her extended family's house for Thanksgiving dinner in a still very racially segregated Texas.

> We were driving over there, and my dad said look at that car sitting next to us—we were stopped at a light. And there was a White man driving and a Black woman in the front seat sitting there, and back in those days, well, you don't know except for studying it, but back in those days, you know, if you're taking the maid home, she sat in the back, or if you're the chauffeur or the person driving, she sat in the back. It was all very very clear what everybody's roles were. And here this car drives up and they're both sitting there chatting—and no, that's just not the way it was supposed to be in Houston, Texas. And I just said, "What's wrong with it?" You know? Well, I got a lecture all the way there. And then, seriously, when we went inside, he said, "Come here, stand up here, I want everyone to hear what I'm raising." (Virginia, 2018)

Virginia then had to stand in front of her disapproving family and tell them what she had said about the White man and the Black woman sitting in the front seat together as her family jeered. Certainly, these were formative memories for her, not just about politics and race, but about politics as a source of *shame*. Virginia took a stance against her family, was shamed for it, and it still stuck out in her mind when thinking about it over 50 years later. This was different than the political shame associated with peer pressure that has been carefully researched with regard to political campaigning and participation.[41] This was shame that was internalized, shame that was associated with expressing disagreement.

Joyce told me a similar story of receiving backlash from family when detailing not only her political beliefs, but also her personal experiences. After complications around a faulty IUD, Joyce had to have a life-saving abortion to remove a fetus that had become embedded, along with the IUD, in her uterine wall. Years later, when she told her family about the abortion, she had many family members ostracize her almost completely, while others prohibited her from interacting with children in the family.

> Years earlier, when they found out—when I told them the story of my abortion, part of those family members quit speaking to me. And I more or less quit going to family events because I couldn't speak up on any number of topics that a progressive could normally speak up on. . . . And in fact, at another person's house, we [she and her husband] were not allowed to give anything to their children or be around certain family members, because of our politics. It wasn't even strictly politics, it was just our attitudes regarding our thinking, like accepting gays, or accepting gay marriage, or anything that would be off of the straight and narrow. (Joyce, 2017)

Others experienced less ostracism from family, and more shock and judgment from friends and members of their social circles. Years ago, when Roberta ran for office in her local county, she recalled having a volunteer who at first wanted to be like her, but upon hearing she was a Democrat, felt differently.

> I had some wonderful volunteers, but we were fighting a real problem from the city, and so, this woman who was the wife of a former mayor, well she went home at lunch and went out and bought herself a T-shirt to match mine because she wanted to be in the same color [laughs]. And she was talking during the time we were sitting out there and, you know, pushing poll cards, and people going into vote and everything,

and the conversation went around to the Democrats and she says, "I don't even know a Democrat," and I said, "Hello?" So here I am, I am a Democrat. And she said, "No you are not," and I said, "Well, yes, I am." (Roberta, 2017)

There was a clear parallel in the stories I heard with the stories of other marginalized identities. For instance, I often heard the women reference their "political coming out," which borrowed the language directly from the experiences of LGBTQ individuals and the often horrific experience of ostracism from families, friends, and even entire institutions.[42] Linda told me the story of her political coming out to a friend from her church.

One person, I was riding in the car with this person, and she was driving, and I said, she says, "Well I don't even know anybody that voted for Bill Clinton," and I said "Well, now you do." And she practically, and this is the truth, she practically ran off the road. She was so shocked. And she said, "I can't believe you voted for Bill Clinton," and I said, "Well, I did." (Linda, 2017)

Many of these women had learned that politics could be a relational-explosive device. Expressing political dissent could lead to isolation from family, judgments of their morality, social distance, and even personal shame. These were formative narratives in their minds that linked being politically contentious with being socially undesirable. Sometimes, as in the case of Virginia and Joyce, dissenting felt like being a bad person altogether. But there were other aspects of their lives that made their politics appear as a source of division and that made them feel the loneliness and isolation they felt so strongly before they found each other. They could always open the local newspaper.

Digital and Traditional Media

"Local people reading the paper love these little fights that erupt."

Just as the members of CWG sought out and self-selected a group of like-minded others, so too did they seek out and self-select like-minded media. This kind of "selective exposure," scholars argue, has become more possible in the contemporary media environment because the sheer volume of media options has expanded over the past three decades.[43] When I asked the women of CWG how they got information about politics, many named news outlets that are typically seen as liberal-leaning. For instance, MSNBC, NPR, CNN, *The New York Times*, and *The Washington Post* were frequently named. That the women commonly cited national news outlets is also consistent with the growing tendency for people to focus on national politics over local politics.[44] Facebook, in particular, was a direct source for many of the women. Some, like Linda, acknowledged that they were likely getting only one side of the story but had no intention of seeking out the other side.

> A lot of stuff on Facebook. I've unfriended a lot of people so pretty much the only streaming I get on Facebook pretty much boils down to being all-political and just the friends I'm in agreement with. I'm really not too interested in trying to convince anybody to believe the way I do. (Linda, 2017)

Others, like Bonnie, were more concerned that Facebook might be exposing them to false or inaccurate information and made more intentional efforts to double-check what they saw there.

> I guess our main information is MSNBC. I get a lot of things on Facebook if it's a source, like the main newspapers, and then I'll go look at the article. I know there's a lot of on Facebook that's very radical and they'll take a little information and make a great big story out of it. Those sources I generally don't even look at. (Bonnie, 2017)

Given that the women live in a place with a large majority of conservatives, they gave special attention and commitment to not only trying to find news that was more balanced, but to "keeping up" with the opposition's argument. Deborah, for instance, said she and her husband read *The Wall Street Journal* to know what conservatives are thinking.

> And then my husband takes *The Wall Street Journal*, he reads it front to back every day and he'll tell me what he read. *The Wall Street Journal* is conservative, so you get another side. So that's how I kind of keep up with what the opposition has to say. (Deborah, 2017)

Perhaps keeping up with the other side was particularly relevant for these women because they so often interacted with people from it. That strategy could serve the women in two ways. On the one hand, intentionally selecting what they saw as conservative news allowed them to know what conservatives are thinking so that when they interacted, they knew what to say. On the other hand, selective exposure to conservative news offered the women information about what *not* to say; that is, it was a way to know what was contentious and to simply avoid it.

Although it was not clear whether the women consumed conservative media for these reasons, it was clear that they consumed it out of strategy and not out of interest. For instance, Barbara, whose husband voted for Donald Trump and remains conservative, mentioned she would read *The Drudge Report* so that she knew what he was hearing and thinking as a result.

> I read *The Washington Post*, *The Atlantic Monthly* is a magazine from time to time that I read. I kind of take a look at *Texas Monthly*, but I don't hold it up as something that's too informative because it's sometimes a lot of fluff. A few issues back they outlined the worst and best politicians in the state of Texas, which is always a good thing. Online, when something comes up, when I want to make sure I have the opposition's views so that I know if it's really what I think it is, I will go online and just Google it. My husband is an avid reader of *The Drudge Report*, which scares me, so I do have to from time to time take a look at it to know what he's reading. (Barbara, 2017)

When it came to news in their local community, nearly all of the women mentioned that they read the local newspaper. The paper, which serves the entire county, went online in the past five years with a firewall prohibiting full articles from being seen without a subscription. As a result, a good portion of the town still subscribes to the daily print paper. Almost all local and election information comes through the paper, which means that to hear about anything going on in the county, you have to subscribe. Given its sheer reach and significance to the community, the women often referred to having your name or picture in the paper as the ultimate public "outing."

The paper served an important role in sending cues about the community because there was so little choice of local media.[45] It was often the thing the women referenced when I asked them to tell me how they thought people in their community think. When I spoke with Nancy in 2018, she saw the county through the lens of the newspaper as a complex mix of people disconnected from politics and people very passionate about politics.

[The county] is just this interesting thing—of people not caring at all and then very passionate or people just concerned about getting their kids to school with plenty of new pencils or do your cows have ticks too bad. (Nancy, 2018)

Cathy, who moved to the county 18 years ago, said she could tell very quickly how conservative the community was from her church and from the local paper.

Well, I don't know that I have the pulse of the whole community. I've not been there forever, and so my contacts, mainly, are through the church. It's predominantly a Republican congregation, but more and more in the last few years, people have either come or they have come out as Democrats. And so, I can't tell you about the whole community, but I'd say just from what I see in the paper, and what I hear a little bit from other people in the community, it is pretty much conservative. (Cathy, 2017)

For others, they felt that the local newspaper not only reflected more conservative views but was also explicitly hostile to liberal ones. In one case, Connie recounted seeing columns in the local paper chastising liberals for not moving on after Trump's election.

C: And you know, just watching the crap that people were writing into the paper that kind of pissed me off. You know, it was like "Oh, poor little liberals, they didn't win, so now they're upset," I'm like, "Are you serious?" I mean that's really what they thought. These people are just ignorant or I don't know what's wrong with 'em.

E: So there was stuff in the paper, too?

C: Oh yeah, it went on for a couple of months. It's finally died down a bit now, but for several months after the election it just went on and on. And also, after the women's march, you know women would write in and say, "You know, I don't . . . what is this all about? What is the issue? I don't feel like I've suffered in my life, I'm perfectly happy." And you're fucking probably White too, you know? I don't know, people were so freaking simple-minded. When they wrote into the paper, it was a lot of this "get over it you people, get over it, he won, let's try to be friends and go forward." I mean, I'm like . . . it's unbelievable. (Connie, 2017)

The women spoke most vehemently and frequently about the local newspaper's letters-to-the-editor section. Paula, while not an avid reader of the section, noted how important the newspaper's letters-to-the-editor section was in the community, if only to bring people into sensationalized conflict.

> They [the people in the community] like the letters to the editor because people do read them. Because local people reading the paper love these little fights that erupt. I don't know how constructive it is, I think that's probably why I haven't jumped into that. (Paula, 2017)

Others were explicitly critical of the kinds of things being said in the letters, not only their ideological leaning, but their hostility toward the other side. Joyce told a story of a schism, of which the county had many, around religion and the town square. The conflict had resulted in mudslinging.

J: Well, the local paper, I read it, but I don't get the news from it. If it's in the local paper, it already happened. . . . The letters to the editor has had an ongoing debate, and that's been going on for a long time about all kinds of things. Oh, we had a big frou-frou last year about [an issue dealing with religion and the local town square].

E: They were against that?

J: There were some people that were against it, some that were against having [a religious symbol], I happen to be one of them, but didn't write a letter. But then somebody did write a letter to the county. . . . But all the local citizens were just nasty, nasty, nasty. "Leave town!" "Look the other way!" "We're gonna stand for God whether you do or not!" All that kind of stuff. (Joyce, 2017)

The women's heightened attention to how their views fit within their community makes sense. People who are worried about being in the minority tend to also be those who pay closer attention to signs that they are.[46] What is less clear is how people form these perceptions, particularly in a time when signals come both from online and offline sources. For instance, how do media and particular messages come to construct people's perceptions of the opinions around them, and which ones matter more than others? For CWG, the local newspaper, and especially the letters-to-the-editor section, is a major signal for what their community thinks.[47] This sits in stark contrast to the focus of journalism research over the past few decades, and to the declining revenue and viability of local newsrooms across the country.[48] Local newspapers, as in CWG's case and especially in rural areas, continue to serve as important signals for public opinion just as they serve as important tools for information.

It also makes sense that, given the signal of the local newspaper to the community, some of the more vocal CWG members wrote letters themselves. For example, Cynthia was a prominent writer to the local paper, and also one of the prominent members of the local Democratic Party in CWG. She told me she often wrote letters to counteract the conservative voice in the paper—whether that was to correct an article in the paper itself or to correct another letter-writer.

> When I write for the newspaper, or write letters to the editor, I try to fact-check whatever I say and make sure it's not wrong... But there's some people who put out there the most ridiculous—sounds like it's straight out of Rush Limbaugh's mouth. And so, when that happens, I will try to write a letter to the editor, you know, saying in a nice way why that is not true and that they did not fact-check it. (Cynthia, 2017)

Scholars would call Cynthia's behavior a "corrective action."[49] She saw the value of the paper as a constructive tool—after all, it informed her *own* judgments of her community's beliefs—and so she also saw value in influencing its message. Cynthia was not alone in her letter writing. Cathy wrote letters to the editor with her husband, also to correct the "rabid" remarks of other letter writers.

> E: So, these are editorials where you say you're a Democrat?
> C: Yes. There are a couple of people in this county that are rabid Republicans. So, we attempt to write reasonable rebuttals to those people. Because they're nuts. You know, they're just off the wall. (Cathy, 2017)

When I asked if Cynthia or Cathy had ever received backlash for their letters, they said on occasion that they did. This was mostly in the form of rebuttals published in the next week's paper. But when I spoke to Cynthia again in 2018, she said that hostility had eased. Several local Republicans, she told me, had recently reached out to commend what she had written.

I've actually had some people who were, [I'm] pretty sure, strong Republicans before, or at least lean that way, say they appreciated what I had written. So that gave me a little bit of hope, not a lot, maybe one or two who said that to me. And which surprised me because I didn't think they would appreciate me telling the truth about what Trump has done since he's been in office. (Cynthia, 2018)

The paper was so central to the women's experience of the community that criticism of the letters-to-the-editor section was not off limits even when it came to members in their own group. About four months into my first interviews with group members, I found out that one of Ann's relatives actually wrote some of the "rabid Republican" letters in the paper.

My [relative] writes prolifically in the [local newspaper] in the opinion section. And I even struggle with—certainly I've run into people who are like, "Are you related to [her relative's name]?" and I say, "That's my husband's side of the family." (Ann, 2017)

This had been a point of contention when she joined CWG, because she shared the "rabid Republican's" last name. When Ann came to the first meeting and said her last name to another member, she had to immediately differentiate herself from her relative.

And as the meeting was about to convene, I guess a little before that, another woman had noticed me after we had convened, and whenever I tell people my name, they always have a reaction to [my last name]. And this woman began to tell the group that "this person knows [my relative in the paper]" but then fairly quickly we all got around to the introductions. (Ann, 2017)

That the women had such strong reactions to just the name of a conservative letter writer shows just how much weight they put on the local paper. Importantly, some of the women, like Cynthia and Cathy, thought they could change that view by writing letters themselves. Others thought they could challenge that view by just existing, in the group they had created, in the company of one another and outside the view of what some considered those "simple-minded" conservatives. Theresa, one of the most active members of the group, told me she thought that the mere existence of CWG challenged all of the conservative ideology in the local paper.

> I personally debate the statement that it's all red out here because that's not what I've seen. The closest town to me has 90 people, that's the total population. We have a women's group that now tops 125, just women. (Theresa, 2017)

For Theresa, CWG not only gave her a separate community, but also redefined the community around her. If there were 125 liberal women, she thought, then the county's conservative veneer may be just that—a veneer. Underneath the surface was a more complex community that had, intentionally, covered itself up. This reflexivity—the ability for a community to affect a group of people and for a group of people to affect a community—is at the heart of political organizing. But it is also at the heart of secrecy and why people hide their political beliefs in the first place.

Conclusion

The development and structure of CWG conveys several things about politics and communication. For one, it says that for individuals who are in the political minority in their community, politics is a source of isolation. Yet CWG also asks us to consider, amid geographic and social sorting, that context increasingly informs one's political experience and one's willingness to engage in politics publicly.

Second, CWG's reliance on the local paper for understanding their community's politics shows just how strong a role local news continues to play, particularly in rural communities. For the women of CWG, the local paper cued a belief that everyone around them had the same political beliefs. This, in turn, triggered a cycle of silence: you stay publicly quiet and fail to find those around you that *are* like you. The processes by which people come to understand the beliefs of those around them, then, become important considerations if we want to understand if and how people express their own beliefs.

CWG's emergence also shows us further proof that digital media can be used to network the minority together. The fluid and more protected features of private email and secret Facebook groups mean that groups like CWG can form out of the view of the public eye and bring people out of political isolation, akin to the groups and movements of other marginalized social identities in historical and contemporary contexts.

The real difference between those movements and this one is that the women of CWG were not marginalized because they are nice White women, but because they are liberal. In fact, CWG is rooted in and largely reflective of the conservative, rural community in which it exists. The members of CWG read the same paper and go to the same stores and churches as others in their community. They are fellow neighbors, patrons, and congregants. The problem is that this similarity is not enough. Their political difference, for some, was a source of shame, even from a young age. This not only made dissenting hard but made a room of fellow teary women all the more shocking and affirming when they organized it.

As much as CWG gave the women community, or at least made them feel less alone, CWG is not its own town. It exists in a larger context that, in many ways, is the reason it was created. More importantly, it is the reason it is secret. In the following chapter I will explore the broader reasons why the women chose secrecy, the ways in which the community necessitated it, and what the secrecy of 136 women tells us about politics in the contemporary United States.

4

Fearing the Other Side

In August 2017, when I drove out to attend my first meeting of CWG, I started counting bumper stickers. At first, I was simply curious if the number and tenor of bumper stickers was different in CWG's area than it was in Austin. In Austin it was not uncommon to see cars with bumpers covered left to right with stickers pronouncing the driver's favorite bands and breed of dog alongside their choice of political candidate. While this was my original curiosity, the stickers later became important symbols of transition as I made my way out of the self-proclaimed liberal bastion of Austin and into the rural countryside that made up 83% of the state's land mass.[1] They showed me not only where I stood physically, but also where I stood ideologically.

When I pulled in that August, I first counted stickers at a local gas station on the edge of town. I drove up to a four-pump station and hopped out of my car. There were three trucks at the station. One had a sticker that caught my eye. "100% DEPLORABLE" it read in big red letters. I counted it.

On my drive through town, I saw several more cars coursing through the main street as they headed home from work. This time I saw two bumper stickers that read "TRUMP: MAKE AMERICAN GREAT AGAIN" in red and blue lettering and outlined with small red stars. When I pulled up to the meeting location outside of town, I counted bumper stickers on the cars parked outside. There were six cars parked when I got there—zero trucks, but two Priuses, one of which had a Beto O'Rourke sticker that simply red "BETO" in black and white on the back window. Then I walked into CWG's meeting.

Although I was aware from the beginning that CWG had a confidentiality component, I was not sure as to the why or the extent of it until I started talking to them. Over two years of interviews showed me that the women had calculated a certain amount of risk to being publicly identified as a liberal, progressive, or Democrat. Nearly all of these calculations happened internally, and nearly all were reinforced by a collective narrative after the group was formed. Many of the members would lessen their fears after finding and interacting with one another. Some of them would ease their fears by simply

Democracy Lives in Darkness. Emily Van Duyn, Oxford University Press. © Oxford University Press 2022.
DOI: 10.1093/oso/9780197557013.003.0004

gaining more distance from the 2016 election. For others, their fear would intensify.

What was clear as I spoke to the women and observed their meetings was that the group's formation was just as much about wanting to do and talk politics with like-minded people as it was about wanting to avoid doing or talking about politics with *different*-minded people. In other words, their formation was not just that they wanted support, but that they wanted protection. Although they expressed fear toward their community, that fear was often hard to tease out. For one thing, these are, like small communities where residents are highly connected and interdependent on one another,[2] women who are deeply connected to the people physically around them. Many are business owners, schoolteachers, and church leaders. In our conversations they first expressed love for their home county, and then, subsequently, their fear of it. What is more, almost all of these women had made a choice to live in the county. Some had chosen to retire there, some had moved back after living in another part of the state, and some had chosen to start or move their businesses or careers there. This meant that to denounce or to speak against their community felt discordant with their own choice to live in it. Kathleen told me her choice to live in a small community—a community where your political opinions were often at odds with the majority—inevitably required sacrifice—a choice between personal expression and social connection.

> I live in [a small town in the county], which is really little, and everybody knows everybody, or at least knows of somebody who knows everybody, we're all connected in a lot of ways. And it would not, in my perception, it would not be good to be identified as being a liberal and an Obama supporter at the time. That would not go over well, and it would more feel like a disconnect with people. . . . You know it's a real balancing act when you live in a small community. If you're in a city you're so anonymous, here you're not, and if you're gonna live here and stay here you have to work with and interact with people here. You have to walk a fine line between how you express yourself and still feel okay where you live. (Kathleen, 2017)

It was clear that the women of CWG relied on their community and their neighbors, perhaps in ways that residents of larger communities do not. When I spoke with Theresa in 2017, she saw neighborliness as a vital part of rural livelihood.

There's a really strong concept for what it means to be a neighbor out here, it actually means something to people. And you know, we're all out here in the middle of freaking nowhere and if you're in trouble there's no 24/7 service that's going to come bail you out. If you can't call your neighbor, you got nobody. And so, it's actually a real meaningful thing out here. And I value that. (Theresa, 2017)

In fact, Theresa relied on her immediate neighbors when her husband was terminally ill, and she could not manage his caretaking alone. Altogether, these were residents of a community who relied on each other. How, then, did women so connected and dependent on their community come to fear it? How did that fear become so significant that they felt the need to hide from those same neighbors? My interviews with the women of CWG portray fear of retribution across three categories: social, economic, and physical. These were fears very much connected to place—the women were worried about ostracizing themselves from the people immediately around them, on whom they relied for support.[3] Although these fears are not mutually exclusive—many of the women feared social, economic, and physical fear while others feared only one—I group the women's responses into these categories and make note of where and if their fears changed over time, as well as how they changed.

Social Fear

"Oh my gosh, you're voting over there?"

When I first spoke to the women, I expected a fear of social isolation or ostracism to drive their desire, and perhaps need, to be secret. I expected this because it is the prevailing explanation for why people withhold their political opinions from others.[4] In the survey data, for instance, fear of isolation was a statistically significant predictor of why people might hide their political beliefs or secretly express them offline or online.[5] In other words, the survey data reinforces years of research suggesting that people keep their politics a secret because they are afraid they will be socially ostracized for them.

This theory holds true, at least partially, for the women of CWG. Many of the women did fear social reprisals or even overt discrimination for "coming out" as a progressive or a Democrat or challenging their neighbors' and friends' political beliefs. This was the case for Joyce, who said she generally remained quiet about politics around anyone in the county because she had experienced social castigation when she said something about politics previously.

> I pretty much would keep quiet unless it was just something terrible. I mean you know, the N-word, you can hear that all the time. I would speak up against that and I would get dirty looks. And I have had, and I can't remember the circumstance, but I have had somebody say, "Well, why don't you go back to California? What are you doing here anyway?" That kind of thing. And so, I kind of would remain quiet. (Joyce, 2017)

Several elements of Joyce's testimony are worthy of note. For one, it took a racist statement for Joyce to finally challenge those around her. It is not clear what might have been said before this statement, any dialogue to which Joyce did not react. It is also striking that the person's response was so hostile, although there is growing evidence that racism has become a topic to which conservatives are particularly reactive.[6] The person's rebuttal also included an implied insult toward Joyce's home state of California—suggesting that Joyce's reaction and implicit beliefs were because she was from California, not because she was against racist language. Their reaction, in a sense, delegitimized her right to be in their community, and even the state—an outsider-versus-insider dynamic that is common in rural areas,[7] and especially between Texans and Californians.[8]

Despite such a reaction, this was not the only time that Joyce spoke out against something she heard, and it was not the last time she received backlash for doing so. In fact, when Joyce did challenge some members of her knitting club, she was kicked out entirely. This time her dissent was not in response to racism but about prejudice against people with disabilities.

> I was in a group, a knitting club, and I liked it because it didn't have anything political about it. It was a group of women that knitted. But when last year, during the election, when they were running and all of that, and I can't remember when it was that Trump made fun of a disabled reporter, and my husband's severely disabled, and he has a lot of conditions that look weird, he's got weird body posture and all of that stuff. And, somebody started making fun of a disabled person, and they kind of went along with what Trump had said, and I went livid. I left the group after they said to me, "you need a break," and I said, "yeah I do," and so I've left that group. (Joyce, 2017)

Joyce's apolitical knitting club turned out to be political. It also turned out to be retaliatory. This kind of social ostracism happened not only face-to-face but also digitally, an occurrence that has become increasingly common and subtle as social networks have moved online.[9] For instance, Gail received judgmental questions from members of the community about her political beliefs after she posted a political statement on Facebook.

> So, I started using social media to draw attention to the issues and to express a point of view. I had several people, a couple of friends in the community, act very shocked that I even felt that way, and that I was willing to speak out on it. A couple of personal friends, long distance, said, "What happened to you?" A couple of other friends unfriended me on Facebook because they thought I was being much too righteous and sanctimonious. (Gail, 2017)

Gail would stop posting on her Facebook account because she did not want to further isolate herself. Like Gail, the women of CWG who were concerned about social isolation denied a very strong part of themselves to people they called friends—a part that had cried when Trump had won the presidency, and a part that had led them to a secret organization.

Linda, for instance, who was and is very active in her church, said she felt the church and the community were always very suspicious that there were Democrats in the congregation.

> Talking politics where I live, including the church, is something that, as a Democrat, I was not very comfortable being very open about. In other words, I didn't want to make any kind of strong statements unless I knew who I was talking to. And there was a lot of kind of suspiciousness I guess you might say, or feeling of disapproval. (Linda, 2017)

Although she wanted very badly to challenge her friends' and even her husband's politics, she could not bring herself to do it because it led to too much "conflict" and "bitterness."

> Like, if I would be in a social group [in the church], I just wouldn't say anything. They would all be talking politics, but they would all be on the same side and I would disagree a lot of times with what they were saying, but I wouldn't say anything. . . . Before this last election there was so much

bitterness, including with my own husband, who was supporting Trump. We just couldn't even discuss it. (Linda, 2017)

When I spoke with Linda again in 2018, she had almost completely retreated from her political activism through CWG and a few other groups she had joined after the 2016 election. When I asked her why she had retreated, she first told me it was because she just did not like meetings.

I don't . . . I just don't like meetings. I don't like group activities very much. And so, I just don't enjoy it. And I don't . . . that's the only reason. It's not anything that I want to do because I am at a place in my life where I don't do anything unless I want to do it. I don't do things out of obligation anymore. (Linda, 2018)

Lind was not alone in quitting. Of the 23 women that I spoke to over the course of two years, two officially quit the group, while three that I know of stopped attending meetings but asked to remain in the Facebook group or on the private listserv. When I pushed Linda on why she left CWG, she revealed that it was also that she was frustrated and a little "hopeless" that nothing was getting done. She told me, through a series of sighs, that it was no longer worth the time and the effort.

L: I just kind of lost interest in the gathering. I'm supportive, I'm happy that they're meeting and doing what they're doing, and you know, that sort of thing. But I just haven't gone. I haven't . . . it's not like I said to myself, "I'm outta here. I'll never go again," or anything like that. I just haven't been motivated to go. I've got . . . part of that is sort of a sense of, well, hopeless is a pretty strong word, but I guess you could say that I don't have very much confidence that we're gonna get things turned around very easily.

E: Why do you feel like that?

L: Well, just, there's been so much that's gone on in the public that has been people complaining and demonstrating and bringing up various issues that initially there was a lot of hope, you know, that that might lead to some kind of change or get other people interested who might have had similar experiences . . . and yet, I don't see any evidence that it's been addressed or fixed.

E: What would it take to get you revived again?

L: Maybe some winning? (Linda, 2018)

Linda, like others in the group, was a woman who had not engaged in politics in a very long time. She had compartmentalized that part of herself to keep the peace with her friends, her congregation, and her spouse. After the 2016 election, she used CWG as a channel for political activism, diving in with a great deal of anger and frustration that Trump had won and that she was not free to be her political self to the fullest extent. Linda had not dipped her toe in the water after Trump's election; she had done a cannon ball. What she found was that swimming in the deep end was draining, particularly when all you had been doing for the past 20 years was sitting on the edge of the water. Being political in her community, then, was socially risky, but it was also simply exhausting.

While I had expected that the women feared social retaliation for their beliefs, particularly after being kicked out of knitting clubs and receiving side-eyes from church congregations, I had not expected that this social isolation would come from what scholars often refer to as the only private political act[10]—voting.

To vote in a primary election in Texas, you must declare a political party. In urban areas, this means walking up to a table of most if not all strangers and declaring a party. In rural areas, this means walking up to a table of neighbors and friends and declaring a party. For a group of women worried about being "outed" to their community, this distinction was paramount. Deborah, for one, told me a story of when she first moved to the county and signed up to help the local Democratic Party at the polls.

I've avoided getting involved in politics here. I was an election judge for the Democratic Party, oh probably 12 or 13 years ago, and that was hard for me to do, but they could not find a Democrat in our little area here. So I said yes, I'd do it, and there were people who came in the voting hall that when they saw me at the Democratic table were rude to me and didn't speak to me for a while after that. So I kind of laid low [after that]. (Deborah, 2017)

Deborah was not the only one who experienced some form of social ostracism after community members saw her affiliated with the Democrats at the voting booth. Ann, who moved back to the county recently, was also judged by community members for having "gone" to the Democratic table during the primary.

> The first time I went to vote, even in terms of a primary where you have separate tables, everyone was kind of like "Oh my gosh, you're voting over there? You're a Democrat? You're for abortion?" (Ann, 2017)

To Ann's neighbors, siding with the Democrats was a betrayal. Even worse, it implicated her views on abortion, which as a strong Catholic, was worse. Ann told me a similar story a year later about a community doctor who, for fear of being publicly outed as a Democrat, did not vote at all in the primary.

> There was one person that, whose wife I was talking to, and someone who is actually a doctor in the community close to us and aware of some of the partisanship, actually did decide not to vote in the primary because you had to essentially declare—very visibly—who you were voting for, and [they] decided to, you know, wait for the general election to vote there. I can see that to an extent, and with the technology and all the things we have these days, seems like there would be a way to ensure that people vote for only one party in the primaries but that they don't have to necessarily declare. (Ann, 2018)

Virginia offered a similar observation based on when she worked as an election judge in her precinct. Instead of voting in person on the day of the primary, Virginia surmised, individuals voting Democratic often voted by absentee.

> In our little precinct, both parties vote in the same room, in the same building, just 15–20 steps apart. And so anyway, everybody who comes in, actually most of the Democrats in our precinct vote absentee. (Virginia, 2017)

These experiences position voting, at least in rural communities like CWG's, not as the private political act it is often touted to be,[11] but as a public and declaratory act. This means that the extent to which voting actually is private depends very much on the social and physical context in which it takes place.

To see if there was evidence in support of Virginia's claim, I looked at data from the 2016 general election, 2018 midterm election, and primary data from both elections. Working with the leader of the county Democratic Party, I analyzed voting method by partisanship,[12] and found that Virginia might be right.

Considering primary elections are where Jane and Virginia cited the most explicit instances of political "outing," I looked first at primary data from 2016 and 2018. If outnumbered Democrats in the county were wary of voting in the primary because it required publicly outing their partisanship, we should see that Democrats are more likely to vote by *mail/absentee* or not vote at all in the primary compared to Republicans. Likewise, we should see that Democrats are less likely to vote in person in the primary compared to Republicans.

The data show that Democrats were more likely than Republicans to vote by mail/absentee or not vote at all in the 2016 and 2018 primaries, and that they were less likely to vote in person—at least in the 2018 primary. Yet Democrats were still more likely than Republicans to not vote or vote by mail/absentee in the *general* election, and still less likely to vote in person in the general election compared to Republicans. In other words, Jane and Virginia's observation was generally right, if not an underestimation of just how much Democrats in their county avoided in-person voting.

Although this analysis is not sufficient to tease out exactly why Democrats differed from Republicans in their preferred mode of voting or in their likelihood of abstaining, it does tell us that Democrats in the county appear to have a markedly different experience at the voting booth than Republicans. Given this is also the county where CWG exists, this offers at least some evidence that being the minority in your community may be related to your political behavior, including whether you vote at all.

Experiences of being publicly outed and subsequently shamed for being affiliated with the Democrats made some, like Jane and Virginia, more resistant to engaging in politics publicly or identifying themselves as Democrats in the future. Yet others continued working the Democratic table at the polls and continued to receive backlash. Joyce, who had recently taken up poll-working for the Democrats, said that social ridicule for her presence at the polls was still going strong during the 2018 primaries.

When I was poll sitting, and other people in other locations told me the same thing has happened, the Republican men come over to the Democratic table and say snide things. And you know we just shine it on because what are we going to do? We're not going to get in a fight at the polling booth. (Joyce, 2018)

When I asked her if she could give me an example of a "snide" comment the men made, she said they referenced the fact that the other woman sitting at the table with Joyce, also a member of the group, had recently gotten a divorce from her Republican husband and was thus moving from her property to a new place. "To the woman who's getting divorced they said, and came over to her, "Oh I guess you're pretty lonely now you had to move." (Joyce, 2018)

Unintentionally, or perhaps intentionally, people were being intimidated from voting, from voting in person, or from working at the polls. The women of CWG, and likely others in their community, were not only wary of publicly declaring a party in the primary, they were wary of telling their knitting club to stop making fun of disabled people, or of letting their neighbor or a member of their church know that they had voted for Clinton.

There were many other instances across CWG's community that made the women reticent to express their political opinions. For instance, some of the women avoided politics for fear of social ostracism not because they felt the other side would not be able to handle their political difference, but because they themselves thought they would not be able to handle the political difference. This was a fear not of what others would do—a fear that you would be kicked out of a knitting club, for instance—but a fear of what *you* would do.

When I spoke with Melanie again in 2018, she first mentioned to me she worried that people would be "ugly" to her and that discussing politics might hurt their relationship.

When you set yourself up for discussing something or you know you're going to be on the clearly opposite side of somebody else, and you already have a relationship with them, I'm thinking of people I already know in town, who I have, you know, an acquaintanceship with. If we were to start talking about politics, it would either change my view of them or change their view of me and there might be a discussion that would get ugly and there might be ill feelings afterwards. So. . . . And to boot, I don't know that I could keep my end of the discussion. I worry about how I would express myself. Whether I would do it effectively or whether I would stoop to being angry or something like that, something negative. (Melanie, 2018)

At first, Melanie was concerned that conversation about politics could fundamentally drive a wedge in her relationships—that either party might "change their view" of the other. Then Melanie recognized it was also that she could not control herself—that her own expression would devolve to nastiness.

Melanie's worries about the conversation getting "ugly" sits in line with research that suggests women are more likely to be attuned and reactive to instances of political incivility,[13] more likely to receive uncivil messages,[14] and also more likely to be punished for engaging in uncivil discourse or expressing anger.[15] The first part of Melanie's explanation was the self-censorship so common in instances of political disagreement—where one withholds an opinion as a way of managing an impression, as a way to avoid rejection.[16] But her second reason had less to do with the other person and more to do with herself. Melanie also self-censored because she feared losing control of her own emotions.

Kathleen expressed a similar sentiment when I spoke with her in 2017. Concerned with keeping the peace, Kathleen said she would avoid politics at all costs, particularly with people with whom she interacted on a daily basis. When I asked her why, she said that not only was she afraid of backlash from them, but she was also worried she would be overtaken by her anger and take the conflict too far.

> I would definitely feel uncomfortable in other people's presence, and I know if I were to say, if I did say something, I would get remarks back that I wouldn't want to hear. Some of the things they say can make me so mad and I don't wanna get mad. I don't want to get in an argument with anybody. It's like, this does not serve a purpose. (Kathleen, 2017)

This fear that one would "lose control" is not an idea that is typically discussed when it comes to why people avoid political conflict or why they self-censor when politics is brought up. To say that these women were withholding their beliefs because they were afraid of the consequences, because wanted to keep the peace, was not the full story. They also withheld their beliefs because they were afraid of themselves.

Beyond a sensitivity to losing social connections in the community, there was also fear of losing social connections within the group itself. Some were concerned that the group would not like something they did or said. For instance, Gail told me in 2017 that she had voted for Trump in the Republican primary because she did not want Ted Cruz to get the nomination, but she also expressed concern that I would tell other women in the group that she had done this.

> You know, I voted against a Republican running in the primaries because I didn't . . . Hillary didn't need my vote, and I didn't think Bernie Sanders, who I really liked better than Hillary, it wasn't going to help him. So, I voted . . . this is confidential, right? I mean, I have not revealed this to very many people in the women's group, but I voted for Trump in the primaries because I absolutely despised Ted Cruz. (Gail, 2017)

While their individual stories were powerful, it was not until I started attending meetings that I saw how the act of coming together had perhaps amplified the women's fears. Meetings would begin with 30 minutes of social activity, which involved sipping wine, eating finger foods, and often sharing the horrors of the Trump administration or hostile interactions with their conservative community. At the meeting in July 2018, in which the women handwrote 1,000 postcards to a Democratic candidate in Ohio, Barbara and Ann exchanged hugs and condolences about how hard it had been at a function they both recently attended. Barbara hugged Ann and asked, "Are you doing okay?" Ann responded, "I am from the perspective of speaking up more, I'm trying." Barbara, in an effort to make Ann feel better about not saying something, said, 'I was at a function with you recently where, if we had spoken up, we'd have been out that door fast."

More often than not, storytelling was a focal point of each meeting. On more than one occasion, time was carved out for the women to tell stories of how hard it was to be progressive in a conservative community. At their June 2018 meeting, there was a designated 20-minute time on the agenda to "share our stories of living blue in a red county, and how the current political situation has affected us." At the November meeting immediately following the 2018 midterms, 30 minutes were dedicated to "members' feelings." Most of these slots amounted to a venting session. The women would recount how conservatives made them feel bad or intimidated, how they had received backlash for expressing a dissenting view, and even how they had responded poorly when someone had brought up politics,

Storytelling sessions often seeped into other moments of the meeting as well. For instance, when the more vocal Democrats discussed outreach efforts, they would often tell tales of Republican sabotage. At the

September 2018 meeting, Cynthia said the Democrats had a table at a major county event to promote Texas's Democratic Senate hopeful Beto O'Rourke's campaign. She recalled that a man came up and slurred insults about Beto, explaining his behavior by saying, "I think he had a little too much to drink." Even worse, someone else at the event had stolen all of their Beto postcards from the table. These were small moments. These were not stories of being physically threatened or attacked, but they carried a lot of meaning for the women—namely, how much they felt their views were accepted in their own community, and consequently, how much they could share with their community.

Not all of the stories that were shared were doom and gloom. Some re-flected positive social interactions around politics. For example, at the meeting in March 2018, the owner of a local bed and breakfast, and a co-vert Democrat, told a story of a woman who came into her business with a Beto button on her handbag. The woman said, "I like your handbag." The visitor responded, "Thank you. I really admire people who have the same taste in handbags that I do." The rest of CWG loved this story. It was like a se-cret code—a way to subtly stand in and share solidarity with others. In fact, after the 2016 election there had been a lot of secret codes for recently active progressives. For instance, members of the group Pantsuit Nation started a practice of turning car magnets upside down when they saw a car displaying the group's magnetic decal.[17] After the handbag story was shared, some of the women of CWG started putting Beto buttons on their handbags, perhaps with the hope that someone would notice and offer them the same veiled recognition.

Other stories were much harder for the women to tell. At the same meeting in March 2018, another member recounted an instance of confrontation at her own store. With an incredulous tone, she recalled a conservative giving praise to the former governor of Texas, Rick Perry. The woman had disagreed with the conservative's remarks and made it clear, resulting in an argument that she described as "heated." As she recalled the exchange, her eyes glassed over and she pleaded with the women around her, saying, "What mistakes did I do? What should I have done?"

The room's answer was this: do not talk about it with *them*, talk about it with *us*. One member offered her own ear in instances where the woman felt the need to rant against some belief or conversation she had encountered. "Anytime you're wanting to talk about the idiot Rick Perry," she said, "you can call me up." "Actually," she added, "you can call any of us up."

The women told these conversational horror stories for a number of reasons. For one, they told them to each other because they had nowhere else to tell them. These were experiences they had kept inside, often turning on themselves and judging their own response to conflict. To share the story was relief just as much as it was a warning to the others in the group. They also told the stories to each other because they needed help, advice on how to respond, and suggestions for how to manage not being complicit with not being combative.

These kinds of stories had an effect, not only on each individual, but collectively on the group. They were now shared narratives of social ostracism and backlash, much like the kinds of stories shared and echoed across generations in other marginalized publics.[18] The shared part of these stories was evident in how often I heard the same ones recited over and over. When I asked the women individually about their own experiences with political backlash in the community, they would recount the stories of other members in addition to their own.

The narratives served two important roles. On one hand, the stories made each woman feel less alone in their experience of conflict or othering. On the other hand, the stories also made the risk of expressing political dissent to those around them more tangible. Each woman's experience of social conflict or isolation was no longer a single incident that happened to them, but something that happened to the women sitting right next to them.

Regardless of whether these stories were made more potent by their repetition, they existed and had power in and of themselves. For many of the women, the fear of being "outed" and losing social connections has persisted even after being a part of the group for some time. This was often evident when some of the group members were comfortable posting a picture of them and a few of the other group members writing postcards to voters, but others were not. Ann and Barbara mentioned this hesitation to me when I spoke to them individually in 2018.

> At the very least there's still some hesitance to be visible because there's . . . even for me at the fundraiser last Sunday, I could feel myself getting a little bit anxious when there was one or more people taking pictures with their iPhone. (Ann, 2018)

Barbara was also wary of having her picture taken by another member at the postcard meeting. When I had spoken to Barbara in 2017 about why she did not want to be identified as a Democrat, she hid behind her job. "I am a realtor," she had said, which she assumed conveyed it all. When I spoke to her again in 2018, she was more attuned to the social ramifications if she were to be "out."

> Even like at the card party—the thing where we were signing cards—and we had a photographer there, I got up and left when they were taking a picture of our table. So, I'm still not fully out there with a comfort level that . . . I'm afraid of ridicule. I'm afraid of people thinking—who all along thought maybe I was one way and now they're finding out I'm another— kind of like, golly, I can imagine what somebody who's gay feels like coming out. You know, something like that. Isn't that stupid? I mean at my age. (Barbara, 2018)

Hiding her beliefs for so long had raised the social stakes for Barbara to "come out" to her friends and her neighbors. To out herself would be hypocritical; after all, she had known them for so long and had said nothing about being progressive. For Barbara, and for other women, it was this fear of ridicule, and a fear of hypocrisy, that stopped them from "coming out" at all. As I will discuss in Chapter 6, some of the women felt emboldened to say something or do something that would identify them as progressive. Yet others remained steadfast in their secrecy. This was particularly true for Barbara and for others who not only feared social isolation, but other types of backlash as well.

Economic Fear

"You'll be sorry when you see me sliding down my cellar door."

Although many of the women in CWG were retired, some of them still ran businesses that were embedded in the local economy. This meant that they relied on their neighbors to either financially support their business or, at the very least, not disparage it to others in the community or to visitors who brought in revenue. Because the county in which CWG exists is far enough away from a large metropolitan area, residents there rely on local businesses for many goods and services that they are not willing to drive far to get— restaurants, grocery stores, hardware stores. Yet the town is large enough that they have more than one of most everything. While choice is limited, it is still available.

The fear of losing business is connected to social ostracism and isolation, but it is also different from it. Losing friends might cause you to lose business, but not always. Some women in CWG, while afraid of being excluded from a dinner party, were more afraid that no one would support their business. While scholars have a reasonably good understanding of how a fear of social isolation causes people to withhold their opinions, they do not have a good understanding of how fear of economic retribution does this.[19]

The members of CWG who were most vocal about concerns of economic backlash were the real estate agents. When I first spoke with her in 2017, Barbara, who has been a realtor in the county since the early 2000s, told me that she had to "sacrifice" her political self to keep her business from suffering.

> In the real estate business, there is great risk. To this day, I avoid discussion with any clients or potential clients. I can sacrifice my need to make a point because of the benefits that are attached to it, and that sounds really crude, but I am self- employed, and so you pick and choose your battles. (Barbara, 2017)

This "risk" was still present for Barbara in 2018. After a long discussion about the trials and tribulations of Facebook, she told me she would never use Facebook to talk about politics. When I asked her why this was such a hard line, she told me her business is too reliant on social media—using it to promote listings and attract clients—for her to bring politics into the mix.

> E: What are you worried about happening on Facebook?
> B: Well, coming out of the closet. Because we use social media in real estate to, you know, advertise and to put our properties out there and talk about our jobs and whatever, and that is really close to home. That would be like stepping out the closet for real. (Barbara, 2018)

I heard that same sentiment of self "sacrifice" from Virginia, another realtor in the county. Like Barbara, Virginia thought it was too risky to express a political opinion, even outside of work, lest potential clients or her employer see it.

I am a realtor. And so, still plugging along. In fact, that's pretty important as far as my experience with the group because as the county is so overwhelmingly conservative and Republican that it makes it difficult to be open about that, you know, about my politics, without jeopardizing my business. And there are several of us in the group that are in that situation, because of that, because we know full well that it would cost us business—to be open about it. So, that makes it awkward. Well, that makes it frustrating, more than anything. It makes it very frustrating not to be able to be yourself and talk about what you believe and what you believe in, that sort of thing. (Virginia, 2017)

Both Barbara and Virginia's reactions contain a similar refrain: to make it economically, they could not be themselves politically. It was not that these women were concerned that being Democrats at the office could cost them business, but that being Democrats *at all* could. Because of the nature of their small community, this meant that the women had to be apolitical, not just at work, but everywhere. Barbara and Virginia buried that part of themselves publicly so they would not turn off a potential client, and sometimes so they would not hurt their relationship with their employer.

If you met Barbara and Virginia, you might be surprised that they hid their politics to the extent that they did. Barbara, though physically small, has a commanding presence. She speaks fast and in quick bursts and uses your name when addressing you, conjuring a kind of warm authority. She is confident and articulate. Virginia, although softer-spoken than Barbara, has a twang and a jilt to her voice that is friendly and assertive. She is quick to laugh and quick to react. In the way she speaks it is easy to tell when she is emotional—angry or sad or excited. These are competent and self-assured women. These are not shy wallflowers.

However, even for Barbara and Virginia, suppressing your beliefs and your identity is sometimes easier said than done. For example, Virginia experienced retaliation from both a client and her employer when she hinted at supporting Obama to a customer over the phone. In 2017, she told me the full story.

Right when Obama was first elected, I got a call on a home that I had listed, from the grandson of the man who had built the home. So, he was talking about it and I said, "Well, are you interested in seeing it the way it is now? Do you have any interest in possibly buying it?" And he said something to the effect that "this new president, we don't know what's going to happen, or how he's going to affect whatever." And I said very simply, "Well, we can hope that he does the right thing." Period. And he said, "Are you a supporter of his? Did you vote for him?" And I said, "I really make it a policy not to discuss politics with clients." And so he ended the conversation and hung up. (Virginia, 2017)

The man on the phone would go on to write a "six-page handwritten letter" to Virginia's broker, who then took her off the listing. When she objected, her broker tossed the letter onto her desk as an unspoken explanation and walked off. Virginia's relationship with her work was only made worse in 2018 when, during a meeting of realtors from across the county, the leader opened a discussion about politics.

Before he [the realtor leading the meeting] started he said, "I want to talk politics for a minute," and I'm like, "Are you kidding me? I pay dues to be in this organization," and I wanted to stand up and say, "No, that's not acceptable, that's not why I'm here" . . . . You know, the county is so overwhelmingly Republican that if somebody says they wanna talk politics then you know that's where it's going to go. (Virginia, 2018)

In Virginia's response there are two complementary assumptions. One, that the man leading the meeting assumed everyone present was conservative. And two, that Virginia assumed he was conservative and remained quiet. These two assumptions work in concert to make politics in the workplace not only seem unsafe for one group of partisans, but also seem safer for the *other* group of partisans. Although the man at the meeting would go on to discuss "how to defeat the Beto O'Rourke campaign," which confirmed Virginia's suspicions, she had played into the same vicious cycle: when the minority withholds their beliefs, the majority goes unchallenged, and when the majority goes unchallenged, the minority becomes more likely to withhold their beliefs.[20]

Virginia did not say anything to the meeting leader. A month after we spoke, I heard her tell Barbara at a CWG meeting just how frustrated she was that she had not said something. Virginia promised she would write a letter to the man leading the meeting to tell him how she thought it was unprofessional to bring up politics at the office.

It was not only real estate agents who experienced and feared economic backlash for expressing their political beliefs. When I spoke with Bonnie in 2017, she mentioned that it would be bad for her job as a counselor to "drive up to somebody's house and have a political statement" like a bumper sticker. When I spoke to her again in 2018, she mentioned that she thought it might actually hurt her business by affecting people's willingness to interact with her at all.

> B: I think the way I see people who are for Trump is that they would just kind of . . . they'd just quit coming I think, if they knew how I felt. You know, I may be wrong on that but that's kind of what I'm talking about.
> E: Because they wouldn't want to interact with someone who identifies as a Democrat?
> B: Yeah, something like that. (Bonnie, 2017)

Roberta, who founded a very popular local business in the county, said that publicly expressing she was a Democrat would have cost her much of her business, especially since she believed 90% of her workforce had voted for Trump.

> I have to tell you, I founded the [local business] here in town, and I can't let my political views in any way harm [the business]. And feelings ran so high that I felt like if I were to "come out of the closet," so to speak, about my Democratic position and supporting Hillary and everything, I felt that there were people in town who would definitely have taken after [the business] because [of] what I said or did. (Roberta, 2017)

Like the women's stories of social backlash, stories of economic backlash were told like group folklore. I would often hear the same stories recited over and over—mostly stories they had heard from others at meetings. Jean, a local restaurant owner and member of the group, told me the story of how she had received backlash for expressing support for Obama in 2012, and how this had only gotten worse during and after the 2016 election.

> During the Obama campaign it became very obvious to me that among Republicans and conservative people, that there really was not any tolerance for having a conversation about the pros and cons of anything other than voting for a Republican candidate. Even during that election, there

were people who let me know that if I spoke openly in my restaurant about being supportive of Obama that they would not come to our place, which was a revelation. . . I was absolutely shocked . . . but that was nothing compared to the 2016 election. (Jean, 2017)

When I spoke to Theresa in 2017, she recounted Jean's experiences, only with greater detail about specific incidents where patrons would publicly announce their boycott.

So, one of our members owns a really popular local restaurant and there was a Trump person really loudly talking about whatever it was to the owner, who you know, has the habit to, you know at restaurants, where the owner will go come around and chat with various people as time allows and that kind of thing. . . . Well she was sort of doing that and he started to say, what she felt like was racist and outrageous remarks, and she called him on it and he proceeded to cuss her out at full voice and stand up and say that he would no longer be patronizing [*sic*] of this place and stomped out of the restaurant. (Theresa, 2017)

Another frequently referenced story was about a member whose employer retaliated against her for posting her political beliefs on Facebook. In 2017, Dawn told me she had been friended by a fellow local employee on Facebook. A few days later she was terminated from her job, for what she claimed was saying too many political "things" on her personal Facebook page.

D: After the election I got fired from a job I had for three weeks because my Facebook was too left-leaning.
E: Oh, wow.
D: Yeah, and that was when I knew, yeah, this can really happen.
E: They confronted you about your Facebook?
D: Yeah, well, I'm so naïve, I just, you know, one of the women there asked to be my friend and I thought, "How nice." Well, she went back to her owner and said, "You know, I don't know what she's saying all these things, and it's going to look bad for our store and people aren't going to come in." And so, he left me a message that it just didn't work out. (Dawn, 2017)

Dawn's story became a shared narrative within CWG and had an effect on other members more concerned with being boycotted or receiving retaliation. When I spoke with Connie in 2018, she referenced Dawn's story with an air of disbelief.

> I couldn't believe that people who owned businesses, if people knew how they felt politically they'd quit using their services, or I've heard of people getting—even getting fired for something they put on their social media on their Facebook account. You know, it's ridiculous. (Connie, 2018)

When I spoke with another member, whom I'll call Sissy, I again heard the same reference to Dawn's experience with the retaliatory employer.

> Somebody got fired somewhere, I forget. I think it was a woman who works at a shop in [a town in the county], and it happened to come out that she was a Democrat. And she was fired from her job. (Sissy, 2018)

While these narratives were both shared and revered, they were also used as a kind of salve. The women would recite horror stories of social isolation and economic retribution from other members in order to prove to themselves they did not have it as bad as other members. No one in CWG wanted to claim that their experience was the worst. Similarly, the women would use others' stories as evidence that the group should be a secret. Sometimes they would do this in addition to their own stories, and sometimes they would reference only the other women's stories as if they were their own.

There was also a sense in the women's responses that this economic retribution was a new phenomenon. Shirley, a longtime county resident, told me she saw economic boycotting around politics as a "sign of the times," that partisanship had turned us against one another both socially and economically. In our conversation about the group being secretive, she told me that while she felt like it should be public and open to challenge the "jackass" in the community who shames them, she could also see that business owners faced a real risk if they were public.

> If I had a business that I was trying to support and I felt like I would lose business, I understand why people don't. And so, I can't be very . . . I'm not critical of them. I'm sorry—what I am is sorry that we can't as a society say, "you know, I don't agree with you, but I'm not gonna shoot you for feeling that way." And by shooting I don't know that I necessarily mean actually but shooting you with not joining in and not buying from you. That's sad to me. But I think it's a sign of our times and where we

are, you know, I want to boycott, so if I'm saying, "By God, I'll boycott you if you don't do it my way," well the other side has that same right. And so that seems to be the rules we're playing by is, "I don't like you so you can't play." You know the old song, "I don't want to play in your yard, I don't like you anymore, you'll be sorry when you see me sliding down my cellar door." (Shirley, 2017)

Shirley was quoting an old tune written by H. W. Petrie in 1894,[21] which was later made famous by the singer Peggy Lee in 1958. The song tells the story of two young girls who did everything together and alike. After the girls had a fight, each hoarded her own play area and prohibited the other from joining, threatening one another by saying they will be "sorry" when they see how much fun they are having in their own yard:

> Once there lived side by side, two little maids,
> Used to dress just alike, hair down in braids,
> Blue ging'am pinafores, stockings of red,
> Little sun bonnets tied on each pretty head.
>
> When school was over secrets they'd tell,
> Whispering arm in arm, down by the well,
> One day a quarrel came, hot tears were shed:
> "You can't play in our yard," but the other said:
>
> Refrain:
> I don't want to play in your yard,
> I don't like you anymore,
> You'll be sorry when you see me,
> Sliding down our cellar door,
> You can't holler down our rain barrel,
> You can't climb our apple tree,
> I don't want to play in your yard,
> If you won't be good to me.

Shirley's metaphor was an apt depiction of the women's conundrum. CWG exists in a county where economics and social life are very much intermixed. To out one's politics in social circles would mean to out one's politics in business. In other words, social life and economic life are all in the same yard.

This made expressing political dissent feel like the kiss of death, particularly to business owners for whom office politics was an echo chamber not in their favor.

To cope, the women of CWG remained like the two little girls at the beginning of the tune. They dressed alike and played along so that they were not sanctioned from their community. But the women were also like the second part of the song, like the turning tables where the one who gets kicked out chants the same thing right back. The women of CWG, as fearful and upset as they were of their own community for threatening to and actually kicking them out of their yard, would discuss doing something quite similar. In Chapter 6, I discuss how, for some, coming out of the political closet meant playing in separate yards and not resolution.

Physical Fear

"There are people on my road that would shoot it."

In my interviews with the women of CWG, I heard not only fear and stories of social and economic backlash, but, to my surprise, also physical backlash. Having driven to and from their county many times over two years, I saw a community that was physically different from the urban area from which I departed. Except for a number of houses in the town's center, most residents lived miles away from one another. They drove more trucks, mostly for utilitarian purposes, and goods and services were often advertised on hay bales or on flatbed trailers. There was a lot of waving when passing by on the road. Over those two years, I also observed a firearm culture that was, at the very least, more obvious than in my urban community. I saw NRA bumper stickers and billboards advertising firearm and ammunition stores.

This is an important detail because I heard this firearm culture echoed in why the women felt the need to be secretive about politics. Simply put, the women saw the prevalence of guns and their high profile in the community as a physical threat. In 2017, I asked Joyce why she felt the need to keep a low profile about politics in the community. She was explicit that she and other women in the group would be in danger if they were to be publicly progressive, pointing to the ubiquity of guns in the community as evidence of, at minimum, the potential for violence.

We're totally surrounded by Republicans, I mean they're the gun toting, bad name calling. . . . And if you speak up you could get literally shot down, but certainly figuratively shot down. (Joyce, 2017)

Often, it was hard for some of the women to admit they were afraid of the people they lived near and knew. This often manifested itself in an amalgamation of defense and admission.

When I first spoke with Kathleen in 2017, she mentioned a fear of being socially ostracized for her beliefs, noting that expressing a dissenting opinion in a small town could cost you the ability to live there, but not necessarily your safety. "Well, I didn't feel any real risk," she told me in 2017, "like somebody might harm me, or come by my house and throw eggs or something." Instead, she said, it was more a fear of "being ostracized—that sort of thing."

When I spoke with her again in 2018, that feeling had changed. Kathleen feared actual physical violence against her property and expressed uncertainty about whether or not she and her family were actually safe in their community. Explicit in her response was that she felt "safe" in her community," yet, implicitly, not safe enough to put a yard sign outside of their home.

We thought of putting up signs at our driveway, but we live on [local road] and we just feel like somebody's gonna shoot holes in it or take it up or something. We don't feel safe doing that. I mean, we feel safe ourselves, well, at least I think we do. . . . I haven't given it all that much thought. But I just feel like the sign will come to a bad end. (Kathleen, 2018)

While Kathleen had originally been wary of social harm should her progressive politics become public, she now saw the potential for physical harm. She feared what would happen to her property and yard sign when she was not there, or by people who were simply driving by. But these were not strangers, they were her neighbors. The people Kathleen feared shooting her yard sign were also the same people she interacted with on a daily basis, the people she had said one year earlier would only socially ostracize her, the people who waved to her on the road that ran through town.

The simultaneity of trust and physical fear was also true for Linda. Even though Linda had written into the local paper espousing her views, she indicated that she had not wanted to put a yard sign out because she previously had two of her animals shot. She was worried she would run a risk of that again if she put a sign in her yard for a Democratic candidate.

I've written several letters to the editor in the local paper. As far as not wanting to put a sign in my yard, that was more . . . that was sort of a fear of the unknown because I think I live in an area with people who carry guns in their car. And I've also had the experience of having two of my animals shot. (Linda, 2017)

While it was not clear when I spoke to her whether Linda had had her animals shot because she had put out a yard sign before, she certainly was afraid of that happening. Both Linda and Kathleen spoke about the potential for violence from anonymous others, but in a place where, they both acknowledged, anonymity was rare. Like Kathleen, Linda feared the "unknown," yet the small nature of her community meant the "unknown" was likely behavior from people she in fact *did* know.

When I spoke with Linda again in 2018, she was not optimistic about politics in general. She had stopped coming to meetings, only following the group from afar. When I asked her again whether she was willing to put a Beto O'Rourke yard sign in her yard for the midterms, she said no. This time, she said, it was about wanting to avoid conflict with her husband and less about having someone shoot at her property.

My husband is supporting the other candidate, so I just don't feel . . . I don't want to put a sign out because if I would put a sign out that would mean he could counter it and put a Cruz sign out. And I just don't want to go there. I don't want to have an argument about it. I don't want to be provocative or be provoked. (Linda, 2018)

Although Linda's concerns about conflict originated more from inside her home than outside of it, her concern with being "provocative" remained true from the year before. Linda grouped being provocative with conflict. As a result, she sought to shelter herself from potential backlash, whether that was a neighbor with a gun or an argument with her husband. Scholars have looked at how the beliefs of family and friends and the experience of political disagreement within the family may affect expression,[22] but the unique qualities of romantic partnerships—their intimacy and dependence—may have unique consequences for if and how someone expresses their political beliefs publicly, as Linda's experience suggests.

The tension between the community as a home and the community as a source of fear was starkly on display for Paula. When I asked her in 2017 if she felt there was any risk in letting people know she was a progressive, she wavered. Initially, she told me she did not think there were threats to her physical safety, but then reversed that statement a mere breath or two later.

> Like I said, this is a nice county, and I don't think . . . unless it was some-body who had too much to drink one night and was riding around a county road and felt like, you know, bashing the mailbox. I don't think generally . . . but there are hate crimes in this county. And you know that fear was defi-nitely palpable after the election amongst this group of women. You know, we were all feeling uneasy. At this point, I don't care anymore. I don't re-ally want to put a bumper sticker on my car, I don't really want my tires slashed. That's another thing I could see happen, you know, like a prank. (Paula, 2017)

Here you can see Paula's contradiction. The community where she had chosen to live was a place where people lived and worked in harmony. At the same time, in the same breath, she thought it held the potential for vio-lence. Paula oscillates between not caring and caring very much about what she publicly shows to her community. She quickly switches between being a bold political activist and expressing concern about her safety and the safety of her property. Like Kathleen and Linda, Paula shows just how hard it is for many of the women to admit their community might be unsafe, or to admit that they limit their own actions out of fear of physical retaliation from them.

Similar to stories of social and economic backlash, many of the stories of actual violence existed as shared narratives among the group. One story, which I heard often, was of a woman in the county being run off the road by men in trucks. I first heard this from Theresa in 2017; she told me there were women in the community who had been threatened and attacked because of their politics. When I asked her to give me an example, she told me the story of a woman being run off the road because of her Obama bumper sticker, told to her by another member of CWG.

> It was to one of the women in the group who was recounting the inci-dent. She had a friend from [a nearby city] visiting for the weekend and the friend was leaving to go back to [a nearby city], apparently she had one of those "O" stickers on the back of her windshield for Obama, you know one of those stickers from 2012 or 2008 that were made that just say "O." And that was the only thing she could figure because there was nothing else that could identify her in any way. She wasn't a person of

color. She couldn't figure out why she would have been targeted for any other reason. And she went to get on the highway to go back to [city in Texas] and these two guys in a pick-up truck pulled onto the highway after her and started driving really aggressively way up on her bumper. And you know, when you're going 70 miles an hour and somebody's up on your bumper that's intimidating. And they started honking and carrying on and yelling at her. (Theresa, 2017)

In 2017, when I asked Deborah why the women felt the need to keep their politics a secret from the community, I heard the same story.

There was a friend of a woman in the group who was visiting from [city in Texas] and she was driving on [a local road]. She was run off the road by some guys in a truck pointing at the Obama sticker. And then other people have had their stickers pulled off their car. You know it's pretty hostile—some of these young guys in particular can be pretty hostile. (Deborah, 2017)

Both women recounted this story with a sense of horror, always with a reference to the assailants being men and always with a reference to them in trucks. As Deborah indicates, many of the women were attuned to the attacks coming from men, often with guns, and often in trucks. Although this specific story had become less top-of-mind when I spoke to most of the women again, that physical fear was still there for Deborah when we spoke in 2018.

E: I remember you talking about how it was kind of scary to publicly be a Democrat or a progressive. Do you think that's changed?

D: I don't. No, I don't. I still would not put a Beto sign on my front gate because I think that there are people on my road that would shoot it— shoot the sign or something of that nature. Or, like having a bumper sticker on my car that some rednecks would try and run me off the road. (Deborah, 2018)

Deborah alluded back to what she said in 2017, to the stories of being run off of the road and having bumper stickers peeled off, this time to justify her own unwillingness to put out a sign or a bumper sticker on her car. She mentioned that "rednecks" or people on her own road would do something to harm her property should she make it public she supports a Democratic candidate.

Other narratives formative to the women's behavior were brought in from outside the group. Connie said she simply avoided politics so she would not have to make the choice between keeping quiet and being public. When I asked her why she did not let others know her political beliefs, she first told me it was a personality trait—that she was simply shy. Later in our conversation, she alluded to a story of a friend who had expressed concern with having her animals hurt because of a political yard sign.

> I've just always been more reserved about it [talking politics]. But then on the other hand, I have a friend that lives near [a small town in Texas] and she also thinks all of this is pretty appalling. And she said she's afraid to put up a sign out where she has horses, what if somebody, a jackass, you know, who knows . . . I mean you know you're dealing with crazy people. (Connie, 2017)

Like Linda and her friend, Connie owned animals. She worried if she put out a Democratic yard sign, her animals would be in jeopardy. That the women alluded to "somebody," "unknown," "rednecks," "bubba," or "crazy people" may be because fearing the anonymous was easier than fearing your neighbor. In a similar vein, to tell the story of others made it easier to swallow, that it was happening in someone else's yard, not your own.

Other members were, at least initially, less affected by physical fear and intimidation. Nancy, a lifelong public Democrat, told me stories of an especially hostile community during the 2016 election. Nancy recalled getting a death threat over the phone when she openly supported an environmental issue in the county.

> I've had some things happen. One time we fought an [environmental issue], and it was a really big deal. And I got a death threat on the phone, and there were some really awful things that happened with people who considered themselves environmentalists at that time, and I've always been a little leery because I know things can happen. You know, weird things left on my doorstep. It ramped up, this nastiness that I see with Republicans, and you know, some man standing on the corner with a photo of Obama with a Hitler moustache drawn on him. People were getting aggressive, and I guess that's what made me not do it [put a political sign up at her office in town]. . . . I put them out [at my house] and I think they got stolen about the fourth or fifth day. (Nancy, 2017)

Although Nancy was skeptical that the community would really engage in violence, when I spoke to her a year later, she had slightly changed her tune. In her mind, there was the possibility that a man driving around—perhaps in a truck—could do something violent. Her scenario sounded remarkably similar to the stories and scenarios of the other women in CWG.

> You know, I was all-in. I decided that I would like to have one thing on my obituary, "[her name] was arrested for public something or other—for hanging a banner down." But then it was in the meeting someone brought up about another incident and I went, "Oh yeah, I still have that little underlying fear of some bubba driving and throwing something or I don't know. It's terrible, but it happens." (Nancy, 2018)

Others shifted their perspective in a different direction after joining the group. Paula, who in 2017 admitted she could imagine hate crimes happening against open progressives in the county, was even more conflicted when we spoke in 2018. Since 2017, she had left the group for two reasons. First, despite seeing the county as "nice," she was moving to another state, and second, she felt the group was failing to do anything but stoke partisan flames. She told me that she personally contested Theresa's claims that at one of their protest events there were men in trucks circling around them while holding guns.

> E: So, there were no people with guns?
> P: Not that I saw. There was an older man in a truck, who was circling around behind the building where we started the protest—where we were gathering. And he circled around, he was hunched down in his truck and he felt that he had to let us know he was there and was attempting to be tough. (Paula, 2018)

Despite her assertion that CWG was "creating a boogie man where he doesn't exist," she did recognize that there was the potential for retaliation, but that sitting around and talking about it was not the solution.

> E: So, you don't think, let me clarify—you don't think that there is any reason to be actually afraid for some of these women, of retribution, maybe not actual violence, but something like peeling off bumper stickers, vandalizing their stuff, something like that?

P: Small-town bullshit? Probably. But you know, if it's going to make you
scurry into a hole that's a bad deal. I would prefer to find a group that
unites—let's say about a caravan that's coming up through Mexico right
now. There's unity in numbers. I mean, they would not travel with individuals and they're so desperate to get where they're going that they're in
a clump of people and determined to go and they're not going to be put
off by whatever. You know, that makes more sense to me. (Paula, 2018)

Paula might be right. The women had come together to share their stories
of fear and retaliation, and it likely did dig, at least some of them, deeper into
a hole. But as Chapter 6 will reveal, for others it did the opposite. It brought
them out, like the caravan, arm in arm, to the surface where they were more
willing to risk that retaliation. The women of CWG did not have to hide their
stories anymore. They had a captive audience.

Conclusion

The existence of CWG, their secretive nature, and the perceived risks and
actual retaliation that led to that secrecy all say this a story not just of social
isolation, but of economic and physical retaliation as well.[23] The women told
stories of social backlash, of being kicked out of clubs and social gatherings.
They told stories where the political system, the trusted sanctimony of
voting, had failed them. They told stories of economic retaliation, intentional
boycotting, and the fear that what had happened to business owners before
could happen again. But the women also told stories of physical intimidation,
often rooted in narratives around firearms and destruction of property.[24]
These experiences and their narrative reverberation in turn distanced the
women from the community they cared so much about.

The experiences of CWG sit in contrast to what scholars know about
why people withhold or conceal their political beliefs. The women of CWG
are not just single-minded seekers of social connection. They did not base
their decision to withhold a part of themselves solely because they are afraid
people will not talk to them or will exclude them from a dinner party. The
women of CWG also made their calculations based on other capacities of
and reliance on community for which being a political minority makes one
especially vulnerable.

These experiences also sit in contrast to who is typically a victim to such behavior. Groups marginalized along lines of race/ethnicity and gender/sexuality have long experienced social, economic, and physical retaliation for being themselves.[25] Likewise, political extremists have previously been and continue to be pushed into margins of public discourse by mainstream society, most often for normatively good reasons.[26] In contrast, CWG—their stories and their fears—are reflective of a new era of prejudice and illiberalism, one that includes the mainstream who, in other contexts, might even be the majority. In other words, the fear, the risk, and the retribution are not new, but the subject is.

While the women of CWG were conflicted about whether or not to express their beliefs, they were also conflicted about the group itself. That is, how they could affect political change while hiding, about whether to include or exclude men, whether they could or should be aligned with a party, and whether it was worth even trying to engage with the other side. In the following chapter I will further explore these individual and group-level tensions and what they meant and continue to mean for the group and their community.

5

Negotiating Identity and Secrecy

While the women were busy avoiding conflict around politics in their own lives, there was conflict abounding within CWG itself. The women had come together around a common feeling: they were all horrified that Donald Trump had been elected president. Outside of that feeling and their geographic commonality, the women had some categorical differences, and most of these had to do with their preferences for the group. Some of this conflict was around their preferences for secrecy, while other conflict was a result of it.

For one thing, a shared dislike of Trump did not equate to a shared preference for the Democratic Party. This meant that some of the women identified as Independents, and some as progressives, but not as Democrats. This made the group's action, particularly in the context of a budding midterm and general election, especially challenging. It asked them to think about political activism and whether it could exist effectively as nonpartisan, or whether it would inherently need to connect to a party.

There was also conflict around whether the group would consist of only women or whether it would include men. Several self-proclaimed, second-wave feminists advocated for CWG as a safe space for women separate from the male-dominated agendas and leadership of other groups in the community. Even those less adherent to the feminist label saw CWG as a place for creating power and a sense of strength. Others were cautious of excluding men, arguing for male friends or husbands who, like the women had before joining the group, felt entirely alone.

Beyond identity, there was a tension around what precisely the group should *do*. Many members saw value in reaching "across the aisle" and engaging in meaningful conversation with conservatives in their lives and in their community. This was not an easy task for a group of women who had compartmentalized politics within themselves and, for many, who disagreed politically with those they loved. The potential for conversation with the other side, they thought, was a redefinition of the words "liberal," "progressive," and "Democrat," and a blunting of the very hostile

Democracy Lives in Darkness. Emily Van Duyn, Oxford University Press. © Oxford University Press 2022.
DOI: 10.1093/oso/9780197557013.003.0005

partisanship that had sent them underground. Others saw attempted conversation as futile, often citing the fears of more reticent members to publicly come out as progressive, or the limited likelihood of changing conservative minds. In some ways, the women's challenge was whether or not they could or would do to conservatives what had been done to them, whether they were willing to look down upon and exclude conservatives from their own lives.

Finally, while Chapter 3 detailed how the women established secrecy and Chapter 4 detailed why, this chapter focuses on how the women maintained their secrecy; more specifically, it looks at how they struggled with the decision to stay secret or go public. Those against secrecy saw the group's power in solidarity. The women could come together to challenge their neighbors and their friends and family to take their side seriously, to back down on their intimidation. Those for secrecy saw the group's power in stealth. They believed that the women had not only protection under the group's coordination, but also strategy in their invisibility from the opposition.

Following CWG over time meant that sometimes these conflicts caused the group to change, and sometimes it caused members to leave the group. In this chapter, I will discuss these conflicts over time, some that were, at least temporarily, resolved, and some that remain ongoing as the group continues to evolve.

Nonpartisanship vs. Democratic Affiliation

"We are not a group of Democratic ladies."

When CWG first formed, their purpose was to mourn Trump's victory. This meant that the group's existence was based not purely on party identification, but on how the women voted in the 2016 election. These preferences, as any purveyor of election data will tell you, are highly correlated, but not perfectly so. For instance, several members of CWG identified as Bernie supporters or Independents. In general, these were the members who expressed concern about aligning with the Democratic Party, even when it came to election activities. This reflected a common concern that a two-party system in the United States grows increasingly inadequate at conveying the preferences of the public.[1]

Paula, for instance, said she was a Bernie supporter in the 2016 primary, and was personally conflicted about how to engage in political activism without going through a party.

> I'm a Bernie supporter, I'm a progressive. So no, I don't walk the line with the party. It's in disarray, and I'm very critical of what's going on with the party. But I did become a county precinct chair. So, it's like I'm straddling two things. It's like I have this attitude, a Bernie attitude, and then I'm sort of trying to see what I can do within the party to raise visibility. (Paula, 2017)

Although she was critical of the party, she had recently participated in party activities through CWG and even taken on a leadership role. This was at least in part because she saw the party as the funnel for most activism in the area. In other words, there were few local political groups for Paula to join at all, let alone progressive groups that were *not* affiliated with the Democrats. Despite her recent participation in the local Democratic Party, Paula did not want CWG to be entirely affiliated with the Democrats.

> There are some people who don't think there should be any distinction between, say, the Democratic Party and CWG, when in fact there is. CWG is anti-Trump and they're progressive. They do not automatically endorse the Democratic Party, and because so few people have been engaged in politics previous to their involvement with CWG, it's hard for them to make that distinction. You know, they don't really understand, [some of them say] "Why can't we all just say we're Democrats?" Some people don't even want people to know they're Democrats. There's a lot of fear. (Paula, 2017)

To Paula, a push for CWG to become a Democratic group, rather than a nonpartisan one, was driven by a lack of political experience among the members. Unlike many of the less experienced members, she saw the gray areas of the left wing—specifically, those between the Bernie supporters and the more institutional Democrats. She wanted the group's distance from the Democratic Party to reflect that difference.

Paula would go on to leave the group and move to another state. When I spoke with her again in 2018, she mentioned wanting to find the right "tribe" in her new state, one that encouraged activism but not along party lines.

E: And you're moving to Massachusetts. Do you have a sense of how en-
     gaged in politics you're going to be there?

P: No, I don't. Because after my year of heavy activism and involvement
     and what have you, I realized that what I must do—because I felt so
     much guilt about leaving the women's group, and that's my own per-
     sonal stuff, that's my psychological baggage, you know, we're not gonna
     go through that stuff, but you know. . . . So, I thought next time, and
     there will be a next time, I'm going to vet whatever I jump—I will not
     jump into—I will gradually introduce myself before I get involved be-
     cause I very much want to be involved, I very much want to find a group
     that feels like my tribe and all that stuff. So, I just have to be patient, wait
     until I get there. Carefully feel my way through things, and then you
     know, jump back in. That's what I'm hoping for. (Paula, 2018)

While Paula resisted aligning with the Democrats because she was critical
of the party, others resisted this affiliation because the label of "Democrat"
was simply too stigmatizing. For example, Ann thought a formal affiliation
with the local Democratic Party could actually cause CWG to lose power in
the community.

It [CWG] really seemed to be heading down this path where there need
to be Democratic representatives, and certainly there is this kind of core
who is involved in the Democratic Party here in the county. . . . Because we
had talked about potentially endorsing a candidate or being out there on
some issue, I thought, "Wait a minute, if we go down this road we're doing
the same things that have been done before and if we begin to endorse,
given the environment, being identified as a group that's supporting this
Democratic candidate—we'll just have lost it. We will be pigeonholed. We
will be identified with the Democratic Party. And so, I think that to make a
difference we have to somehow be a part of the narrative, help change the
narrative, really focus on the issues and doing that in a way that doesn't get
us back into beating our heads against the wall or against each other. It has
to be more strategic. (Ann, 2017)

Despite that the group was a secret from the community, Ann was worried
about what the community would think. She was worried that CWG would
never be heard if their message came from a Democratic pulpit. If CWG
one day wanted to use their power to amplify their shared concerns about

their country and their community, she thought, then a Democratic group would only be adding to the cacophony of partisanship and not rising above the noise.

In contrast, there was also a strong insurgence of CWG members who had been lifelong Democrats who wanted the group to be completely aligned with the party's efforts. Cynthia was one of these members. When I spoke with her in 2017, she described the Democratic Party as an arbiter of universal values—something that all the women in the group should be able to get behind.

> Some people felt like we were going more towards a Democratic, you know, a Democrat's view of things, and some women felt like that was not appropriate—that we should, you know, be open to other ideas. I'm not sure I agree with that. Because most of the women are Democrat or Independent, and actually, no one's come right out and said that they were a Republican, or that they voted Republican, but for me, I think we should move toward universal values that everyone can accept, and for me, that's the Democratic values from the Democratic Party. And it's just a difference of opinion I think with some of the women. (Cynthia, 2017)

Like Cynthia, some in CWG felt that aligning with the Democratic Party was the only way to affect change. Alice, who had originally identified as an Independent, said after joining CWG she had changed her mind about the Democratic Party. She was tired of feeling compelled to take action. The only way, she thought, to have any long-term effect on her community was to support the Democratic Party and its candidates.

> I don't want to be 92 years old and still having to make daily calls to action and fight. At some point I want to elect someone who really represents the rural people like us, what we need, what we desire in our representatives, so I would much rather be proactive getting people we need elected as opposed to having to protest and fight. (Alice, 2017)

For Alice, party support was essential for the long term. The group would inevitably have to pick a party and support it. Joyce and Deborah felt this inevitability, too. The midterms would require them, Joyce thought, to make a choice between Democrats and Republicans, and with the Trump administration at the forefront of the Republican Party, she could not imagine their choice would be the latter.

We may be shifting over to kind of being a Democratic group, even though we're not all Democrats: we feel like we have to align with the Democratic Party because we can't start a third party. . . . So that may be the biggest push in the group. I don't know if it's going to split up, but I think we're going to have a big part of the group that's going to work on that and the other part may not. (Joyce, 2017)

Joyce thought that partisan choice could split the group, or at least fissure the cohesiveness of their activism. When I spoke to Deborah in 2018, she attributed this partisan tension to a difference between two kinds of CWG members: members who just wanted to be *engaged* and members who wanted to be *established*. Those who wanted to be engaged did not need a party to do so. They could protest and make phone calls without going through a party. Those who wanted to be established needed a structure. They needed the institutional weight, the state and national associations that the Democratic Party offered.

There were people in the beginning that didn't want to be identified with a party, per se, they just wanted to be in a group that was politically concerned, but I think that was just unrealistic. It's impossible because we only have two parties and we certainly don't identify with the Republican Party. (Deborah, 2018)

The group would, as Deborah mentions, make a decision to side with the Democrats. This gradual shift from nonpartisanship to Democratic affiliation is most evident in the shift in language at their meetings over time. Earlier meetings often included a section in which some of the active Democrats in the county would give an update on the local party's efforts. This was an ordained section of the meeting for how the group could help the Democrats.

For instance, at the December 2017 meeting, the minutes mentioned an update from Cathy and Cynthia, two CWG members also in the local Democratic Party, about their efforts to campaign for Beto O'Rourke before the primary. The minutes read as follows:

Cathy and Cynthia also reported that the [county] Democrats have been working in conjunction with the [neighboring county] Democrats and will continue to do so regarding block walking and getting out the vote for Beto, [other local candidate], and others who will be on the Democratic ticket. We were invited to block walk with them, a rewarding task since we will visit only known Democrats, who have so far welcomed our visits and information. Call Cynthia or Cathy to participate. (Each person walking will have a partner).

At some point during these early meetings, the Democratic faction would often advocate for CWG members to come to meetings. At their fourth meeting, in February 2017, the minutes explicitly mentioned the vocal Democrats in CWG encouraging those who were interested to join and support the local party:

> Many sources nationwide have reiterated that we progressive/liberals are too late in the game to start from scratch before the elections in 2018 with a new party. No matter our affiliation we are urged to stop scattering our efforts over many possibilities and instead concentrate on our common strengths to revitalize the Democratic Party. Locally: attend the meetings of the local Democratic Party. Be a precinct chair. Register people to vote. Knock on doors. Run for office. Support someone we (collectively, state-wide) choose to run against Ted Cruz. Be part of changing and revitalizing the local Democratic Party. Meetings of the [county] Democrats are held in [town] on [day and time monthly]. ATTEND!

This push from the group's vocal Democrats would, over time, work as an effective recruiting tool and ultimately bring many of the women out of their political and nonpartisan shells. While Chapter 6 will address how the women's behavior shifted toward the Democratic Party, this language change does convey that the group had originally compartmentalized the vocal Democrats into a section of the meeting and had resisted that label across the group more broadly.

I spoke with one of the youngest members of CWG after her first meeting in August 2017. In our conversation she mentioned that at this meeting, it was clear the group did not want to be entirely affiliated with the Democratic Party.

> So yeah, I went to a meeting and it was just wonderful. These women all kind of feel the same way. They're not . . . I won't say they're off the top right, they're not all Democrat I guess is what I'm trying to say. But they all

are opposed to a lot of stuff that's going on politically and with the current administration, so that's the common thread there, which is awesome. But they're real careful about not saying Democrats in that meeting I noticed. (Audrey, 2017)

I recall this meeting because it was the first meeting I attended as well. The group had discussed a potential fundraising committee and there had been a brief and rather vocal argument about what the purpose of a fundraising committee was when they could not even say who they were. One member shouted, "We're a group of Democratic ladies!" and Alice retorted, "We are *not* a group of Democratic ladies," and another added, "This is not semantics." At some point in the argument, Alice had been hushed by another member of the group, and five minutes later she picked up her things and left. This was not semantics, it was personal.

Audrey and I had come at a time when the group was facing down a divide: a divide between those wanting affiliation with the Democratic Party and those wanting partisan distance. By their meeting in June 2018, they officially recognized CWG as holding a Democratic affiliation, precisely for the reasons that Theresa, Joyce, and Deborah had predicted. "No matter our political identification, we agreed that voting the Democratic ticket at this time is the best way to win seats," the minutes read. They did not forfeit that there were members of the group who were not Democrats, only that they had to pick a side and they chose the Democrats. This would prove to be monumental for their future and for the future of their local party, as will be discussed in the next chapter.

All Women vs. Mixed Gender

"Because what happens when you have men in a meeting? Have you studied that? They take over."

One of the more obvious and important aspects of CWG is that it is open only to women. This exclusivity makes sense considering that marginalized groups often seek out those who are similarly marginalized to form groups for social connection.[2] But CWG's exclusivity makes sense for two other reasons. For one, the group's original purpose was to serve as a "therapy" session following Trump's upset victory over Clinton. And that election was, in many ways, an election *about* women—the first female candidate for president from a major party, Trump's own admissions and accusations of sexual harassment, and the ongoing misogyny of his rhetoric made the election returns burn tenfold for women across the country and across the world. Finding a group of women with whom to gawk and cry was a natural response to an election that had very much become a referendum on women's place in society.

CWG was also exclusive to women because of a norm in their community that women avoid talking about politics. Outside of a political party, men and women in their community did not sit together to talk politics. If anything, it was the men who did the talking for the women.

Connie experienced this firsthand. When I spoke with her in 2017, she told me a story about her neighbor, a strong Trump supporter, who would sometimes come over to talk politics with her and her husband. Yet the neighbor directed all political conversation at Connie's husband while the wives had a separate conversation that circumvented politics.

> I've never been particularly political, but you know our neighbor would come over and would, you know, he and [her husband] would discuss the election and it was just—I've never seen him just get his back up so much regarding Hillary Clinton, and you know, for me, I was voting—we were voting—against Oba- I mean against Trump. . . . His wife just kind of . . . like I said they're Republican, I don't know who she ended up voting for and I didn't ask her, cause I just didn't want that to even come up. (Connie, 2017)

Perhaps some of the women in CWG, like Connie, saw politics as a male topic of conversation because they had been socialized to equate the political sphere with men. In fact, research across several decades has found that women are more likely than men to avoid political conversation, and that this avoidance is most common among topics falling into the political sphere rather than the domestic sphere.[3] The propensity to view politics as a decidedly male topic made having a political conversation taboo. It also made finding other people who shared your political beliefs difficult. It was hard for the women to find political compatriots when the ones who talked openly about politics were unwilling to have a political conversation with them. As a result, the women were left to find political similarity with other women and through means other than an unabashed conversation about politics.

But the women of CWG gravitated toward other women because of the 2016 election itself. The nature of the election as a centrifuge for public opinion on women's rights was especially apparent when the women talked about watching the 2016 returns. Linda, for instance, mentioned she had a group of five friends from across various counties who were "all on the same page," and who watched the 2016 election results together.

> We checked into a motel and we spent the night together to watch the election returns. And in the beginning of the evening, we were just real high, we were just so sure that this was gonna be a big victory for Hillary. And so, of course, it didn't turn out that way. And I'm telling you we were just every one of us so devastated. We all just went into these depressions. We just cried, we just felt helpless, and we felt like the world was coming to an end. We felt afraid. Afraid for the future. Afraid for our children. Feeling that, you know, we were just going to lose what we had fought so long and hard for in terms of civil rights. And also our own individual liberties. (Linda, 2017)

Cathy also had a couple of Democratic friends with her on election night who stayed at a (different) motel to watch the results together. Cathy even wore a "nasty woman" T-shirt and chilled champagne as she sat with her friends and watched the numbers roll in.

> Some friends and I got together on election night in a hotel in [a local town] with our Hillary signs. And I had on my nasty woman T-shirt and we had a bottle of champagne, and we were fully expecting to be celebrating. And I went to bed sometime during the night knowing that it was—that she had not won and we never opened the champagne, and it was like a funeral the next morning. (Cathy, 2017)

Linda and Cathy wanted to be among women and outside of their own homes that night because, to them and to many others, it was an election *about* women. The women were not with their husbands or their families, they were with their female friends, because, on the night when they either celebrated a major victory or cried because of a devastating loss, they wanted to be with people who would understand.

All of this is to say that the women of CWG had many reasons to want a group of only women. At the beginning, and even currently, most of the women prefer the group to remain this way. As I spoke with them over the years, they often justified their desire for a women-only group as a necessity to keep it secretive. For instance, in 2017 Joyce mentioned that the women were actually worried that if they opened the group up to men then they would also risk being infiltrated and exposed to the community.

> I think, ultimately, we need to not just be all women. But important, I mean it is important, maybe to the same women who wanted to keep it secret, but it's important to ones that have husbands or relationships that are on the opposite side. And they've had worries that we'd be infiltrated or that the Republicans might send some spy out or something and that if we had men that we'd run a greater risk of that. (Joyce, 2017)

There was also skepticism about the role of husbands in the group. Given the tendency for politics to be a male-dominated conversation in the women's own homes and friend groups, many women were resistant to bringing this dynamic into CWG by allowing men into the group. Melanie told me that the women's initial push for men joining the group was related to their desire for some husbands to join.

> We had a social around the holidays, and it was brought up, "Oh should we bring our husbands"—somebody said, "We should bring our husbands," and a couple of people went "No." And then it was pretty quickly that it was decided that it would not include spouses. (Melanie, 2017)

Theresa was especially perplexed why the women would want men, particularly Trump- supporting husbands, there at all. She speculated that the women advocating for men to join were receiving pressure from husbands who wanted to control what their wives were doing.

> T: These guys don't care to hear our voice at all, and I'm really sick of that. So, I very much want it to stay a women's group.
> E: Do you think that there are some people that want it to be mixed?
> T: Yes, and a number of women oddly enough, said, "I would love to bring my husband," who, 20 minutes earlier were complaining about how their husband voted Republican in the election, and how they feel so distanced from them, and how they feel like they're sleeping with the enemy—I've heard that phrase I don't know how many times. And yet they want them to be included in this kind of meeting? No way. . . . I find that a really odd thing to be saying,

because they're the ones that are saying, "Oh, can't we bring the men?' and I sort of wonder if the men aren't putting pressure on them, saying "Can't I come?" or "Why are you doing this without me?" (Theresa, 2017)

While appeals to the group's secrecy and to safeguarding the group from suspecting husbands were frequent, the most common justification for the group being all women was that the women were afraid they would lose their voice if men were allowed to join. This idea was most commonly alluded to with one expression: the men would "take over."

For example, when I asked Deborah whether she thought it was important that the group was only women, she cited research that found men often talk over women in deliberative settings. This was why, she said, the group should remain only women.

Somebody mentioned at the meeting—that third meeting which was at [location]—about inviting guys. And I just, oh no. Because what happens when you have men in a meeting? Have you studied that? They take over. They monopolize the conversation and we women turn into wimps. That's probably a big exaggeration, but I remember a study that I read when I was in graduate school about some graduate students that observed couples—groups—in restaurants. And this is back in the day when you had tape players, and they taped the conversations. And then went back and studied the conversations and they did this several times. And what they realized was that women ask questions and encourage men to talk and men talk. Men were the ones talking like 70% of the time. So, I just want it to be women. (Deborah, 2017)

Deborah was concerned the conversation—and who and how much each person participated—would be affected by men's presence. She was likely right. In fact, Deborah's reference to research on men and women's different styles of communication is part of a well-documented pattern of gender differences in discursive participation. Women do tend to accommodate their conversation partner more by asking questions or engaging in what researchers call a "facilitative" style of communication.[4] In the context of political discussion or political deliberation, men are also the ones most likely to speak and to speak most frequently.[5] CWG safeguarded themselves by setting rules around membership, which they thought would help set the rules around conversation sharing.

Deborah was not alone in these thoughts. When I spoke with Cynthia in 2017, she advocated for an all-women group because such a composition would distinguish CWG from other political organizations, like the local Democratic Party, of which she is a part.

> You know, women have a camaraderie with each other that I don't think extends to men. You know, I have close women friends that I enjoy being with in mixed groups, but I prefer, you know, when I have really things that I want to talk about with just a woman I think they would only understand or maybe have experienced, I just think that's important. (Cynthia, 2017)

When I spoke with her again in 2018, she mentioned more explicitly that the gender exclusivity of CWG was not only essential to keep men from "taking over," but also to keep their current membership coming to meetings.

> C: I just feel like if we opened it up to some men that some of the women wouldn't come.
>
> E: Why do you think they wouldn't come?
>
> C: I just think they feel like the men might take over. You know, women and men just have different ideas I think about the way they express, you know, their feelings. And I guess how they work toward their goals. I don't really know. I just think it should stay women—that's how it started, and I just think it might fall apart if we opened it up. And I don't think anybody's gonna vote to do that. Cause they've mentioned before, you know, well should we invite men to some of our events and things? And usually the women say no when there's a vote. Now the social that's coming up, we're going to open that up to men, husbands if they want to come and to other people that we know would like to support a money-raising thing for the Democrats. (Cynthia, 2018)

Cynthia was referring to the fundraiser the women would hold in September 2018, where husbands did attend, but sparingly. I attended that fundraiser and saw how clear it was whose husband supported whom. The stark contrast of women walking around solo compared to the women walking around with a partner spoke to the various experiences in the group and a reminder of why they had excluded husbands to begin with: opening it up to husbands was "othering"; it was a reminder that in other parts of their lives, they were politically isolated.

When I spoke with Melanie in 2017, she also mentioned the potential for men to "take over" meetings when we discussed why it was important that the group stay all women.

> I think that women need to take a stronger and bigger part in the important things that happen in our country, whether it's at a political level or a business level. I think that when men get in the mix, we have a tendency to defer to them and they have a tendency to take over things, so I think this allows women to develop a stronger side of themselves. (Melanie, 2017)

Likewise, Dawn expressed the concern that men would "take over" when I spoke with her in 2017. Citing her experience as a feminist in the 1960s and 1970s, she saw instances where men took over and shifted power away from women.

> I was very active in the women's liberation movement in the late sixties and early seventies. First in the Vietnam War, SDS, all that. And then I started seeing how people were treating women and that's when I got onto feminism. . . . And I feel like in a group, the dynamics totally change when you get men in a woman's group. They tend to take over. It's just a different mentality if you will. I feel like there's a power shift and I don't think it's a good one. I think we need to stay a women's group. I think that if we could be a co-ed group, it would be great. But personally, I've been to several meetings that are co-ed, [other statewide group] and all that, and the guys take over. (Dawn, 2017)

Her response echoes what any critical scholar would consider a strongly "second-wave" perspective, alluding to the era of women's rights activism that focused on creating "women's spaces," which served as their own form of resistance.[6] Rather than having men change their behavior, the solution, at least temporarily, was for women to find a separate space.

Melanie's and Dawn's evaluations of the group as a place for women to feel "stronger" was a sentiment I heard from other members as well. Shirley saw CWG as a place for women to practice independence and leadership, and she referenced women's own susceptibility to being overpowered as a reason to keep it open to only women.

I see these women who—it's like those women who won't fight with their husbands about it. We just—we are peacemakers, women are, and so it is very difficult for us to say, "this is not right and I'm going to stand be very vocal about it and I don't care what you say." So, I think we will stay much more independent and much more aggressive and show much more leadership if we remain a women's group. (Shirley, 2017)

Like Shirley, Roberta saw the value of an all-women's group as a tool for "training." As a group exclusive to women, CWG members could practice talking about politics, especially those who had little experience with politics coming into the group.

This issue [the gender of the group] just came up, just at this last meeting. That question was asked, and everybody felt strongly that it should stay all women. I mean, after all, one of the things that it's doing, Emily, is the training. And you know, it's good if you bring some guy to help teach you something, I think that's terrific. But I think the membership in the group should stay all female. I think women who are not particularly versed in politics are not necessarily comfortable speaking out in a group, but that's easier for them if it's a group of women than if it's a group of half and half, so to speak. Because they're used to having their positions put down or they're used to having to put themselves down to present their positions so that it does not antagonize men." (Roberta, 2017)

Virginia also mentioned the fear that men would "take over" as if it was an inevitability, as if once they let men into the group that the women would lose all control. This fear of losing control was inherent in the repeated phrase of men's "taking over." Remaining only open to women allowed the group to continue building a sense of strength and power without men disrupting their progress.

E: Do you think it's important that it stays all women?
V: I think that for now, I do think so. There were a lot of people who said, "Look, we know what happens if you get men involved—they take over." And too often, we let them, you know. And so, we're not ready to do that. And I think that it adds strength to our group for it stay women, for now anyway. Because there are plenty of things that other groups and we as a group can get involved in that do have men as members. And so,

I think that in that we can work together. But I think this is a good group to stay all women at this point, so we begin feeling, learning, about our own strengths. (Virginia, 2017)

In this response, Virginia also references the ability for the women who want a mixed-gender group to join other groups, like the local Democratic Party, where men and women could both act and meet together. When I spoke with Cathy in 2018, she said the Democratic Party was the place "where men and women can be involved," but that CWG "oughta stay just women."

Others used the examples set by the local party or other local or statewide groups as an example of why CWG should be all-women in the first place. Theresa told me in 2017 it was important to her that CWG was open only to women, particularly after she saw how the local Democratic Party meetings were run when there was a mixed gender membership.

I see it in our local Democratic Party. I will not go to the [county] Democratic Party because what I see is that the men there are acting like a microcosm of what Trump is doing, but with his behavior. So, while they're on the side of the right issues, their behavior is no better than Trump in a lot of ways. They dominate and control meetings. They want to do all the talking. They don't want to hear what other people have to say. They're not interested in consensus building. They're interested in dominating and controlling and telling the group what the decision is going to be. (Theresa, 2017)

Often this dismissal of women was explicitly connected to men's dismissal of the women's fears. Theresa told me that men in the local party would often dismiss the women's concerns about being public Democrats in the county. In her response, she references the story of the woman being run off the road that had become a symbol for physical intimidation in the CWG narrative.

They [men] tend to put down and be dismissive of the fears that all of the women are verbalizing. So, when there was this woman who stood up and talked about her friend from [a nearby city], one of the men who had been invited by the [county] to speak on a specific issue stood up and said, "Well now, aren't you just getting all worked up for nothing?" He diminished a very real incident that had just happened the weekend before. And so, I'm sick of that. (Theresa, 2017)

Nancy told a similar story in 2017, of telling a man in the state level Texas Democratic Party about an "anonymous" group of which she was a part. In response, she said, he went on to chastise her and the others of CWG for keeping it a secret and thus failing to help Democrats get elected.

> I told him a bit about what we were doing and that there was this anonymity, and he was surprised. He goes, "Well, how are you gonna elect Democrats if you're not going to say who you are and what you're doing? How are you gonna get anybody to do that—to vote for Democrats?" (Nancy, 2017)

Despite Nancy walking the line of group confidentiality, she had uncovered a man, even on the women's own partisan side, who failed to understand why they were secretive. It struck me that I got this kind of reaction from men when I told others I was studying a secret group of progressives in rural Texas. Women commonly responded with understanding. Men commonly responded with skepticism.

But there were also women in CWG who saw value in including men. Most notably, even the women who were *against* excluding men were aware of the "take over" narrative so prevalent in the group. Gail, who thought the group should be open to men, recalled a time when a woman showed up to her first meeting and brought her husband, who was not allowed to stay.

> At one of the meetings a woman and her husband showed up and she was new. And the people sitting around me said, "Oh no. He can't stay. We don't want men here." And I said, "Why? Why are we discriminating against men? What's the difference?" Because I have a friend who would probably enjoy being part of it. And that's what they said, they said, "Well, because men won't respect us, they'll just talk down to us. They'll take over." And I don't necessarily agree with that, but that was the general consensus, so I didn't argue with it. (Gail, 2017)

Gail saw the exclusion of men as unfair, particularly as she thought of a person who needed a group of their own. Ironically, though she disagreed that men would "take over," Gail herself was being overpowered by a group of women.

Most obviously, there appeared to be different perspectives on the group's gender composition that depended on age. Most of the women who strongly advocated that the group stay only women are, as Kathleen mentions, of an age where men often did take over, and where women often let them.

I'm liking the women energy, the "we're in charge and we're leading the show." You know, I grew up when men did run the show and that was the way it was. And most of us, you know, are my age group, so we all grew up in that era where men are the leaders and you do what they say, which I know right now sounds crazy, but it was in fact the way it was. So, I think we're all perhaps more guarded about keeping us in control than I'm imagining perhaps a woman of your generation might be. (Kathleen, 2017)

Kathleen was right. There was generally a different perspective from the few younger members of CWG. Alice, who was open to a mixed gender group eventually, saw the relationship between age and gender driving the group's current decision to exclude men.

I think that it works well, being all women, given the women who are participating. I think if it were a younger group, I think it would be much less important that it be all female. I think that the generation of women that are participating in this group have been conditioned to act a certain way with men around. And I think that a younger group could be, you know, both genders more easily than an older group can be. I don't think a lot of these women could be comfortable speaking the way they speak around men. (Alice, 2017)

Likewise, Audrey, one of the youngest members, thought the group could benefit from being mixed gender, at least occasionally. Like others, she referenced wanting her husband to have someone "on his side."

I'm a big fan of anything women run or led, I just like girl power. But at the same time, my husband doesn't have anything equivalent and, you know, he would love it. And so that's a little thing that I kind of think about sometimes. Because the men in this county, in [county], are very right-leaning and they have their beliefs and he smiles and nods and drinks his beer just to not have to say anything, but he doesn't really have anyone on his side as well. So yeah, I mean, it'd be nice if we could, I don't know maybe once a quarter, bring anyone. (Audrey, 2017)

Despite arguments for a mixed-gender group, CWG has remained all women, and the issue has become less of a discussion point over time.

Importantly, the women who saw value in men joining, notably Alice, Audrey, and Gail, have all stopped attending meetings. Either CWG had come to a consensus that excluding men was best, or perhaps, like their community, it simply weeded out those holding a dissenting opinion.

Talking to the Other Side vs. Talking to Each Other

"If you think you're going to change their mind, good luck with that and have at it."

Just as the women experienced division around whether to be partisan or whether to exclude men, so too did they struggle with how they would interact with the broader community. Early on, it was brought up that perhaps the women could learn how to talk to the conservatives that many of them feared. The first mention of this was in their February 2017 meeting, with an agenda item on "private conversations of consequence." The minutes from that meeting mentioned a discussion that focused on the importance of listening and communicating with the other side.

> Jane led the discussion in group four about how to best engage one on one with ultra-conservatives that are against all that we believe. Suggestions about approaching conversations gently and not falling into upset and anger were made. Listening well would perhaps promote understanding and an ability to work together might be gained.

That discussion would generate some talk between Jane and Deborah, the therapist cofounder of the group, and a plan to learn how to talk to conservatives and then to teach the other women. Ultimately, that plan did not come to fruition and the women went several more months before it was ever brought back up to the group.

At the meeting in November 2017, there was another push for the women to reach across the aisle and talk to conservatives in their lives. The women first discussed holding a Knock on Every Door campaign in the county, and when the facilitator asked for volunteers to raise their hand, only a few hands popped up. Several of the women who had kept their hands down expressed concern that they would encounter conservatives and not know how to talk to them. Several other women complained they had little knowledge of how to talk to conservatives about politics. "I would like to know how to talk to the people I know who are Republican," one member called out.

From this comment came a five-minute exchange about how to engage with people from the other side. "You just ask questions and listen," Deborah said. Others suggested you connect on a different issue before bringing up politics. There were only a handful of people who did not express concerns that talking to conservatives could not only bring on conflict, but also be counterproductive to the vision they had for turning their community "blue." "We should have a class for ourselves so that we can learn how to talk about these things without agitating," proposed another member. Others saw the need for this strategy and practice in order to change how people in their community vote. "We need to know how to persuade people to vote for our candidates," said one member.

What is striking about this debate on reaching across the aisle is how much the women focused on communication and not on the logistics of political action. Nearly one-third of the meeting time had been spent on political issues, candidates, and courses of action like protests and calling members of Congress. The other two-thirds had been spent purely on communicating with others in their community and in their lives outside of the community, including how to keep the group confidential and how to talk to others unlike them.

When I spoke with the women individually, I heard this same mixture of perspectives, between talking to the other side and only talking to like-minded others. A number of women saw the value in speaking to the other side, despite how hard it could be. Ann, for instance, was a strong advocate for speaking to conservatives in the community. In 2017, she recognized that, in the past, she spoke about politics very little because she said there was a "level of bashing" that was unproductive.

> But I also knew that just trying to engage on a level of the bashing wasn't going to be very satisfying to me and I wouldn't be making much of a difference . . . I think I did temper some discussions in terms of at least some of that recognition [of partisanship] . . . because they just go into this frenzy and there's no real communication happening, and especially if there's already been some drinking happening. I'm picking my battles. (Ann, 2017)

By 2018, she saw even more value in having conversations with the other side that were meaningful. She told me she had even started doing this with her husband. I spoke with her briefly about this at the fundraiser in September of that year and we finished up our conversation over the phone a few weeks later.

> And again, I think I've talked before of how, in some respects, my own spouse being a pretty staunch Republican, I am used to figuring out what works and what doesn't. And just as we kind of started talking about at the fundraiser, that idea of really listening and wondering, being curious, kind of asking questions more so than necessarily getting in someone's face and/ or commenting at everything that comes up. Just kind of, you know. . . . Because I really think that when it's this kind of constant butting heads or feeling like I have to take a stand on everything or everything that comes up in the news or comes up in a conversation, which then just causes that person to get even more entrenched. They have to defend their candidate, their party, their whatever. But being aware of the kind of what's important to them, doing that listening and engaging in a conversation when I think it might make a difference, or when you know they actually might listen. Versus me being anxious in that, so I've got to defend my side, and my issue on everything. (Ann, 2018)

When I asked Ann whether or not she was having more of these conversations now than she had before, she told me she was. The group had made a big difference, she said, because she now had a sounding board—a safety net—for if and when those conversations went awry.

> E: Yeah it does. Would you say you're doing more of that now? More of this engaging in conversation about things?
> A: Yeah yeah.
> E: And what do you think has made the difference with that?
> A: I think it started with the group and knowing that there are others out there who are experiencing a lot of the same things. Knowing that, you know, there are people that I can go to, to have those deeper conversations when I really get frustrated with what happened and/or there's support out there. And there's people out there who . . . I mean, who have credibility is kind of where I was going with that, I guess. (Ann, 2018)

For others, there was value in talking to conservatives, but the secrecy of the group limited that possibility. One of the reasons Paula ultimately left the group was because she felt the women could not do the work of reaching across the aisle while remaining secretive. She was adamant that the secrecy had been "counterproductive" to effecting true change in the community's politics.

> You know, I dropped out a while ago. I don't know how things have evolved, but the secret group thing always rubbed me the wrong way in that I don't really understand how you get people to understand or communicate when skirting around in a secret group. I just found it counterproductive. Now, there are people in there who felt strongly that they needed to keep it that way, and so I respect that. You know, then they should be in that group, but I couldn't be a part of that group. (Paula, 2018)

Instead, Paula thought CWG should have been engaging with the community to change others' minds. In the same conversation, she referenced another fundraiser that the group had done under the guise of the local Democratic Party, at which she had valuable conversations with locals at the farmer's market happening nearby. "And I truly wanted to continue on with that," she told me, "and I just was not able to."

Others were more explicitly against reaching out to and speaking with the other side, not because the secrecy limited them, but because they felt it was a waste of time. Theresa held one of the more extreme perspectives on this, arguing that Republicans in their community were incapable of hearing truth or could not be reasoned with.

> There seems to be within every group a small contingent that say, "Oh we need to have empathy for these poor Trump people, they're uneducated, they're ignorant, they don't get it. They—whatever it is. We need to understand and be empathetic and blah blah blah." And there's others of us going, "If you think you're going to change their mind, good luck with that and have at it. Glory be if you can accomplish the task." But these are people who are—they absolutely don't want to hear facts. They don't want to listen. (Theresa, 2018)

Dawn felt similarly, although her objection was more active indifference rather than active disdain toward and distrust of Republicans. "There's no way I can change their minds," she told me.

Likewise, Cynthia saw potential for talking to some Republicans, but thought that conversation with the "die-hards" would be futile, given it would likely fail to change their minds.

> I know we're not gonna change the minds of the die-hards that are just, you know, voted Republican and who want to remain, even though they may not like Trump and what he's doing and what he's done, but because of what they consider their Republican values will not change their minds. But I just feel like this group could be a force in this county at least . . . to change the minds of some people, to educate them to the values that I think are values that all people feel, you know? (Cynthia, 2017)

Ironically, the extreme partisanship that had pushed CWG underground was the same partisanship that was pushing some of them away from their community. This was the insulation of like-minded groups that scholars have feared as media and communities have become more politically insular.[7] In some ways, CWG members had reason to disengage from a community that had stigmatized and ostracized their beliefs. In other ways, they were contributing to the gulf between the two sides by painting the "others" in their community as incapable of change or unworthy of interaction. The group ranged on a spectrum between taking an eye for an eye or turning the other cheek, with most falling somewhere in between.

In March 2018, the women finally had the "training" they had discussed back in February 2017, and that many women had again called for in November of the same year. The members who had been the original co-facilitators, Jane and Deborah, put the training together, which focused on how to talk to conservatives and was based on "current knowledge and research."

In her PowerPoint presentation, Jane approached the essential question of this training as "How do I talk to my bridge club? How do I talk to my church? These are my friends." Jane, who was for talking with the other side, saw this interaction not only as imperative for turning the county blue, but also for keeping the country alive. "If we continue to look at them as evil," she said, "we will lose our country."

Jane oriented her presentation around George Lakoff's research and his book *Don't Think of an Elephant!: Know Your Values and Frame the Debate— The Essential Guide for Progressives.* Jane's main argument was that liberals and conservatives have structured information differently, and if the women wanted to reach conservatives, to get them to think in a different way, they would have to communicate differently from how they might communicate automatically. Her most compelling point, and the one that the group reacted most positively to, was her charge to "access the nurturant, not the authority part of the brain." By this she meant the women would do well to engage conservatives with care and to pose progressive politics as a solution to their problems. As she talked through this, the women nodded in furious agreement.

Outside of this moment of understanding, the rest of the training was bleak. As Jane went over the need to rationally engage with conservatives, and to manage their own emotions while doing so, one member called out, "But conservatives don't want a rational answer!" In response, Jane said that while conservatives may not seem rational to the women in the room, they believe their political positions *are* rational. The goal of conversation, she said, is to bring them to their rational mind and not their emotional mind.

But the comment had already led the women to a different head space and the feeling in the audience had changed. The remaining conversation devolved into a pessimistic back-and-forth in which the women recounted and gawked at stories of conversations with conservatives that went poorly. One woman told a story she had told previously about an instance where she got into an argument with a conservative person visiting her shop. Another woman told a story of when she hired someone to paint her fence, which at the time had an Obama sign attached to it. The man asked her sarcastically, "Should I paint over your sign?" At that, she told the group, she "went off the rails."

The women were emotional about this topic. Most had a bad experience interacting with a conservative to recount, and those who did not had likely been too afraid or concerned to even engage.

This would be the last time I saw or heard the group discuss how to talk to the other side. Some members, like Ann, continued addressing it when I spoke to them individually, but the group had put it, at least temporarily, to rest. Instead, they set their sights on mobilizing Democratic voters in the county and letting individual campaigns do the persuasive legwork.

Yet their struggle in communicating with conservatives, even conservatives with whom they had already interacted, is telling in many ways. For one, it shows how big of a hurdle communication feels when you are afraid either of the process of communicating or the outcome of it. Many of the women had been scorned, and that experience had dug them deeper into a communicative hole. For some it had dug them deeper into secrecy.

Second, their struggle shows just how much help the women needed and the potential of their group to address that need. They had a resource in each other as a tool for practicing their responses and hearing best practices, whether they were able to use each other or not. Their struggle also shows a need for information on how to talk about politics in a way that will not ostracize, stigmatize, or polarize their community further. The women sought information on how to talk to their neighbors in ways that do not subject them to danger or hostility and instead connect them to the humanity of their neighbors, and their neighbors to their own humanity. Whether they were unwilling or unable to fill these needs is unclear. What was clear was that the women's experiences with conservatives had affected their willingness to communicate. As a result, engaging with the other side was more aspiration than reality, and when they were faced with the task, it felt impossible.

Remaining Secret vs. Going Public

"Look, it's me, I'm your neighbor and I'm not some commie."

Although division around the group's partisan affiliation, its gender composition, and its efforts to engage conservatives popped up from time to time, no other issue was more divisive for CWG than that of the group's secrecy. Secrecy was the issue that caused the most turbulence over the first two years of the group's existence, and the one that sits at the heart of this book.

When I spoke with the women in 2017, most of the concerns with the group's secrecy related to its effect on their power. Some of these concerns were from those who had previously been quiet about their political beliefs but had become more vocal after joining the group. Joyce was one of these women. Although she "kept quiet" because of bad experiences with expressing her views to friends and family in the community and because of her local business, she found her voice after joining CWG. When I spoke to her in 2017, she was ready to use that voice, and the voices of other members, to the fullest extent possible. Secrecy meant that could not happen.

J: I honor it being secret, but I wish it wasn't. I think we'd have more power
     if we weren't secret.
E: Like political power? Manpower?

J: Yeah, political power, yes. Because in order to shift Texas anywhere we're going to have to move some people on the right. We're going to have to. We can get new voters, that's good, we can get our old voters to come out and vote, that's good, but we still might not have enough to win some of the elections that we want to win unless we get some Republicans converted. (Joyce, 2017)

Joyce saw value in talking to conservatives, in attempting to "convert" them, and she saw the unique power of doing this together as a group. To her, secrecy made that less possible and weakened the ability of CWG to change how the county votes.

Cynthia, a long-time Democrat in the county, gave a similar prognosis. In order to take action that she felt would "affect the political climate in the United States and Texas," she thought the women would have to come out as Democrats. She told me that there were others in the group who felt this way but had quelled those feelings to the needs of those who were not ready to take a public stance.

And it has been suggested that eventually we be very open about the fact that we meet and are active in stopping Trump's agenda. It's been suggested, and I think at some point that we'll have to. Not all the women in the group agree that we should remain, you know, not open about what we're doing. (Cynthia, 2017)

Like Joyce and Cynthia, Cathy saw a chance to change the community's perception of self-identified Democrats in the county. While she understood some members' hesitation in becoming "public" Democrats, she also thought it hurt those in the group who did want to be more publicly engaged, that it kept them from "using their power."

I don't know, I'm not one of those women who has a business. So, I'm sure they have their reasons. But I would prefer to let people know what I think and what I belong to. It's important for me . . . I guess it kind of—it kind of feels a little, for people not to want anyone to know, it's not using their power, it's not using power as a group to let other people know how many of us there are and who we are and what we stand for. But like I said, I don't have a business and I can't speak about that. (Cathy, 2017)

This potential for the group to change the hearts and minds of their community was rooted in power the women already held. Nancy was especially convinced that "coming out" to their community could help to assuage others' ideas of who is liberal and what it means to be a liberal in the minds of conservatives. After all, the "conservatives" the women spoke of were their neighbors, friends, and family, not strangers.

> When it became the topic that we would have this anonymous stance I just went, well wait, we're a room full of what I'm thinking is a room full of influential women in the county, and we should say that. We should be public and stand up and say, "Hey, look, it's me, I'm your neighbor and I'm not some commie. (Nancy, 2017)

Nancy had a point. The idea that meaningful contact with someone from a different social or political group is one that has received growing support from a variety of research. In fact, there is evidence that direct and meaningful social contact can help decrease political polarization and change people's political attitudes, and that this is especially likely when this contact is facilitated in apolitical contexts.[8]

Shirley also saw this potential. There was value, she thought, in challenging outsiders' perspectives, in presenting counter-evidence to the idea that their community was "all Republican," and in challenging insiders to see their group as a "coalition" with real influence.

> I think it's better if we were very open so that we could say, "Listen, you jackass, this is the way we—we really have a coalition here." And I think that would make us a bit more powerful or influential or whatever. (Shirley, 2017)

There were also concerns about the group's power in recruiting more members if it stayed secretive. Bonnie thought being open to the community might allow them to find and bring more like- minded people into the group, the same challenge inherent in the "secrecy-efficiency trade-off"[9] from Chapter 3.

> B: I think for some of the people it is. I think we'd have more power if we were not hidden.

E: What kind of power do you think that would be?

B: Hmm . . . maybe to get the word out more so that if there are other people who don't know about the group, but have like-thinking, would feel comfortable joining us. (Bonnie, 2017)

Dawn was attentive to Bonnie's concern when considering how to bring more young women to the group and how to diversify their membership overall.

I mean it's all older women . . . where are the young women? We need to talk about that. And I said yes, I agree, because if we're private, if we're secret, how are young women even going to hear about us to know that there's a place for them? (Dawn, 2017)

Arguments for going public, like those from the women discussed thus far, were about finding others who were like-minded, about changing the community's perspective of liberals, and about attenuating conservative beliefs by giving a viable, and even nonthreatening, alternative. The women wanted to show the community that being a Democrat was safe, even normal, in the hopes that one day, when the right Democratic candidate came along, they would not be held back by the social and cultural stigma of the party label in the voting booth.

But CWG ultimately voted in favor of a confidentiality agreement because most of its members wanted the group to be confidential. Many of these were the women who were not comfortable being publicly "out" as a Democrat and worried about the social, economic, and physical consequences associated with that decision. The business owners like Barbara, Roberta, and Virginia, and the self-protective members like Ann and Connie, were all part of CWG precisely because it was a secret.

Beyond their fears of retaliation, there were other, more strategic reasons why the women wanted CWG to remain a secret. Unlike those who saw power being limited by their secrecy, there were other members who saw power in the group remaining a secret. Much like other marginalized groups who help change mainstream narratives by creating their own counternarratives,[10] some members of CWG saw potential and power in shaping what is public by doing things in private. For instance, Roberta viewed the group's secrecy as a way to subvert the Republican Party, arguing that going public opened them up to attack and the Republicans counteracting their efforts.

As long as the Republicans don't exactly know us, don't know what we're up to, don't have a clue, then they can't really do too much about it. But the minute we go public they will start saying everything is a lie, that we are just, you know, the trash of the earth, or we're so stupid, we don't understand the importance of everything, blah, blah, blah. And I think it is better, until we are stronger, I think it is better that we stay private. I really do. Not everybody feels this way. (Roberta, 2017)

Barbara agreed that there was a certain strategy in remaining secretive from the community, namely from the Republican Party. She describes this strategy like a hunting tactic—to sit and watch the prey before attacking.

I want to see a change, but I want to take this stealth look at it because the Republican Party is so strong, and I would like to remain anonymous for a while to see if our numbers grow and if we get impact in the coming elections. So, that's the reason why I would like it to remain anonymous for a while. But having said that, the majority rules and I will go along with what the majority says. I won't be ready to come out of the closet, boldly, and I would have to fall back. . . . But I would prefer to remain anonymous so we can watch, sit back and watch what's going on, so that when we decide to support someone [a candidate] we are successful. (Barbara, 2017)

There was also an argument that the group filled a political niche, serving as a private alternative to the Democratic Party. Those who wanted to be public-facing Democrats could join the Democratic Party, while those who wanted to remain private could stay exclusively in CWG. Audrey saw this division in visibility. In 2017, she mentioned she felt the group should stay secretive, not only to make her feel more comfortable, but because there were simply other places where one could be publicly progressive, but none where she could do so privately.

E: Do you think that the group itself should be hidden?

A: I don't know. I don't know the answer, how I feel about that, just because I personally feel more comfortable when it is, like as it is right now. So, like, I think if they want to be out and open and loud about it, not loud, that's not the right word . . . there's other organizations that do that, like the [county] Democratic Party and the other ones. So, if you're cool with that, and you want to do that, and, you know, scream from the rooftops, that's badass, go do that. But do that with them. (Audrey, 2017)

Like their stories of social, economic, and physical fear, the women often used others' stories as a justification for secrecy. Theresa was one of the more outspoken members, but also one very sensitive to the risk many members felt in publicly coming out.

> I don't have much to lose. I'm retired. I'm not trying to hold down a job any-where. I'm older, and so I don't have those concerns. So I can sort of sit from a lofty place and say, "Yeah, I think this ought to be happening," but in prac-tice, whenever somebody says, "Oh come on, this is ridiculous," I'm the first to say, "No, we can't do that because it's not about you and what you think it's about the people who feel most threatened and most at risk that we need to stand and protect because nobody else is doing that." (Theresa, 2017)

Theresa felt the same way in 2018. Unlike many others in the group who wanted to remain confidential, she thought there was strategy in coming out to their community. Specifically, she saw the benefit of being public in that it challenged existing narratives about liberals in their community received about liberals. When I asked her about the value of being public, she said she thought it had the potential to change the community's minds about liberals.

> I think it's a really good statement to be making to the community. Like, "What? Here we are having a damn bake sale, what? How radical is that? I mean come on, man." That kinda thing. Because it's the whole Fox News hype that make up the "all these liberals are wackos that aren't supportive of the Trump agenda," you know? "They're bad people." And then, you know, to have all these white-haired women out there selling cookies just kind of contradicts that, and I think that's really important. (Theresa, 2018)

In 2018, Melanie still believed that the women should remain secret. She thought it was "sad" this had to be the case, but always spoke to the collective group fears and not to her own.

> I can completely understand why some women just have to keep it under wraps. People with businesses that would probably put their business in jeopardy if they were to let that [their partisanship] out. So, unfortunately, I think there's a place for it. I wish it wasn't that way. . . . I think it's tragic that we feel like we have to keep this private because we're not comfortable with expressing that we have a different view. I just think that's really archaic and unfair. (Melanie, 2018)

Given how essential the distinction between going public and remaining a secret was to CWG's existence, these concerns were brought up often at meetings. In November 2018, after the facilitator read aloud the confidentiality agreement, Cynthia mentioned the need for the group to go public. There was a two-minute discussion, the majority of which was occupied by Cynthia's argument that the group was "a force and people need to know about us." But the group had little response, and this tended to be the case whenever secrecy was brought up. Although I spoke to many who were against the group's secrecy in theory, when it came time to discuss a change in the confidentiality agreement, they were noticeably silent.

Many of the references to the group's secrecy happened when the women spoke about photo opportunities in the community. At the meeting in November 2017, Nancy mentioned they would be taking a photo with the county Democratic Party for a donation they had made. Since CWG had helped raise some of the money, Nancy offered the opportunity to join the photo for the local paper. "There's going to be a photo op," she said, "so if you want to come out as a Democrat, you can join me for the photo op."

This reference to a photo op was also in the minutes from July that same year, which read, "It was also mentioned that we will not mention CWG in the newspaper photograph. Anyone willing to be in the photograph is welcome to participate as an individual, not as a representative of our group, which will remain incognito." I later found this picture in the local paper and saw only a few faces from CWG in the back row.

That some women wanted to be out and some wanted to remain secretive posed a challenge to a group trying to accommodate both. In March 2017, CWG attempted a solution by creating a "press co-ordination committee," whose goal was to find "appropriate newspapers" in their area and write letters to the editor that would challenge the conservative narrative. There was hardly a report following its creation and the committee quickly died.

At their meeting in January 2018, over a year after they were formed, the focus group that included Deborah, Theresa, and Joyce announced there would be a subcommittee of CWG, which would do more public-facing work with credit directly attributed. I spoke with the subcommittee's champion, Theresa, about its development. She considered it a third space for women wanting to be out and remain a part of CWG but also wanting to be separate from the local Democratic Party.

It doesn't have to be either/or. We can still serve everybody's needs. How about if I just create, you know, a wing of the group that is comfortable being out. We can put an actual name on it so people can refer to us and then we can actually do things like what I was saying in the meeting—make political endorsements and be on people's campaign materials, for other rural people to see "oh hey, there's this group of rural women that support this candidate" kind of thing. So, it's not just, you know, city people that are supporting a certain candidate. (Theresa, 2018)

Theresa thought it was important, particularly for the upcoming mid-term election, that the women be able to publicly endorse candidates as a distinct entity from the Democratic Party. Her argument was that in rural areas, where people know you outside of your politics, an endorsement can go a long way when it is independent from a party. "There are advantages to us being ourselves in public" she told me.

While Theresa wanted CWG to be public, she was still sensitive to the fact that many of the women did not. She told the group at their January meeting, "Whoever you feel you are—you can be as out there as you wish in this new wing, or you can stay right here and do exactly as you feel comfortable." She emphasized that the subcommittee was to be a front for CWG's efforts that was distinct from the local Democratic Party. This was particularly impor-tant for those who wanted to remain nonpartisan. To manage membership in both CWG and its public-facing subcommittee, the group created a sheet where those interested in joining the subcommittee could sign up. The day they unveiled the new subcommittee, four women signed up, and only a few followed after.

When I spoke again with Theresa about the subcommittee's development, the photo op related to the book donation was brought up. This time, Theresa argued that the subcommittee could have replaced the local Democratic Party getting all of the credit and challenging the ever-present publicity of the "Republican women."

We had to hide behind the Democratic Party. And so, we wanted a photo op in the newspaper to publicize the fact that we were doing this to sort of counterbalance the Republican women, who are constantly in the paper because they have so much money to throw around donating this and that to everybody, and you know getting all this press for it. But we had to hide behind the Democratic Party, which, you know, I don't personally define myself as a Democrat. And I dislike doing that. You know, I'd rather be who I am, and I feel more of who I am is the women of CWG. You know, that's me. And so, it would have really felt good to do that, and as it was, I had to hide behind somebody else's name. (Theresa, 2018)

Although the women still used the public-facing name for events in which they partnered with the local Democratic Party, the subcommittee itself became obsolete over time. For one thing, no one wholeheartedly joined. Such a disinterest suggested that despite some of the women claiming they were now comfortable "coming out" to the community, they remained reticent to do so. The committee also fell flat because the women would increasingly rely on the Democratic Party as their front. After announcing that in advance of the midterm election CWG would align with the local Democratic Party, the group turned their attention to supporting the party's efforts and not inventing their own. This made the subcommittee less necessary, and in some ways a detractor from CWG and the local party's joint effort to turn the county blue.

That increasing alignment with the local party also meant that, as time went on, the general conversation around remaining secret or going public changed. I heard their secrecy mentioned less and less at meetings, and as I spoke to the women again in 2018, I started to hear less hesitance when I asked about their confidentiality.

Some of the change in how much they talked about CWG's secrecy was because the women who had been skeptical of being public now saw a path forward. CWG was increasingly leading people to become public, not through the group itself, but through the local Democratic Party. It was not that these members saw the secrecy as good, but that they saw it served a purpose. Cynthia, who in 2017 thought the secrecy was a missed opportunity for the women to connect with potential swing voters in the county, had come around to the secrecy more when I talked to her again in 2018. Some of this was because she saw more legitimacy in the women's fear of losing business, but also because she saw that the group offered a niche for Democratic political activism that the public nature of the party did not.

C: I've always thought we should be loud proud and open. But I understand, I'm beginning to understand more about how businesses and women in business don't want to be vocal about supporting Democrats.

E: So, do you now think it should stay secret?

C: No, I don't. But I'm in the minority, I think. Well, they want to try to keep the group together the way it started with women who feel safe coming there and being able to share their feelings and maybe work behind the scenes, whereas they couldn't if they were in the party. So, I think that's a good thing. (Cynthia, 2018)

Similarly, Nancy had previously thought that the only path forward was for the women to come out together as a distinct progressive entity. When I spoke with her again in 2018, she said she still believed there was power in going public but was less convinced it would or should happen with CWG as separate from the party. This change came as the women were now well-aligned with the Democrats—many joining, coming to meetings, and holding leadership positions—which afforded a natural front for their efforts.

I don't think we'll do it [go public]. I still think we'll do it in other ways. Like, there's probably going to be an ad in the paper and we'll just identify ourselves as the Democratic Women and not the group. But it still leaves a good portion of those women unaccounted. (Nancy, 2018)

Although Nancy was right that not all the women in CWG had joined the Democratic Party, the pipeline was growing. The midterm election had brought many of the women to the party in big ways, and in the last meeting I attended, in November 2018, it was clear the membership was starting to see the value of the group for the local Democrats. One member who is actively involved in the party's field operations committee said that CWG was the party's "secret weapon,"—that it helped to engage people who were unwilling to do so publicly with the party. As Chapter 6 will reveal, there were many members for whom the group's secrecy was still troubling, but those feelings were overshadowed by the fact that the group's secrecy had also rebuilt the party itself.

Conclusion

CWG is a group of human beings, and, as such, things were not always cohesive or consistent. The women faced tensions within the group and within themselves about how to exist as a collective and how to affect political change. For one thing, the group was conflicted about how to contain those who desired to be nonpartisan and those who saw the Democratic Party as the most viable option. Ultimately, the group would decide to align themselves with the party, and that choice would fissure their membership, alienating the strict Independents and the progressive wing that was too critical of the party to support it, even covertly.

Second, the women faced a tension between being a group exclusively made up of women or being a mixed-gender group. The nature of the group as a response to Trump's win and an election that was overtly about women made the appeal of an all-female group strong. This was particularly true given the ages of the majority of members who still saw and clung to ideas that men would "take over" should they be allowed to join.

Just as the women faced tensions about their identity, so too did they face tensions about how they would function. One of these concerns related to the group's willingness to engage and communicate with conservatives in the community. This discussion about how to treat their community was juxtaposed with how they had been treated by their community. There were many moments within the group's collective and individual discourse where the women demonized conservatives in ways that were similar to how conservatives in their community had demonized them. This was made harder by the fact that the group was secretive, which meant horror stories of exchanges with conservatives were not tempered by an outsider perspective, much like the insular narratives of other like-minded groups.[11]

Finally, and most consequential, was the group's negotiations to remain secretive or to go public. The coexistence of vocal and public Democrats with reticent progressives was a challenge the group addressed through a myriad of attempted structural solutions. Unlike the typically loose and ungoverned forms of social movement organizations in the "connective" age,[12] the necessity of protection required clear rules and structure. Fueled by fears of social, economic, and physical backlash, the women had strong reasons to resist going public. Yet of the 12 members I spoke to who were most reticent about publicly expressing their beliefs, exactly half of them ultimately did, not through the group's public-facing wing, but through the local Democratic Party itself. In the next chapter, I will unpack just how CWG revitalized and fueled the local party, and how secrecy was paramount to that success.

6

Political Incubation and Infrastructure

Over the two years of their existence, CWG had become a space for shared narratives of backlash and fear, but it had also become a space of shared action. The women, who had originally banded together to express anger and sadness at the 2016 election results, realized quickly that they wanted to do something more than cry—they wanted to act. Some of that action would require little to no public identification as a progressive, but other actions would require a great deal of political "coming out."

Such a range of activity allowed the women to be selective in how they participated. More reticent members could choose anonymous postcard writing over local phone banking for the Democrats, while more outspoken members could participate in local canvassing or working the Democratic table during primary voting. These actions varied in their degree of publicness and afforded political engagement for those who were still wary of being publicly political.

The women who participated in these types of action, however, did not remain the same. In fact, some of the more reticent members started phone banking, knocking on doors, and attending local Democratic Party meetings. Some of them were appointed the Democratic chair of their precinct, and some of them ran for local city council. The women were slowly matriculating into the local party and rebuilding its infrastructure. Just as the group had promoted *insulation*, so too had it promoted *incubation*.

The fluidity of their publicness and the resulting incubation from CWG to the local party can be largely attributed to CWG itself. The women avowed that knowing others like them gave them a sense of safety in their "coming out," allowing them a place to practice talking about politics, which many had not done in 10 or 15 years, and a confidence and security in their identity as a progressive.

Importantly, although CWG had funneled some members into the local party, it offered, and continues to offer, an alternative space for those who remain unwilling to go public. CWG as a place for reticent partisans continues to afford the party both help and protection from community intimidation

Democracy Lives in Darkness. Emily Van Duyn, Oxford University Press. © Oxford University Press 2022.
DOI: 10.1093/oso/9780197557013.003.0006

and counteraction. Put differently, CWG gave life to the local Democratic Party by providing avenues for engagement to those unwilling to be public Democrats while also giving them strategic protection from view of the opposing conservatives. They could gain (wo)manpower while also holding a competitive edge.

In this chapter, I uncover just how CWG served as an incubator from secrecy to publicness, and how it helped to rebuild party infrastructure in ways that would not have been possible were it a public group. I highlight many of the women's transitions from secrecy to publicness, the interconnection between CWG and the local Democratic Party, and how imperative CWG's secrecy was to rebuilding local party infrastructure, which had remained stagnant for decades.

As I speak about this incubation and infrastructure, I speak about the Democratic Party. This does not mean that the Democratic Party is the only party affected by political secrecy. It is, however, the party that is affected in CWG's case and the party most affected by political secrecy in rural communities. Still, the survey data suggests that at the national level, Democrats and Republicans alike are both likely to engage in political secrecy,[1] and the implications of this chapter remain relevant to both parties.

Coming Out of the Political Closet

"That's why I have insurance."

Joining a group of like-minded people was important for the women of CWG. That importance was made greater by the fact that many of the women previously believed there were no other like-minded people in their community at all. Finding one another meant a number of things that would end up shaping how the women engaged in politics from then on. For one, CWG offered a space for the women to find emotional support after an election that was a source of great anger and sadness for many women across the country,[2] support that most of the women did not find elsewhere.

CWG's role as an emotional watering hole was evident in how the women talked about its influence on their lives. Prior to the 2016 election, Theresa had lost her mother and husband. The election results became the last straw, sending her into an emotional upheaval that was both debilitating and isolating. The group, Theresa said, was her way out.

The other thing that's been really important for me, I just lost the love of my life a year and three months ago. And I was having a horrible time—I lost my mother the year before that—and so I was pretty much a basket case when [her husband] passed away. And just had a horrible time trying to get it together, and when Trump got the election, I just felt like that was the end of the world. That was Armageddon for me. It couldn't have gotten any worse. I lost my mother, I lost my husband, and I lost my country all at the same time. And I just wasn't sure I was going to be able to sit up and get out of bed again. It was really really bad at first. I had god-awful nightmares— it was just awful. The group gave me—the social part of it was really im- portant to just get me up and out of the house again—but it also gave me concrete and specific ways to focus all that anger, because my crying wasn't going to change anything. And I knew that, but I didn't know what to do. I was so overwhelmed. (Theresa, 2017)

Theresa used CWG as a container for her emotions but also as a channel for them. It gave her a place to engage with others who were angry about how the election had gone, but it also gave her "concrete" ways to "focus" that anger to political action.

For others, CWG was more than a channel for their emotions; it was also a validator for their identity. In 2017, Shirley spoke to me about CWG's first meeting, which she attended. Upon finding other progressive women in the county, Shirley felt that her beliefs and her feelings about the election results were validated—salvaged from conservative friends who did not understand her devastation.

It [CWG's first meeting] was very affirming. Because we all looked around and went "Oh my God there's more of us than we thought," and it was won- derful in that all of a sudden, we went, you know. . . . It was very verifying, like we're not crazy. There are people who think the same we do. You know, my Republican friends, particularly the men, they couldn't understand why we were so upset. I remember a very good friend of mine, who said, "You know Shirley, my daughter cried for a couple of days" and I said, "So did I." And he said, "Oh, come on." And I said, "This is a tragedy." And he didn't get it, you know, he didn't understand. He still doesn't. (Shirley, 2017)

Beyond its emotional impact, CWG also provided a channel of polit- ical information from which the women were previously disconnected. As many of the women were intentionally wary of and removed from politics, reengaging required a heavy lift. For Karen, CWG provided an entry point into politics and a place to discern political action within her comfort zone.

> For me, beyond the education, the connection, and the solidarity, is getting information about those opportunities where I can make a difference and I can decide if I want to be a part of it. How I might be able to use my voice because I have more information. (Karen, 2017)

This was also true for Connie. In 2017, when I asked her what she thought the purpose of the group was, she too brought up CWG as a source of political information and action that was within her "comfort zone."

> It's [CWG] a way to be with other like-minded women, and I mean it was really nice to see that there were so many. And also, to see what was going and to see what I could do in my comfort zone, cause some of the women, you know, they go to Austin, they bring letters to the congressman, that sort of thing. And you know, that's not anything that I would really be interested in doing. But you know, just by going [to the meetings], and also afterward reading the minutes that they send out, you can kind of pick and choose what you'd like to do. And also, they let you know of other ways, other outlets, to find out what's going on. (Connie, 2017)

Connie felt little pressure to take action she did not want to take. CWG offered opportunities for engagement that were scaffolded, not only from little to substantial commitment, but also from completely private to completely public. The women who did not want to visit their members of Congress, go to marches, or canvas with the local Democratic Party could find another outlet that required less of a public face. "I don't want to block walk or work at the polls," one member boasted at the meeting in February of 2018, "but I can look up stuff online!"

This emotional, informational, and scaffolded support in turn had an effect on members' public partisanship. Over the two years I followed CWG, of the women who were reticent to disclose their beliefs publicly when I first spoke with them, about half shifted from secret to open Democrats. Those who had previously been unwilling to engage in public-facing action were now increasingly willing to do so. As I have referenced throughout this book, the women referred to this as their political "coming out," like the coming out of previous marginalized movements and identities, which was already evident when I spoke with them in 2017.

Deborah, who had been part of CWG's formation, expressed her willingness, and surprise, at taking a more public stance through the Knock Every Door campaign.

> At the last meeting I presented this thing called "Knock Every Door." When I introduced the idea, I said "If I had known, if somebody had told me eight months ago that I would be willing to knock on doors in this county, I would have said no way. I would have been terrified." And I'm still nervous about it, but because of the support of the group and because I think it's going to do a lot of good, I'll do it. It [CWG] has given me courage. (Deborah, 2017)

CWG's scaffolding had worked not only as a political gateway, but also as a political ladder. The women could find an entry point to political engagement within their "comfort zone," and that entry point could lead them out of complete secrecy and into public engagement. For Deborah, that was a change in her willingness to engage in public political acts, like door-to-door canvassing. Importantly, it is not that Deborah's concerns about public identification changed, but that, through the group, her courage had. When I spoke to Deborah again in 2018, this bravery had increased. She was not only more willing to take a public political stance, but had actually done it.

> D: A lot of women have registered to be deputy voter registrars. Some write letters to the [local paper]. I've actually written two, which is unusual for me. I've never written political opinions to the newspaper before, so for me that was a big deal, it was like I was coming out.
>
> E: Did you get any backlash for that?
>
> D: No, as a matter of fact, the first article I wrote I had one phone call from a neighbor, I just assumed she . . . I mean she is one of the original [local] people, and she said "Deborah, is that you? Are you the person who wrote the letter about immigration?" I said, "Yes, it is." And she said, "Well, thank you so much you really did a great job." I was floored. I thought she was going to say I'll never speak to you again. (Deborah, 2018)

Her assumption that the local woman would ostracize her suggests that Deborah wrote the letters to the local paper not because she thought the community would not attack or isolate her, but because she did not care if they did or not. In other words, it was not that fear of a backlash had gone away, it was that the women of CWG started to care less. It was also possible that such a positive reception to her writing made Deborah feel more comfortable in expressing her opinions in the future—a feedback loop of positivity chipping away at her fear.

I heard a similar openness from Dawn when I spoke with her in 2018. She had recently put Beto O'Rourke and anti–Ted Cruz stickers on her car. In this case, it was her husband who feared that her car would be vandalized by the community, not Dawn herself.

> My husband was really upset with me, cause I've got a Beto sticker on my car, and I've got a Humans Against Ted Cruz sticker, and for a while he said, "You know, you're gonna get your car vandalized." I said, "Well, that's why I have insurance." Nothing's ever . . . people have looked at it and looked at me, but I just don't know. . . . [CWG's] county is pretty bad. (Dawn, 2018)

It was not that Dawn saw the community as safe, it was that she did not care whether it was safe. She was willing to risk her car being vandalized both because she wanted to express herself and because she knew she was insured if she did receive backlash. And while Dawn had car insurance to protect her physical property, she also had CWG as a type of social and emotional insurance, a group that would listen to, understand, and validate her experience of backlash should it happen, and that made a difference for her as well.

Some of the women went as far as directly addressing their earlier fears of community backlash by improving the circumstances for Democrats in the community. For instance, Ann had previously had bad experiences voting in the open primary and declaring she was a Democrat to friends and neighbors working the voting booth. After joining CWG she decided she could help with the situation by volunteering to work the polls during the primaries. When I spoke with her in 2018, she discussed the ways she had publicly engaged because she felt "more supported" by CWG. She also mentioned she was recognized by others in the community when she volunteered to work the voting booth during the primaries in 2018, something she had been concerned about a year earlier.

> One of the things that I've, or couple of things maybe, that I've done differently, because I do feel more supported or I'm aware of other in the

community who believe some of those same thing and are working towards some of those same behaviors and policies and kind of the whole nine yards—one of the things I have done is volunteer to help with voting in the primaries. . . . I think there was a bit of uneasiness sometimes as well. You know, for people as they walked in the door, you know, in terms of having to declare by going to one or the other, probably more among the Democrats. But, you know, some of the Republicans would pretty much just look that way [toward the Democrat's table]. But then coming back out, it was kind of like, "Oh, I know Ann, I know [the other woman working the poll]" [laughs]. (Ann, 2018)

Ann had been informed by her own experience of voting in the primary and, with the comfort of knowing like-minded others in CWG, sought to make that experience better for others. She could offer a friendly face when others made their declaration and were publicly sorted to the Democrats. But although she had been willing to help alleviate the experience of voting Democratic in a primary, she remained reticent about other public-facing events. She still balked at having her picture taken at group meetings or their fundraiser in the fall of 2018, for instance. In some cases, the women's "coming out" still had limits.

While CWG had lessened, to some extent, concerns of social and physical backlash, it had also lessened concerns of economic retaliation. Joyce, who runs a small business in the county, said she never told anyone in the community her political opinions, and had thus avoided backlash against her business. Since joining CWG, Joyce had become more active, "out of the political closet," and cared less about what the members of her former knitting club said behind her back.

Since I've come out of the closet, come out of the political closet [laughs], now I'm like super active. Now I say anything to anybody, I just don't care. And people have unfriended me on Facebook, and I've seen some of those women since the election [the knitting group], and one of them has shopped with me before, but the last time I saw her she kind of raised her chin and went by my booth. (Joyce, 2017)

Joyce attributed this newly embraced political confidence, at least in part, to CWG. She noted while she had previously been paying attention to politics, she was now participating in politics in ways she had never participated before.

> E: And what are some of thing you see yourself doing now that you would
>   not have done before the group?
> J: Oh, I'm doing everything. I went and became active in the Democratic
>   Party. I'm active in this group. I practically call someone every single
>   day, one of my representatives . . . I just—I cared about things, I followed
>   things, but I was never involved to this extent. (Joyce, 2017)

Some of these changes in fearing social, physical, and economic backlash were happening because the women had become more confident, not only that their beliefs were shared by others in their community, but also in how to express them. This was important considering CWG is a group with many who had suppressed their political beliefs for years. Flexing atrophied political muscles would require a kind of communicative conditioning.[3] It would require a rebuilding of external political efficacy, or what scholars call a belief in government responsiveness to the public, and of internal political efficacy, or the degree to which one believes they can affect political change.[4] But, because the women of CWG had not only taken little political action over the years but also spoken about politics very little, this rebuilding would also require increasing their communication efficacy, or what scholars would label the belief that one *can* communicate with others.[5]

CWG was the place where that rebuilding and practice could happen. For one thing, it was not under scrutiny from anyone outside of the group. This eliminated the potential for interjections and attacks from disagreeable others, whether these were online or in person. CWG was also a community within a community. The women were socially and emotionally connected to one another, which moderated the risk associated with practicing. The women could say something wrong or poorly communicate their beliefs without the extreme embarrassment of a more public stage. The community nature also meant that there were varying levels and areas of expertise and experience in the group. If the women misunderstood or miscommunicated something, there were others who could correct or respond to their statement with the right information or language. In this way, CWG served as a communicative backstage,[6] a known place where rehearsing one's identity and communication was possible without the scrutiny or pressure of frontstage performance.[7]

I observed this practice at the meetings I attended between August 2017 and November 2018. Much of it was explicit, resulting from inquiries such as "How do we talk to Republicans?," as well as efforts related to the women's "talking to other side" initiative discussed in Chapter 5. On one occasion in February 2018, one member asked how she should talk to a Republican if she accidentally reached one during phone banking. Cynthia offered her advice, telling her to say, "Read up on Beto O'Rourke, and leave it at that." The women also celebrated their perceived successes when talking with those from the other side. Vicki boasted at the July 2018 meeting about standing up to her Republican mother. "My mother is a Republican" she told the group, "and told me 'you know, Vicki, you shouldn't be talking about political things,' and I said, 'you know, everyone is allowed to have an opinion.'"

Practicing and recounting with one another made a difference. It allowed the women to talk about politics after intentionally avoiding the topic for a long time. In turn, the women got better at communicating about politics and more confident in doing so outside of the group.

But this dialogue with one another at meetings also put them in a place where it was *expected* that they talk about politics. That expectation served as a kind of communicative accountability for members. They talked about politics more, not only because they felt more comfortable doing so, but also because they felt it was an expectation. Paula mentioned the group's accountability for political talk when I spoke to her in 2017. Before joining CWG, Paula was not confident in her ability to express her opinions. After the opportunity to and expectation of talking politics with the other women, Paula's confidence changed.

P: I'm not afraid to say write a letter to the editor of the local paper and put my name on it at all. And you know, before I might have thought twice about that. You know, before the women's group got together.

E: What do you think it is about the women's group that made that feel better for you?

P: I think it's just that we're all there. And I think, for me, being able to articulate where I'm coming from, uh, and having to articulate where I'm coming from by being in a group who sort of talk about this stuff. I've gotten more, I would say, or equal amounts of support from being involved in these—I've been very active in [other local group]—I don't think you get to talk enough, which is why I was so willing to talk to you, about my thinking right now. . . . So, it's just *having* to talk about stuff and *being able* to talk about stuff. (Paula, 2017)

For others, practicing politics within the group encouraged them to engage in political conversations outside of the group that they were unwilling to have before. For instance, when I spoke with Barbara in 2017, she was adamant that she could not and would not talk politics with others in the community. As a realtor who feared she would lose business if she were public with her political beliefs, Barbara focused purely on her fear of being publicly political and the role of the group in helping her feel solidarity in that fear. When I spoke with her again in 2018, she spoke about feeling "emboldened" to have political conversations with others.

I haven't talked politics outside of my family with anybody before. I would not have done that before. But now, I'm feeling emboldened and empowered and whatever. I'm getting to the point where I might say, "People have to accept my beliefs for what they are and to heck with trying to stay in the closet for a long long time." I'm not out yet, by any means, but I am speaking a little more freely when I might detect a receptive ear. (Barbara, 2018)

When I asked if she had an example of when she had discussed politics with others outside of the group, she told me a story of a photographer she works with, who resides in the county, and on whose political post she recently commented.

I've really gotten a little bit more brave. For instance, on Facebook, I would never have forced my opinion on Facebook. But we have a photographer that we [her real estate company] all use. And he is, you know, he posts things on Facebook that I find he needs to have an attitude adjustment about. So, he says, "Maybe I oughta quit discussing this on Facebook," and I'll write, "Good idea." Because it is. (Barbara, 2018)

To Barbara, telling the photographer it was a "good idea" to stop discussing politics felt like "forcing" her opinion on others. This was not, technically speaking, an admission of her opinion, but it was an indirect hint, which she felt was a significant step toward being public with her beliefs.

Before we ended our conversation, Barbara told me she was going to do something "brave." She told the story of a local business that had previously had a Beto sign up but had been asked to take it down by disapproving patrons. In response, she decided that she would go around town and find businesses that had posted Ted Cruz signs and ask them to post a Beto O'Rourke sign alongside it.

> B: I'm going to do one thing on my own. I'm going to—there are a couple of companies that I see that have Cruz signs stuck out in their yard, and in their business, and I'm going to go in and ask to put a Beto sign out. There are two that I have in mind, because I pass by them every day and think, if they could put a Cruz sign out there, we could put a Beto sign out there because they're open to the public.
>
> E: So, you're going to ask these other people with the Cruz sign to put up a Beto sign?
>
> B: Absolutely. I've got the Beto sign in the back of my car, ready to stick in the ground. I bought it, but I can't put it in my house. (Barbara, 2018)

The irony was that Barbara did not want to put a sign up in her yard, but for different reasons than those in the community with Cruz signs. It was not that she did not feel like putting a sign up, it was that she was afraid of what would happen to her property and to her business if she did. I followed up with Barbara a little over a month after we talked to ask if she had asked the owners to put up the Beto signs. She had asked the business owners and they had put up the signs. This was, I thought, a much more public act than her comment on Facebook only a few months before.

But "coming out" as Democrats or progressives did not mean the women entirely embraced their community or that their community entirely embraced them. In fact, there were a number of instances where although the group had led the women to take more public political stances, it had also insulated them further from the community, from conservatives, and even from their own families.

In 2017, Virginia was one of the most reticent members of the group. As a realtor, she knew that she could and would receive backlash from others in her business who disagreed with her politics. In fact, as outlined in Chapter 4, she had received backlash from a client and from her boss. When I spoke with her again in 2018, she told me she had started to feel like a "new person."

E: Yeah. And do you think that it. . . . Are you worried about other people finding out about your political opinion?

V: Well, no. As a matter of fact, I just got real brave at the last two functions or two. I have this very colorful necklace—it was made by a local, one of our local artists, who would be a member, but she sold her house and she moved to [a city in Texas]. But anyway, it's all colorful and all of the little things hanging on it—oh I can send you a picture or show it the next time that we have a meeting. Anyways it's got all these little things hanging onto a chain, so I just picked up my little Beto pin and worked it into the chain and I wore it. And every Democrat that I knew of that I was in their presence when I had it on said something to me about it. I mean they spotted it immediately. And I saw a couple of other people that I know are staunch Republicans that saw it and just eyes fixed on it. And I thought, "Well, there you go." And so—I tell my husband, I said, "I'm just tired of it." So, there's a Beto sign at the end of our driveway. I put up one once before and it got taken down by someone and hauled off. And so, I now have another one. So, I've just . . . you know, I just think this is silly. I mean my close friends know who I am. And I have close friends that we've all agreed to disagree. And so, it can be done. And so, I'm just—I feel like a new person all of a sudden. (Virginia, 2018)

Although Virginia had become more public after joining CWG, she was not exactly looking to embrace her community. In fact, in some ways, she was looking to isolate herself from it. For instance, in that same conversation, she told me of her plan to start targeting her business to only Democrats.

I have just finally gotten to the point that I just feel absurd not just speaking up. Although it, you know, it probably will cost me some. But just very recently there was something on the Internet, it was about a group of people who had a realty company in I don't know, Wisconsin—no, no, Seattle— and they were very vocal. And they were identified as one of the most outstanding groups in the nation. So, I looked at their blog, and they're all gay and lesbians and they are very vocal, and they are very out there, you know, as far as their politics. And I got to thinking, you know, maybe I've just been thinking about this totally wrong and not worrying about . . . don't worry about the Republicans, but make sure every Democrat in this area knows that you're a Democrat and that you're a realtor. And so, I'm about to do something along those lines and just start targeting those people that

I know are like-minded and just forget about the rest of them and see what happens because I've been in this business a very very long time, and you know it has ups and downs and all of that. And right now, most of my business is referrals anyway. So, it's worth a shot, I think. (Virginia, 2018)

When I followed up with Virginia a month after we spoke about her new plan, she told me she had yet to start. She was hopeful it would not be long before she got it underway. It struck me as ironic that Virginia had been the same member who complained that she could not express her opinion at work because conservatives would not do business with her. Now Virginia had posed her own plan to avoid business with conservatives.

Melanie also experienced a kind of negative insulation after joining CWG. In 2017, she mentioned she and her husband had very different views on politics but was vague about the degree to which their relationship had been strained. When I spoke with her in 2018, she admitted that she had been "drowning" after the election and that she and her husband had recently gotten a divorce.

When I said I was drowning, I was in a marriage where I didn't feel like I had any . . . you know, we were on opposite sides of what was happening, and I was devastated and he was like, "Well let's, you know, let's give it a chance, " kind of attitude. So, by the time I got in the group, and that was probably four to six months after the election, I didn't know anybody in my community felt like I did. I felt like I was in a community of all Republicans. As it turns out, I wasn't, there were others, maybe not real close by, but as it turns out [CWG's] county does have Democrats. I just didn't know they were there. (Melanie, 2018)

The group gave Melanie a place to talk about these feelings, to share experiences, to commiserate about husbands or family members whose politics were drastically different from one's own. It gave her a place to incubate, and that incubation did more than bring her into political action, it also influenced her marriage.

M: It [CWG] gave me, you know, people to talk to and people that I could, you know, that felt the same that I did, and wanted to. . . . It wasn't even as much about doing something as much, in the beginning, as much as it was, you know, just being horrified of what was happening and it's comforting to be around people that feel the same way you do.

E: Do you think that may have had an effect on what you were going through personally with your husband?

M: Yeah, it did. Well, it probably wasn't a positive thing, because then I felt like I had—I don't want to say a right to feel the way I did, but it made me feel more convicted about how I felt and it kind of probably made the wedge a little bit larger. (Melanie, 2018)

Melanie saw the wedge between she and her husband grow after joining CWG because it had made her more "convicted." Her experience reflects the experience of CWG more broadly, of a coexistence of incubation and insulation. CWG equipped the women with the support, tools, and practice to publicly express their beliefs, but it also made them more likely to stay within their own circle and to leave out those who are not of the same political mind. To do, in some way, the same thing that had been done to them.

One way in which incubation and insulation coexisted was in the funnel from CWG to the local Democratic Party. Several women came out explicitly as "Democrats," and joined the local party. Cathy, who identified as a Democrat before the election, said she had not been active in the local Democratic Party because she felt it would be useless and because the party itself had very little going on. Before joining CWG, she felt she could do little to influence the local party's practices.[8] After joining CWG, she joined the local Democrats, attended meetings, and when I spoke with her again in 2018, was helping with the field operations committee that coordinated door-to-door canvassing.

C: Well, I've been a Democrat for I guess almost all my life. But I never went to the meeting. It wasn't a very active group and I was kind of half-hearted about it. Like I said, I put signs in the yard and that's about it in terms of being active in the Democratic Party. But now I'm going to the meetings, I'm much more active in that as well . . .

E: Yeah. And you feel like after joining the women's group that kind of pushed you to be more active in the [local] party?

C: Yeah. Actually, I started to think that there's a lot more activism in general, and that was sort of the impetus for me to . . . I could see that there were things that I could do. Before the election, like I said, Texas is such a Republican place, [CWG's] county is such a Republican place, it just didn't seem like much was gonna get accomplished by anything I did. Now I have reasons to be involved and that my involvement is going to make a difference because I'm doing it with other people. (Cathy, 2017)

After joining CWG and seeing those in the county who had been equally horrified by Trump's election, Cathy saw hope for the local party. The same was true for Dawn, who reengaged with the local party through CWG after her frustration with the "older guard" of local Democrats caused her to leave. When talking about trying to pose new ideas to the local party, Dawn expressed how draining it was to suggest changes to party operations and to time and time again be met with opposition.

> D: A lot of my stuff was met with hostility from the older guard, the older women.
> E: In the party?
> D: In the party. Because I was asking for change. And everybody had been doing the same thing for so long, the same way that, you know, they didn't want change. So, I just got tired of it. I felt like I spent six months, I don't know what the word is—Sisyphus? When you roll the rock up the mountain three times and it rolls back on you? And it just got really tiresome. (Dawn, 2017)

Dawn got more involved in the local party after joining CWG. With her came a number of others from CWG who had previously not been connected with the party, and who brought with them a new energy to the party's fundraising.

> After the election, I got very involved in the Democratic Party here. And they had never had a fundraiser, they had never had anything. A lot of it now has come out of CWG joining the party: we got a lot of people there. We were like, "Sure, let's do a bake sale," and we raised $87—we almost doubled our treasury. (Dawn, 2017)

How a bake sale that raised $87 could double a party's treasury was one thing, how it took a secret group of women to host the first fundraiser was another. The funnel between CWG and the local party was robust precisely because CWG was a secret. For the women to make a change in their county, state, or in the country at large, they would have to act through a group that was public. In their community, that meant the local Democratic Party. This relationship would bring (wo)manpower and life to a party that had been run by the same people for over twenty years. It would also give the party a strategic advantage over their opponents because, in many ways, what was invisible was also undetectable.

Covertly Fueling the Local Party

"The women's group will remake the Democratic Party in this county."

As CWG developed and drew closer to the 2018 midterm election, the group chose to fully align with the Democratic Party. In fact, CWG kept all of its fundraised money in the local Democratic Party account, earmarked for their use. Although not all members wanted CWG to be tied to the Democratic Party, as discussed in Chapter 5, most believed it was the only answer to the constraints of a two-party system in the United States and the only answer to taking political action while remaining undercover. Because parties are inherently connected to very public acts (e.g., public fundraisers, campaign rallies),[9] in order to raise awareness, the group's relationship with the party not only helped people "come out," but also offered a tertiary space where members could be engaged in what the party was doing without having to be public "members."

Roberta, who had previously been active in another urban county in Texas, had since become politically dormant in CWG's county. But Roberta saw CWG as a way to "be active in the Democratic Party without actually becoming public" (2017) and recognized that she "would not have done that if it had not been for the group." In fact, for a while, Roberta tried going to some of the local Democratic meetings after joining CWG.

R: And you know, what, I'll tell you also, the women's group will remake the Democratic Party in this county. It has already started. I had never been to a Democratic meeting in this county until after the election and until after several meetings of the women's group. And then I said to myself, "You know, what are you doing? You're hiding. Why are you hiding? Are they really going to hurt the [her business] because of this?" And I thought, "Well, I don't know." . . . And I thought at that time, I will at least go to a few meetings, you know, the Democrats themselves have no reason to put out any of our names. There are a number of people there that it would hurt in the school district, for example, and in other places, I'm not the only one. So, I started going to some Democratic meetings and lo and behold, do you know who the majority of those people were? They were from [CWG]! And almost all of them were women who had not been active in the Democratic Party until that point.

E: That's huge.

R: It is huge. It is huge. And you just wait, Emily, we're gonna end up—it'll take some years, and I may not see it—but you'll see it. We're going to elect some Democrats in this county and we're going to elect women. (Roberta, 2017)

The same nudge from CWG was also true for Barbara. CWG served as a secret intermediary to the local Democratic Party. It let her be a part of Democratic efforts without being public. Barbara acknowledged that she could not fully "migrate" to the Democratic Party—that is, attend meetings or events— because she cannot do it publicly.

I think I've become aware that I need to be more active in some kind of Democratic movement. And maybe I will be one of those that migrates to the Democratic Party, but I can't do it openly. So, it would probably be better that I didn't—that I stayed with [CWG] if they continue to meet on a regular basis. (Barbara, 2018)

It is important to note that the relationship between CWG and the local party was not always amicable. Early in the group's history, women who had long been active and public Democrats in the county were frustrated with the group's creation and size. Cynthia told me of an early schism between the old Democrats, who in many ways had faced down fear and stigma around being a Democrat in the community, and CWG, which was filled with more reticent progressives, many of whom had not been connected with the party at all.

C: Well, when the women's group started coming to the Democratic Party, a little incident happened where they decided they [members of CWG] were gonna say that what was wrong with it [the party] was the core group—the executive committee and the chairman hadn't done enough to keep it, you know, inspired and going, and we were the only ones keeping it going so we—all of us—did not feel like that was a warranted complaint. I mean, we felt they should have said, "Look, we want to come in and help y'all out." . . . And when they heard how we felt about it they apologized for that and said they had made a mistake but some of the people that have been coming didn't feel like it was sincere and they stayed away from the women's group. (Cynthia, 2017)

Their frustration made sense, given that some of the women in CWG were the same few women in the local party fighting to keep a Democratic presence alive. Nancy, another longtime Democrat in the community, was originally upset that the women had been in hiding and not active in the party. "It's kind of like, where have you all been all of this time?" she told me. "There were five of us at the Democratic club, you know? I can count everybody on my hand."

Still, Nancy saw the arrangement between CWG and the Democrats as a viable option for maintaining and engaging the group of women who wanted to remain hidden while also supporting the party.

To say that we [CWG] would never endorse a candidate or something, I really can't say if we will get there like that. We may just always funnel it through the Democrats, and those of us who are already active in the party, we are the face of that. But I want them to realize that this is really something exceptional. (Nancy, 2017)

This model would lead to more growth, activity, and success than the party had seen in decades. Some of these actions were small. As mentioned before, CWG raised money and made local donations under the pretense of the Democratic Party. They organized a bake sale benefitting the local party. These were efforts that were attributed to and benefitted the local party but organized and carried out by the members of CWG, many of whom were not official members of the Democratic Party.

But there were also larger successes. CWG coordinated three efforts in particular that in part benefitted the local party and in part picked up its slack. The first of these was a series of advertisements in the local paper and postcards to local voters. The idea for advertising in the local paper came up at the meeting in February of 2018. Joyce, who had read the county paper from the week before, noticed that the paper had published the 2018 midterm polling locations for Republicans, but not places where Democrats could vote on Election Day. This was either a large mistake or an intentional oversight. In the state of Texas, political parties run primary elections and make decisions about whether or not their polling location will be open to both parties.

In the county in which CWG exists, any person may vote at any polling location during early voting. On Election Day, however, polling locations can be party-specific. In other words, Republicans and Democrats may not vote at the same polling location during Election Day voting.

All of this meant that when the newspaper published only Republican polling locations for the primaries in 2018, about half of those locations were ones where Democrats could *not* vote on Election Day. Given the newspaper was the main source of information about poll locations, this left potential Democratic voters unsure about where to vote.

Upon hearing Joyce's concerns at the meeting in February 2018, the group became incensed that locations for voting were limited only to Republican voters. Dawn suggested the women write up an advertisement in both English and Spanish listing the polling locations for Democrats. Joyce announced she had determined it would cost the group $300 to publish the bilingual ad in the paper before the midterm primaries, and, of course, with the county Democratic Party as the ad's listed sponsor. Within two minutes the women had taken a vote on approving funding for the ads and it had passed unanimously. They circulated a cup for women to donate money and nearly every member put a bill into the cup as it was passed around. They raised $170 for the ad on the spot. Surely, I thought, if the room had a median age 20 years younger, no one would have had cash in-hand and they would have had no such luck.

The ad ran two weeks later in both Spanish and English. The Democratic Party had visibly, but not financially, sponsored the ad. At the group meeting in March 2018, Gloria, the member who had been the liaison between CWG and the Democratic Party, reported that the primaries had gone well. Numbers at the Democratic polling locations seemed higher than years before. Moreover, the party had, for the first time in recent history, fully staffed each Democratic polling location. Cynthia, who had been a key liaison with the party, boasted that many of the staffing positions had been filled by women from CWG.

The second "advertising blitz," as CWG would call it, was more explicit in its promotion of the Democratic Party. At their August 2018 meeting, the women decided they should take a more proactive effort to promote Democratic ideals before the midterms in November. Gloria and Theresa proposed mailing postcards to voters in the county with a pro-Democratic message, information about Democratic candidates, and information about where and when to vote. Gloria had designed the postcard and offered to pay for a portion of the mailings. At the meeting, Roberta and Nancy agreed they would contribute their money as well. By the September meeting, over a thousand postcards were ready to be labeled and mailed to voters in the county who had previously voted Democratic. At the end of the meeting, the women sat at tables and labeled all the postcards, which were attributed to the local Democratic Party.

At the October meeting, the women decided they should promote something similar in an ad for the local paper. With midterms approaching, the women hoped the ad could help minimize Democratic stigma that could keep some community members from, at the very least, voting for Beto O'Rourke. Once again, the women would run the ads under the auspices of the local party.

Although the women had recruited a friend, who was also a graphic designer, to create the postcard for free, running the ad for a number of weeks would require substantial financing. In response, the women made their second significant push, which was a fundraiser for the local party. At their August 2018 meeting, the women started planning.

A relatively new member named Beth was put in charge of the fundraiser and bounced a few ideas off the group. They settled on a ticketed event open to 50 "like-minded people," including men, although Beth suggested that "if your husband is Republican, don't bring him." They decided to charge $25 at the door and to conduct a silent auction to raise extra money. They agreed on a member's bed and breakfast for the location, as it was big enough and remote enough not to attract attention. Beth mentioned that she would contact everyone on the CWG Facebook group to get help planning and recruiting for the event. The event would list the public-facing name of CWG, which was developed several months prior, and all payment would be made to the county Democratic Party. Because CWG is not a PAC, every donation must be connected with an individual. In other words, each woman's donation would be public information. Beth suggested that "if anonymity is your thing, you might want to get someone in your family to donate for you" or on your behalf.

I was allowed to observe the fundraiser without donation in mid-September 2018. About 60 people came to the event—around 20 men and 40 women. For the first time, I met some of the women's husbands, and also made note of the many whose husbands were not in attendance. There were signs and posters from previous protests where CWG members

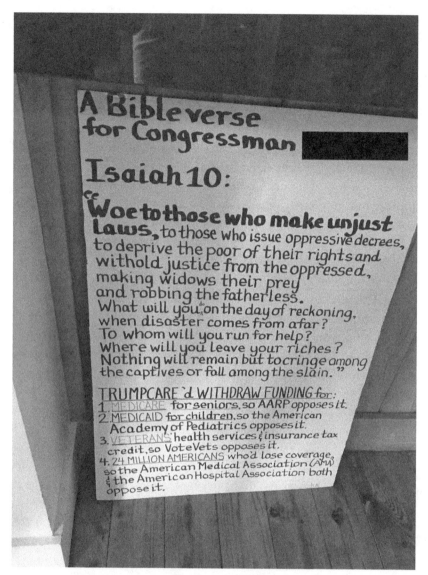

Figure 6.1 Sign at CWG Fundraiser, September 2018.

had participated (see Figure 6.1). There were also around six different silent auctions, all including different goods or services donated by CWG members. One woman sold her custom-made jewelry, another her original art, and another a private lesson on birdwatching. A representative from a local Democratic candidate's campaign attended to address the group, and the chair of the local Democratic Party made an impassioned plea for those in attendance to join the party. I overheard several women asking others why they do not attend party meetings. "I can't get anyone to come to meetings," Gloria said while gesturing around the full room, "but look at this."

At the CWG meeting shortly after the event, the group announced they had raised $5,517 through tickets and silent auction sales. It is unclear the extent to which all of that money was credibly tied to each individual donor. It is possible that each person who gave money can be reliably tracked, but it is also possible that there were those still afraid to make a direct and necessarily public donation who in turn had someone else make a donation on their behalf. As usual, the group stored the money in the Democratic Party account, but under agreement with the Party, the funds were only usable by CWG.

The amount raised was large enough to fund their ad blitz before the general election. The women were proud of their success. For one thing, they had heard from many that the fundraiser had been one of the best attended Democratic events in the county in decades. At the same meeting in September, Deborah recalled hearing an "old-time Democrat" at the fundraiser remark, "Wow, look at all these people." Of course, "all these people" were those members of CWG who had never been to a Democratic fundraiser before. Such a tightly controlled, private, and remote location was reassuring and brought those members, at least temporarily, out of hiding. It also raised a lot of money and morale for a party that had been struggling to stay alive.

Beyond raising awareness and money for Democrats, CWG also made an effort to get more Democratic voters. They did this through two efforts: one to register more voters altogether, and another to call and mobilize voters who had previously voted Democratic in the county before the primary and before the general election.

To aid with voter registration, many CWG members, including Cynthia, Deborah, Theresa, and Joyce, became deputy voter registrars. The women helped the local party distribute registration cards at major county events between January 2018 and the general election in November. The women also called around 2,000 voters in the county who had previously voted Democrat before the March primary and placed another 1,700 calls before the general election. One voting bloc the women specifically targeted were those eligible to vote by mail, including voters over the age of 65 or voters who were disabled. The women saw this group as an opportunity to engage potential Democratic voters who were unable to make it to the polls or were unaware they could vote by mail.

Their efforts seemed to make some difference. Overall, CWG's county saw steady growth in the number of registered voters and voter turnout. The number of registered voters was larger in 2018 than in either 2014 or 2016. The overall number of votes in 2018 was also substantially higher than the number of overall votes in 2014. Nearly as many people voted in the 2018 midterm election as voted in the 2016 presidential election.[10]

The women of CWG suspected they had something to do with the growing numbers. When I spoke with Ann in 2018, she felt the increase in voter registration had been a symptom of the women's hard work.

> In the [local paper] a week or two ago, they had an article about registered voters, and if I am recalling correctly—the number of registered voters in [CWG's] County increased by [moderate percentage] versus statewide by an average of 1 percent. And so, you know, that as well, I'm going hmm . . . I expect we had at least a little bit to do with that. (Ann, 2018)

At the meeting in September 2018, Jane mentioned the same article and thought immediately it had something to do with CWG. "I bet they think the Democrats have really been beating the bushes," Joyce told the group triumphantly.

In terms of Democratic voter turnout, the county also saw a significant jump in 2018. Compared to the 2014 midterm election, CWG's county saw between a 75% and 90% increase in straight-ticket Democratic votes. For comparison, a neighboring county saw only an increase of between 45% and 60%. One of the newer and younger members, Michelle, the daughter of another CWG member, reflected on the numbers at the meeting in November shortly after the election results came back. Having been an integral part of the field operations committee with the local party, Michelle saw the value of CWG for rebuilding a party that received very little from the state and national offices. "The Democratic Party in the county doesn't get what we need," she said to the group. Michelle saw that CWG had been vital to the Democrats' growth. CWG, she thought, could be the "secret weapon" for rebuilding the party while keeping Republican opposition at bay. In fact, this had already started.

Revitalizing Party Leadership and Infrastructure

"It's energy trickling up."

All of CWG's efforts were under the auspices of, and often a joint effort with, the local Democratic Party. But CWG's work did more than give credit or muscle to the party; it also helped rebuild the party's entire infrastructure. In order to target postcards to potential voters, CWG, along with the Democrat's field operations committee, went to great lengths to contact and update the Voter Activation Network (VAN) records, which had been out of date for many years. They also supplied the party with a new batch of leaders willing to serve as precinct chairs and even city council members.

When I first spoke with the women, the connection between the Democratic Party and CWG was not strong. For one thing, the group had originally taken a nonpartisan stance, which limited them from entirely overlapping with the local party. Still, there were inklings that the local party might recruit from an underground group of reticent progressives.

Early on in CWG's existence, Cynthia told me she saw the potential for it to revitalize the local Democratic Party's membership. At that point, the women had only started to collaborate with the party. And, as Cynthia notes, some of the women had since become members. Unlike many of those in CWG, Cynthia had been a staunch Democrat in the county for many years. Seeing new faces at meetings reassured her that the party could go on when previously its membership had been dwindling.

This mattered in a small county where options for membership were already small, and options for membership in the Democratic Party even smaller. But CWG was not only influencing the size of membership, it was influencing leadership as well. Cynthia saw this happening when I spoke with her in 2017.

Well, I'll tell you how it's influenced the Democratic Party. The Democratic Party was a pitiful little group of us of about six or seven who never gave up, who stayed together, who kept the party going with a little help from anyone. And so, the women's group [CWG] has energized the [CWG's] County Democratic Party, in the fact that they are coming to some of our meetings now and getting involved. Some of the women, one of the main things that women coming to the Democratic Party has caused is for many, several of the women, to become voter registrars, you know, to be able to be out and registering voters. And also, they have become precinct chairs; it was kind of sad that we only had six or seven that were the precinct chairs when we have so many precincts. Right now, I can't think of the number of precincts in [CWG's] County, but there's a lot. And there was no precinct chair. So, we were a band of Democrats who were holding together the [CWG's] County Democratic Party, meeting once a month, trying to do everything we can, you know, to be public, to be out there to be showing the values that we support. And from the women's group, several have started coming and gotten involved. So that has been a big difference . . . it [CWG] really helped infuse a new life into the Democratic Party. (Cynthia, 2017)

It was true that the local party was dying. Nancy, another public Democrat in the county, knew that the party's leadership was suffering burnout. Having more members in the party not only reenergized those who had been there for decades, but also fed leadership into precinct chair positions that had been vacant for an equally long time.

Right now, the party . . . someone's in there because nobody else would take that position, and those who are still there have suffered burnout. [Secretary]'s been the secretary for 10 years and that's where I hope this group . . . because already the meetings are much more fun to go to because we've got more people in the audience and it's all these women. We had trouble even having precinct chairs and now I don't think there's a single empty precinct anymore. And it's because we kind of shamed people at this meeting that "look, if you're . . . if you have complaints about the Democrats you better be there at the meeting," and then damn if one or two came. Joyce came and then more. Then Roberta came. So, we've breathed life back into the club. (Nancy, 2017)

When I spoke to Nancy again in 2018, she described the continued movement from CWG to the local party as "energy trickling up." The party had been fighting to keep their membership for a long time. CWG's movement brought energy and fun, particularly to a group that had felt continuously rejected from the community.

E: I want to revisit the thing you said about the trickling up to the Democratic Party. What do you think has been the challenge for the Democratic Party? Why has it taken this trickle up to get going again?

N: Because everybody had gotten worn out. It was the same bunch of us at every meeting. You know, I've been precinct chair for something like 30 years. And there was nobody new coming in. And people who'd been doing it for that long got tired and said no more. And [local Democratic leader] has resigned a half a dozen times from different positions, and here he is back again. Because he's got the bug and he gets sucked back in. To have a little more . . . you know we kind of shamed some of this group and said, "Look, you've gotta get involved," and a couple of people had their feelings hurt because someone said how terrible the Democrats were, and I looked at the room and said, "Well, we're the problem because y'all aren't showing up to meetings and you can't put down a group whose been working like this forever and is worn out." We've lost our spark. . . . So, to get some like-minded and fun—we try to keep it fun—I'd never been much for getting together with women (laughs) and this has proved me wrong. The importance of women's groups and what it can do. (Nancy, 2018)

Dawn, who had previously been active in the local party, saw this "new life," too. She attributed the revival to CWG's direct pipeline: women joined CWG and then they joined the party. "Honestly," she told me, "I think if it weren't for the women's group, the Democratic Party here wouldn't be doing anything."

In fact, while some of the old guard Democrats were upset the women of CWG had been in hiding, they were also eager and even proud to show them the ropes of political activism. Nancy, for instance, told me the feeling of being needed—of showing CWG members how to get involved with the party—in turn made her feel more confident. Guiding the members of CWG into politics gave her a sense of purpose.

It gives me confidence because now . . . I like to be needed, so it fills that. And I do feel like we're doing something. And it was hard . . . I'm a little, you know, the group gives me confidence to try a little harder and where I'd gotten kind of lazy and lax in the last election, that's not happening again. (Nancy, 2017)

Beyond precinct chairs with the local party, there was some push for CWG members to run for office themselves. Given that CWG and its membership are a secret, it is understandable that hardly anyone in the group was willing to do this. Yet one CWG member *did* run for office. Melanie, after being unwilling to "discuss it [politics] with others," decided to run for city council in May 2017, shortly after she joined CWG.

> M: So, I went to the [city council] meeting, and then I ended up going to a couple of more meetings, a few more meetings and in those meetings, I witnessed this man, the mayor, just being so unbelievably. . . . Oh my God, I can't even . . . I mean, just childish, rude. And he, on two if not more occasions, I saw him rip two women separately up one side and down the other. Criticizing them, belittling them. You know, it was just jaw-dropping for me. And I thought this cannot go on. And it just so happens a seat opened up on the board and I just put my name in there and no one else was running, so I got on the [city council] board. Because I was not going to stand by and let this—I wasn't going to stand by and let him do that. (Melanie, 2018)

Melanie's choice to run was most obviously about standing up to the "childish" mayor. Perhaps she had felt emboldened by her new membership in CWG. Running for city council was a way to use that energy, and to combat the same things, the same type of man, that had brought her to CWG in the first place. Although running for city council did not require a public partisan stance, it did ask that she dive into the political world, which was quite literally a man's world, and stand up for what she felt was unjust. It required that she be political, which carried with it some commitment to politics, even if her partisanship was allowed to remain latent. CWG rallied behind her, strategizing and encouraging her at meetings. Melanie won the election.

Because CWG is in a county where many Democrats feel like they cannot be publicly "out," it makes sense that there would also be very few Democrats running for local office. Cynthia told me in 2018 that leadership and candidacy are some of the hardest issues that the Democrats face in the county. Specifically, seeing no Democrats running for local positions makes it harder for local Democrats to break down the stigma toward them in the county. That there are few, if any, local candidates running as Democrats also makes it harder to get any down-ballot effects of Democratic candidates running for higher office. That is, in order to vote in some local races, residents often cannot vote a straight-Democratic ticket.

I push when we call, and we go door-to-door, to ask if you will vote a straight ticket. That's one of the major questions we ask. If they say no, there's some other questions we can ask them, like "Are you undecided? Do you lean Republican? Do you vote a split-ticket?" We don't say do you lean Republican—we say do you vote a split ticket? And a lot of them do because of the fact that there are more Republicans running for local places than there are Democrats. There are some places where only a Republican will be the one that's running. Naturally, a lot of people, even Democrats have voted, like in the primaries, I know of many Democrats that voted in the Republican primary because they wanted to get their local people that they wanted to be in office, and there were only Republicans. They were more concerned about the local races than the state. (Cynthia, 2018)

In fact, the local party had to work to keep the few officials who had remained with the local party over the years. Nancy knew that if they did not continue interpersonal relationships with the few remaining Democratic officials, they might lose all institutional presence in the county. What is worse, they might lose a few of their candidates to the more active, and supported, local Republican Party.

To say that the county's Democrats had to fight for what they had would be an understatement. For one thing, there were very few local candidates who would run as a Democrat. The officials who remained seemed to be hanging by a thread. Prior to CWG's pipeline, the party had consisted of the same six or seven people desperately grasping for members, let alone leadership. But to say that the party was entirely to blame would be an overstatement. Their trouble came down to two interrelated factors: stigma and support. As CWG's entire existence shows, being a Democrat in an overwhelmingly conservative community was intimidating and risky. The growing hostility between both sides was one reason that the group was formed as secret and distinct from the local party, which by its very nature was trying to be public and persuasive.

But the failure of the local party was also a result of the national, and even state, Democratic Party having given up on the county, offering them little, if any, support. Nearly all of the local Democratic Party's funding came from local fundraisers, and recently through the work of CWG. Many of the active Democrats in the group saw the disconnect between the national party and their local party as the result of a "hopeless" attitude toward Texas. Dawn thought that the party failed to provide support because it was believed that a Democrat could not win in Texas.

> I think the Democratic Party is set up . . . it's not set up well. And you know, we don't have any money, and I'm not just talking about [a town in the county], I'm talking about Texas. And I'm not quite sure why. . . . I've had a lot of talks with people about it. I think a lot of people feel hopeless about it. I know the National Committee feels like why put money into Texas? They're not gonna win. (Dawn, 2017)

Theresa saw the need for a secret group, like CWG, because the Democratic Party failed to provide support specifically to rural areas.

> The recent history, if you talk to anybody around here, is that [decades ago] this area was all Democrat, it's more the failings of the National Democratic Party not to perceive that rural people are important and to give them some time and get out here and do some legwork. And so there hasn't been a presence, and so there hasn't been a noticeable population in response to that. So, I think that it's a lot less red than they think it is. And that's in my opinion personally some Republican dogma, so you know there's only a few of you out here so you may as well throw in the towel and give up, because we're told that all the time, and we're like, no actually, there are a lot more of us than you think. We're not throwing in the towel, suck it up people. (Theresa, 2017)

One glaring example of how the state Democratic Party had failed to support CWG's county, and other rural "nonviable" areas, was its maintenance of voting records across the state. In fact, data management had become a key role for the party as voter databases, like the VAN, were housed and maintained within the party itself.[11] In 2018, CWG members started their initiative to contact vote-by-mail eligible voters in their area. This would require that they use the state Democratic Party's records for their county through the VAN. The only issue was that these records were abysmally out of date. It took a lot of effort for the local party to maintain these records, and the state party perceived little incentive to do so, considering their success rate in the county. I first heard about this when I spoke with Theresa in January 2018.

So, you have to be 65 or older or disabled to get this application in the mail. Well, we got our numbers from the state, and we got our list, and there were [number less than 500] people on it. So, Joyce looked at that, Joyce is a precinct chair, and she said that's not right. I mean, I know how many voters over 65 I have in my own precinct and that that number is way low. We're missing a bunch of voters—what's going on? So, she questioned the Texas Democratic Party and they said, "No no no, that's the list, that's the list, we don't know what you're talking about." And she said, "You know, to hell with this. I'm going to figure this out." So, what she did was she got into the VAN, which is the Texas Democratic Party database, and she has access to that as a precinct chair, she dug back three election cycles and found indeed, that whenever somebody didn't vote they didn't reappear as a voter in the next cycle—that they were getting dropped. And it went on and on and on. (Theresa, 2018)

When I asked Theresa why voters had been dropped from the list, she said it was voters who had missed voting in a recent election, which could even include small referendums or school board elections.

T: It was an additional 2,000 plus voters. 2,000 plus that had been dropped that were Democrats, registered Democrats.

E: But just hadn't voted? They hadn't voted in the past election?

T: Well, they had missed even one or two elections over the last, like if you went back in 2008. So, it isn't that they voted Republican, but [that they] somehow missed voting. But let's be plain about this, they have referendums for school board things and local bonds. So, this isn't like they're missing voting in a presidential election. You know what I'm saying? So, we actually had [number less than 500] plus 2,000 and some and that was the actual total of voters we were supposed to be phone calling. (Theresa, 2018)

When this was brought up at the meeting in February 2018, the women were indignant and demanded that the records be cleaned up and that those eligible to receive a ballot-by-mail be notified. But this was only after a number of conspiracy theories were thrown around that there was a "Republican in the system" who had tampered with the records. One member suggested that they publish what they had found in the local paper, but another expressed reluctance to go public with "critiques of the Democratic

Party." I later confirmed with Joyce that the records had been out of date and that the women were working to correct them.

> It's [the VAN] so out of date in terms of addresses and phone numbers. It's not out of date on whether they voted or not, that is accurately updated, although there's people that have to sit there and do it. . . . So our group contributed money to pay for a search, like white pages, that got results. I think there were 10 of us. I organized it and divvied it up, so I got the list of all the bad phone numbers or bad addresses for all the Democrats in [CWG's] County, that had either the mail had come back or the phone number because we had called them. . . . So, we researched and brought it all up to date and then I corrected the records along with this guy [local Democrat], who's the man in the Democratic Party who does all the computer work and he's the one who trained me. . . . And then when people went out, we call it "car driving," but you've probably been at some of the meetings, we can't really block-walk around here [laughs], it's a lot of driving. So, then those people turned in the corrections that they found; they went to some places and the address was simply nothing but a field. Or, they went, and the mother would answer the door and say the kid doesn't live here anymore, whatever. So, those records got reported back to us and we corrected it. (Joyce, 2018)

By September 2018, they had cleaned up the entire VAN records for the county, making over 3,000 phone calls, updating the system with individual's cell phone numbers rather than landlines, and verifying records on the ground as well. Cynthia, who did a good amount of "mile-driving" across the county, often went to locations that the records listed as the homes of former Democratic voters but now contained no more than an overgrown field. She mentioned that this kind of validation work proved challenging, given that many of these locations were remote and often hard to reach.

C: You know what the VAN system is?

E: I do. And it was it was really out of date, right?

C: Yes, and that's another thing. The first part of the spring and summer we mainly were trying to get the correct phone numbers and addresses for these people. Some of them had either moved—we don't know where they are if they've moved. But some people only had their landline phone, or they've gotten rid of it, so we tried to get as many cell phones as we could. And the people who are calling also did that. So that is helpful. We're trying to update the VAN, in other words. . . . And it was quite challenging because a lot the places are not just right on the country roads, you go down another path, and it's quite challenging to get to the house, I'd encounter several dogs, which we usually get unless a person comes and we know they're friendly, and many times there would be gates and we couldn't get in. (Cynthia, 2018)

It is important to acknowledge that while CWG did a lot to rebuild the local party's infrastructure and leadership, they did not do this in a vacuum. They had the support of the local Democratic Party, for example, which had several strong advocates, like the local Democrat Joyce mentioned, who helped the women of CWG learn about the party's tools and structure, and coordinate efforts.

They also had help from a Democratic group in a neighboring city. Sissy, a member who had grown up in the area and still owned land in the county, found out about the group through one of her friends and another member of CWG. I spoke with Sissy in 2018 about how her group had helped CWG and two other rural counties nearby. Specifically, the neighboring city group had a "campaign professional" visit with the group's leadership and helped the women figure out who to target using the VAN. "If we do the targeting, and we pay for that," she told me, "they do sort of on-the-ground work, like door-knocking, like having meetings, like writing postcards."

Outside of this original funding and strategy, the city group did little else. This was mostly because they lived many miles away, which made supporting CWG's efforts on the ground harder. Moreover, the city group was not the Democratic Party itself, but another group of engaged, wealthy citizens who saw potential in "awakening Democrats and encouraging them in this part of rural Texas," as Sissy put it. Interestingly, the group had chosen to go through CWG and not the local party—a testament either to the party's shortcomings or the advantages of a secret group that could covertly do some of the heavy lifting for them.

But the women of CWG had something else going in their favor in 2018: Beto O'Rourke, the Democratic candidate running for Ted Cruz's Senate seat in the midterms. Beto was first mentioned at CWG meetings in August 2017. The group had agreed to partner with the local Democrats who were organizing a meet-and-greet with him and his campaign. In general, the group's reception to his candidacy seemed equally as warm as it was skeptical.

By December 2017, it was clear that Beto had grown a presence in CWG's county. He was talked about more frequently at CWG meetings, members started putting signs in their yards and bumper stickers on their cars, and they started seeing his signs around town and in the countryside. When I drove in for the CWG meeting in January 2018, I even saw a hay bale with a giant Beto sign along the highway.

Dawn, who had just returned from a summer away in New Mexico when I talked with her in October 2018, saw that things had changed in the community in the months she had been gone. Still, she was worried that if Beto lost, Democrats in the county would be back to square one.

> And then I came home and yesterday, and I was going for a walk, like a six-block circle kind, and there were five houses with Beto signs and [local candidate] signs, and I was shocked because it's like all of a sudden people aren't afraid to put those things up. And it made me feel pretty good because I've had to replace my Beto sign, because I've had it since last December and I got a new one. . . . I'm really worried about the election because I'm afraid that here in Texas, if Beto loses, I don't want it to throw everybody back into where we were November 16. That concerns me. (Dawn, 2018)

Most of the women in CWG felt Beto had a fighting chance in their county. Barbara admitted to me in 2018 that "if there's ever a time for it to happen, this should be the time." Cathy told me that "if enough of them [Democrats] come out, he can win." Joyce was also optimistic when I spoke to her in 2018. She thought it was important to residents of the county that he simply showed up and listened during his campaign.

> E: What do you think it is about Beto that is appealing to these communities?
>
> J: Well, first of all he shows up. He's visited every single county in Texas, and he made it a point. And he's—you can tell he's honest just by being around him. He looks at you. He listens to what you're saying. He's addressing what people are interested in. And he's had Republicans show up all around the state. I've been watching his Facebook page and all that and I've seen the videos and he's had a lot of Republicans ask him about this, that, and the other. He never engages in mudslinging. He focuses on what's positive about what he wants to do. And I think that appeals to people. (Joyce, 2018)

Beto had visited CWG's county, the first statewide Democratic candidate to do so in 20 years. Joyce recalled that his first event in the county had been standing room only. "The place was packed—standing room only" she told me.

Nancy was a little less optimistic about Beto's chances, although she knew that even getting close to electing a Democratic candidate in the state of Texas, let alone a Democratic victory in her county, would be monumental.

> Well anyone who's heard him speak is just taken with him. I know that one of the last rallies I went to there were a couple of people doing a little yell, "Republicans for Beto," so in [neighboring] County, to get somebody to do that, that's good I thought. So, yeah, I just hope he can get those extra Democrats. I don't know if he'll convert the people in [town in CWG's county] because they're not that tied to who they know, Ted Cruz, or what is Ted Cruz doing for you? They're just gonna vote Republican. (Nancy, 2018)

Beto got close to winning Texas in 2018. He would take 48.3% of the votes in Texas compared to Cruz's 50.9%. In CWG's county, he was not nearly as close.[12] At their meeting in November 2018, after the midterms had ended, the women reflected on the results. Nancy, the meeting's facilitator, read a statement from an article in *The New York Times* recounting the number of women who had run for office in Texas. At this, the room erupted in applause. I had come to the meeting expecting the women to be somber, even distraught. Instead, I found them energized and elated that they had helped their state come close to putting a Democrat in the Senate. Theresa, who did not attend the meeting, had someone read aloud all the accomplishments of the group over the past year and distribute a document titled "The Hidden Numbers." The women's 3,000 phone calls and 3,000 postcards to local voters, newspaper advertisements, and over $8,000 in fundraising were all listed on the page in a bright blue font.

Once they came to the section of the agenda entitled "member's feelings," the women were too invigorated with their own accomplishments to engage in their normal venting. They spent only 10 minutes on the agenda item before turning to "new business" and forging the plan for 2020.

Conclusion

About two years after CWG had formed, it had affected political change in its members and in the county. The group had rebuilt the women's confidence in their own abilities and their ability to influence politics—what scholars call external and internal political efficacy. They had also gained confidence in their ability to talk about politics at all—what scholars would call communication efficacy. All of this practice and improvement had led many in CWG to "come out" as Democrats to friends, neighbors, relatives, and themselves. They had taken public stances, knocked on doors, made phone calls, and campaigned for Democrats in their community. A handful of them joined the local Democratic Party, even becoming precinct chairs or running for city council.

The women did these things because they felt a sense of confidence that they were not alone. They did these things because they knew *how* to talk about politics and *how* to take action. The group had also given them different channels for activism that remained in their "comfort zones." They could engage in politics under the auspices of the Democratic Party without being officially affiliated. Although Chapters 4 and 5 showed CWG's role as an *insulator*, this chapter offers evidence for CWG's role as an *incubator*, which sits in line with existing evidence that like-minded groups can and do encourage people to engage in and practice political conversation.[13]

Through their actions, the women of CWG rebuilt their local Democratic Party. They increased the membership and provided important local leadership, a ground game, and support in updating an entire system that had been largely abandoned by local, state, and national Democrats. CWG had given life and structure to the party, an energy that started not from the political inside—institutional structures like parties or advocacy organizations—but from the outside in.

CWG did these things all while keeping their group a secret. Although they funneled their activity through the local Democratic Party, they remained independent from it. Members of CWG were not necessarily members of the party, which suited those who remained reticent about being publicly political. In many ways, this strategy gave CWG an edge. Importantly, the Republican opposition could not ascertain exactly who was behind all of this action.

The relationship between CWG and the local party is novel when compared to decades of research on political parties that has generally overlooked local-level party infrastructure.[14] In contrast, CWG's experience shows that the *county* party plays an important role in mobilizing voters, creating competitive elections, and combating partisan stigma. It shows that the relationship between local, state, and national parties varies dramatically depending on where each of these are situated. CWG's rural and Republican county was not a priority for state and national Democrats because it was not seen as viable. CWG's experience also shows that a focus on public politics—the yard signs, the advertisements, the block-walking—while beneficial in the long run, can be a short-term failure for the Democrats in rural communities like CWG's because it overlooks the growing privilege of being publicly political. As parties address the need for a ground game that is both online and offline, communicated through mass media and interpersonally, CWG shows just how it important it will be for parties to also address the tension between private and public politics.[15]

The women of CWG and their local Democratic Party had changed over two years, and so too had the state of Texas. Although rural communities in Texas went decidedly for Ted Cruz in the 2018 midterms, Beto O'Rourke did receive more support in these areas compared to Democratic candidates in 2014 and 2016.[16] As a result, predictions of a Texas "blue wave" that were common before the 2018 midterms persisted even after, especially the idea that Texas is and will continue to experience a shift toward the Democratic Party even in conservative areas. But if CWG is any indicator, that blue wave may start as an undercurrent.

Although the 2018 election had been an important litmus test for CWG's progress since their formation, it was a comma, not a period. The women had their sights on 2020, which offered the national reclamation they had been waiting for since Trump was inaugurated. The women did not and could not know how much their country and their world would change between November 2018 and November 2020. They only knew it was time to get to work.

7

2020

"This year," Jane says to a screen full of squares, "gets the prize for most challenging year since we've been in place." Heads nod in agreement as Frances calls out, "How do I show my video camera?" and a couple of members deliver instructions. Joyce, one of the cofounders of the group, has moved to a northern state but is able to attend the party virtually. She gives an update on her experience in her new home. "It's a red state here. The Democratic Party isn't well-formed, but then COVID didn't help that," she says to the group. "Well, we know how that is," Deborah retorts. A couple of others on the call snicker. When she tries to speak again, Joyce's screen freezes and someone else on the call exclaims, "She's frozen." "Well, it is cold there," Jane says, and all the women laugh.

CWG is meeting for their annual Christmas party, which like most things in 2020, is taking place over Zoom. As Jane notes, the year was challenging, but it was also remarkably successful, all things considered. The women had navigated a pandemic and an election, a Democrat had won the election, no one in the group had gotten COVID, and only one of them had to go the hospital for high blood pressure on Election Day. Of course, none of them saw any of this coming.

The women of CWG had closed out 2019 with optimism. They dedicated a section of their meeting in November of that year to "brainstorming how we want to proceed in the all-important 2020 election year." During this session, they asked each other what they felt the group had done well, what they should stop doing, and what they should focus attention on in the year to come. In the minutes from this meeting, the women commended themselves on "working well as a team," and they hoped that next year they could "stop complaining about those that don't agree with us." In looking to their efforts for the 2020 election, the women promised to make "voter education" a priority—continuing their outreach and exploring new ways of reaching possible Democrats in the area.

The first few meetings of 2020 maintained this optimistic momentum. At their meeting in January, the women discussed a texting project facilitated

Democracy Lives in Darkness. Emily Van Duyn, Oxford University Press. © Oxford University Press 2022.
DOI: 10.1093/oso/9780197557013.003.0007

by the county's Democratic Party and spearheaded by a member of CWG, Michelle. According to the minutes in January 2020, the program allowed "volunteers to ask voters if they are Democratic or not" and subsequently target them with information about upcoming elections. The minutes championed the texting program as a way to mobilize and build a presence in rural communities. "Finding like-minded voters is so important, not only in getting more people to the polls," the minutes read, "but also in giving the few Democrats moral support and the courage to step forward." This sounded very familiar.

At their February meeting the women discussed local candidates running as Democrats, a project to donate books to the local library, and a local forum on environmental issues the group had sponsored under the Democratic Party. One member brought up a new term, "intersectionality," which she had learned from watching a Ted Talk. The group discussed how they could better educate themselves on issues of race and class. This year they would expand not only their political awareness, but their social awareness, too.

The group's March meeting focused on the 2020 primary, which had happened a few days prior. The women celebrated the increase in Democratic primary voters in the county compared to 2016 (an increase of nearly 10%). In anticipation of a busy general election season, the women set dates and appointed facilitators for the remainder of their meetings that year. They started putting together the details on a fundraiser slotted for September to help fund ads before November. One member who had been absent from the last few meetings due to a mobility issue arrived in her new accessible van. On this, the minutes read: "it is a sign that good people still exist in our county, because this van was entirely donated." Things for CWG—their politics, their county, their members—were looking up.

COVID-19

"What do you think you are, the Lone Ranger?"

It was not until the end of March that the group's correspondence began reflecting the impending reality of the COVID-19 pandemic. On the 27th of March, the group's founder and acting secretary, Deborah, sent an email effectively canceling the April meeting for "obvious reasons." "Our first concern was the welfare of our members," her email read, adding, "is anyone feeling extremely anxious or lonely?" Like she had done nearly four years earlier, Deborah looked for CWG to offer connection. "We urge anyone who needs connection to use our confidential Facebook site" she pleaded, "But certainly we can do more than Facebook." The email went on to ask members if they were interested in doing a phone or "virtual conference," and to email Deborah expressing their interest. "We will try to figure out a way to organize this," Deborah assured them.

A few days later another email came from Michelle, the volunteer working closely with the county Democratic Party. Michelle urged the women to join a county volunteer training over Zoom that would brainstorm ways to mobilize voters during a pandemic. Michelle assured the women they were going to "get organized," even if that meant they had to "fight this war from our desks and our phones."

By May, the women were back in full swing. The focus group had met virtually, and successfully, over Zoom, and created a few priorities for the coming months. Energized by the state Democratic Party's declaration that Texas was in play for the presidential election, the women decided to focus on activities they could do from home—postcard writing to mobilize Democratic voters and a virtual fundraiser to help support ads they would run in the local paper.

The focus group had scheduled a meeting on Zoom for the following month. Anticipating that the membership might struggle with how to access it, several Zoom coaches were appointed to offer assistance for members unfamiliar with this technology.[1] At the bottom of the email in all-caps was a statement of energized anticipation: "IT WILL BE GREAT TO SEE EVERYONE'S FACES, SHARE GOOD NEWS, DO SOME BRAINSTORMING AND GET REVVED UP ABOUT DEFEATING TRUMP."

The group's first Zoom meeting was a success. By the accounts I heard, the women were thrilled to be back together, even if it was virtual. In Deborah's words from the minutes, "twenty-one women were anxious to get started since we had not met since March." Despite how excited they were to be connecting, even virtually, there were a number of things working against the group's virtual pandemic meetings. For one, rural areas are some of the communities least likely to have access to the high-speed Internet required for reliable streaming.[2] This meant that even if the women of CWG could access Zoom, the connection was often choppy, unclear, or unstable. Nancy told me the glitches in her connection sometimes caused confusion when she tried to communicate with other members during their meetings. Even with the "glitches," Nancy was glad to see the others, to socialize, and to share a virtual glass of wine.

> I'm out in the country and when the teenagers next to me get on their computer after school, my bandwidth lessens. And there's been a couple of times they're [CWG] like, "Nancy, you're not coming in. We don't know what you're saying." So, there's little technical glitches. . . . But we still do our 30-minute happy hour—social hour—and you'll see someone sitting on their porch with a glass of wine with the laptop set up." (Nancy, September 2020)

At their first meeting back, the women had a lot to talk about. They were working again with the local Democratic Party to phone bank, calling voters over the age of 65 in the county. They had plans to launch a postcard campaign like they had in 2018, sending cards to mobilize Democratic voters in their county and across the country.

As I heard them recount these first few Zoom meetings, it struck me that it might be hard for some of the members whose husbands were not aware they were in the group to attend these meetings at all. Hiding your participation in the group was a lot easier when it meant leaving home, but a virtual meeting did not provide that same level of physical cover. I asked Ann, one of the members whose husband is unaware she is in the group, whether or not she was attending the CWG's Zoom meetings at home. She was not.

> E: I know he's [her husband] not familiar with your work with the group [CWG]. . . . Have you been taking the Zoom calls at home?
>
> A: Actually, I have not been doing it here—you're right. . . . One of the convenient things is that he has an [local community group] meeting on that same evening . . . so now that they have reason to meet in person, that actually helps. I'll be able to do it [attend the CWG meeting] from home tomorrow. (Ann, October 2020)

My conversation with Ann showed both how difficult it is to navigate political differences in such intimate relationships and how the pandemic had made this maneuvering even trickier. Previously, Ann would just leave her house for CWG meetings, providing a different excuse for her exit. Everyone in attendance was on the same page, all gathering in a neutral space and all removed from the trappings of their domestic life. But the pandemic had redistributed the membership to home. While everyone Zoomed from their porches or their kitchen tables, Ann Zoomed from her office at work.

I had talked to Ann about her husband for several years now, but it seemed that the conversation on this topic had gotten tougher. Ann stopped and started more than she had before when discussing her husband and their differences. "How best to answer that?" she would say when I asked her if they had talked about the upcoming election and how she was feeling about their disagreements. She had even called me back when we finished our conversation, looking to add more to her depiction of her marriage and of her spouse in general. There was something else Ann had mentioned more over my years of knowing her. Increasingly, she spoke about her differences with her husband and her community not just as a discrepancy in partisan preferences, but that there existed a true *moral* imperative to vote and work against Trump's policies and what he stands for.

A: For the people who are working hard now, putting themselves at risk, who are trying to feed their own families—that should not be happening in the United States of America. And the violence, the disparities in terms of justice and what is happening to young Black men, it's just unconscionable. . . . I will be fine here. I'm one of those people of privilege. And as much damage as Donald Trump could do in the next four years, I will probably be okay, but for the longer-term, and for so many other people, they will not be okay.

E: So, it sounds to me like this has almost become increasingly more of a moral imperative to not support him [Trump]. Am I right?

A: Absolutely. Absolutely. (Ann, October 2020)

The intensifying public and personal reckoning for Ann—the public realization of injustice and her personal realization of morality and politics—was perhaps why she so often felt the need to justify her husband's beliefs and behavior. For every negative story, stories that showed prejudice or callous thoughts, there was a story that showed sensitivity and compassion—where he filled someone's gas tank when they asked for help, for example. Perhaps the co-occurrence of these two trends, her entanglement of indecency and Trumpism and the instinct to defend her husband's moral compass, were related.

CWG's role as a place of political shelter for women married to Trump supporters had continued during the pandemic even for those new to the group. Nancy told me the story of another woman using CWG as a secret channel for participation during the pandemic. The story was brought up when I asked Nancy how she was feeling these days about the group's secrecy, of which she had long been critical. Despite her earlier misgivings about the group's secrecy, Nancy told me she had started to "get it." As evidence for her change of heart, she mentioned she had recently dropped off some postcards to a woman who was looking to get involved in Democratic politics in the county. The catch was that Nancy had to drop the cards off in an "unmarked envelope" so that the woman's husband would not find out what she was doing.

> N: I get it now [the group's secrecy]. I totally understand it. And I worked with a woman on these postcards . . . she called and said, "I reached out to a Democrat who said I should call you. My husband is leaving on a hunting trip on Thursday. And if you'll put the 40 envelopes—cards— in an unmarked envelope and send them to me, I'm going to do them while he's gone."
>
> E: Is this someone in the group?
>
> N: No, we may pull her in now because she knows now that we exist. And what a sweetheart. She's doing it all alone in a house full of men who are Republicans. (Nancy, September 2020)

The rise of COVID-19 had changed more than just how the women could do politics at home; it also changed how they would or could do politics in public, because the pandemic had brought with it a new display for and consequence of partisanship: the face mask. Mask wearing was not recommended by the CDC until early April. Scholars have since found that rates of face mask use are highly correlated with percentage of support for President Trump in the 2016 election.[3] For the women of CWG, the publicness of that partisan display mattered. Going into a store or a restaurant as one of the few wearing a mask was not only a threat to one's physical safety—a threat of contracting the virus—but also a threat to one's political privacy—a threat of exposing oneself as a Democrat. It was not only bumper stickers, yard signs, pins, and verbal declarations that explicitly declared one's partisanship, it was now a previously *apolitical* tool for health and safety that did so.

When I spoke to Nancy in September of 2020, she said it was clear to those in the community that the people who wore face masks were Democrats and those who did not were Republicans. "You might as well have communist written on your forehead" she told me, "because they're sure you're a Democrat because you're wearing a mask."

Virginia, Deborah, and Theresa noticed the same thing. When I asked Virginia whether she felt mask-wearing differed across party lines, she said she can typically tell someone's political leaning based on the consistency of their mask-wearing. "I can tell" she said, "once they come in and they don't have masks on and they don't intend to wear masks, and then you start picking up on things in conversation that are pretty indicative." Deborah saw this difference, too.

> Republicans, most of them do not—I don't know if they are now—wear masks. "We're not gonna get it," was their attitude, "because we're so spread out and there are so few cases here," even though people *were* getting it. (Deborah, October 2020)

In her typical form, Theresa was incredulous that Republicans, whom she equated to "idiots" in the county, would be so brazen as to refuse a mask. She even noted that when required to wear a mask in a public space, they would intentionally leave out their nose in defiance.

> So, all these idiots are out there making my life a lot more difficult by refusing to do the most basic things. Refusing to give me some space. Refusing to wear a mask. And then there's those Republicans that, that is the cool thing for Republicans to do around here is when a place requires a mask still, they'll have their nose hanging out over their mask. . . . That drives me absolutely crazy. Well, you know, hello? How do they test for COVID-19? Well, it's a nasal swab. And, why is that? That's because there's enough of a source of the infection to get a good sample, okay? Cover your damn nose. (Theresa, October 2020)

But for Nancy and Deborah, this difference in approach to safety was not just a difference of opinion, it was enough to hurt their relationships in the community. For example, when Nancy went to her local printer to print the postcards for CWG's mailing effort, she found him maskless and on the offense about Nancy's own mask.

> I went to the printer, my longtime printer I'd worked with in [local town], and no mask on. So, I said something to him . . . I had to go back a second

time to kind of further the project. By then, the county had mandated a mask. No mask on him. And he's asking me about the man that just died in [local town] from COVID. And I'm saying, "Well [man's name], look you're asking me about someone who died and it's a perfectly good reason why you should wear a mask . . ." And he goes, "Well, you know, you Democrats," and I said, "Are you about to call me stupid?" . . . And I picked up my cards and I haven't been back." (Nancy, September 2020)

Likewise, Deborah had received commentary on her face mask when she attended a local event outside. Confrontation about mask-wearing had happened between Nancy and her longtime acquaintance, and Deborah had received "ridicule" about wearing a mask from her friend.

And those of us who did wear masks were . . . commented upon or to. . . . For example, this summer there was an outdoor movie at [local town], a big gathering place outdoors. And [her husband] and I went to that, and we had masks on, and somebody I thought was a friend ridiculed me: "What do you think you are, the Lone Ranger?" (Deborah, October 2020)

Just as comfort levels surrounding social distancing and mask-wearing varied across the country, they also varied within CWG. Some members never left their houses. Others went out to eat once a week. What was consistent in how the women spoke about the virus and their community's response was that they were outliers—no longer just in their politics, but in their personal health practices as well.

Racial Reckoning

"We want to elect Democrats, but what else?"

In June, at CWG's first meeting back since the pandemic, there was also a lot to talk about that did not involve getting out the vote. Since they had last met, not only had hundreds of thousands died from the novel coronavirus, but there had also been a number of high profile cases of Black Americans killed at the hands of police officers. The outcry surrounding these killings had resulted in a national reckoning with how Black communities are disproportionately mistreated and discriminated and retaliated against.

In the section of their June meeting minutes entitled "reflections," the women of CWG spoke about their horror at the murder of George Floyd. They encouraged members to attend a local vigil and prayer rally sponsored by a Black church in their community. When I asked the women I interviewed this year what their own and the group's response had been to this reckoning, it was a mixture of disgust and paralysis.

> E: What is the women's group's response to this kind of moment of reckoning with racial injustice? What has the group's response been to this?
>
> A: Even before this happened, we had initiated some conversation around that with our one Black member about our group and had actually had two convenings around dinner and food and just kind of—the focus group—to try to figure out how we might have the conversation with the larger group. And then, the pandemic hit and it disrupted that. (Ann, October 2020)

Deborah told me a similar story when I asked her how the group had responded to the growing tensions around race, particularly in their county. Like Ann, Deborah's example of how the group was grappling with racial injustice was confined to their interactions with their "one Black member," Robin. Their reliance on Robin to educate the small focus group was positioned as a tactic for knowledge-building, but also as an excuse for action.

> E: And how about the kind of tensions coming up around race this year? Have you guys had any discussions about your role in how the county is reckoning with racial injustice right now? Has that been a topic of conversation?
>
> D: Yes. Yeah, well, we have one Black member, and she's very outspoken and we—she has really kinda helped us wake up to the reality of this. We talked and talked and talked about what can we do, and we just—people had ideas; they wanted to have a—some kind of a presentation or awareness exercise or whatever. . . . So, finally, I think the focus group decided that we—I'm very close to her. We've been good friends for a long time. So, we decided that I would approach her and say, "What can we do?" So I did. And she ended up inviting us to her house and giving us dinner, and her husband was there too. He's very—a great guy. And so, we've met two or three times, just the members of the focus group and her, and we've hashed this out . . . but then COVID hit and we couldn't do

that anymore. And it got close to the election and just—so busy with that. I think maybe once the election's over we're gonna try to revisit that. (Deborah, October 2020)

Theresa told me that CWG, while supporting the movement in defense of Black lives, had not organized a response to any of the deaths because they felt it was already handled by the community. She mentioned a local event that took place in response to protests around the world. The event had been led by several local teenagers, mostly Black, and their families.

There ended up being a really cool thing and it was only because there was this group of high school seniors that had graduated and had some sort of sensitivity training or something like that and they were a group of real popular kids like athletes and cheerleaders and stuff like that.... They called it [the event] something really positive, like a rally or whatever, and they had speakers and ice cream and they got all their families real involved ... they made it like a real community event, but in a really positive way. ... So, our group didn't do anything specifically because it was already happening in [local town], which is where we would have gone to anyway. So, I know there were people that participated in that, but it just went real well. (Theresa, October 2020)

Across their responses was a similar locus of responsibility. The women of CWG relied on other Black people in their community to lead the way—to support, to educate, to organize—for issues grappling with race. CWG was good at recognizing and taking charge of their own plight. When it came to the plight of others, of experiences different from their own, the women were not as reliable. If anything, they were not sure it was their place.

While the women I spoke to said they were eager to fight for justice, it was also clear that they struggled with how to incorporate this message into their existing one about political marginalization and mobilization. The minutes from June mentioned someone asking the group, "What do we want to do? We know we want to elect Democrats, but what else?" The women understood that George Floyd, Breonna Taylor, and the countless others before them were not killed because they were Republicans or Democrats, but because they were Black. This was not the women's experience of political marginalization, but of systemic marginalization along the lines of race—an enduring prejudice that Black Americans paid for with their lives. The women knew this was a problem that could not be solved through postcards or phone banking or simply by electing more Democrats to office, but they did not know the solution. A couple of books were suggested as "recommended reading" on the issue of racism and antiracist principles. Considering that only a few months earlier several members had only been introduced to the concept of intersectionality, the women—like most of America—had a long way to go.

The Road to 2020

"It's the election of a lifetime for people that wanna keep their democracy."

CWG's Zoom meetings continued in the months to come. In July, they announced a rollout of 1,000 postcards to go to Democratic voters in the county and an upcoming internal fundraiser to gather monetary support for newspaper ads. They encouraged those who were interested in going public with their beliefs to join the public-facing branch of the group, which had been in existence since 2018 and allowed more reticent members to remain under the CWG cloak.

At their meetings in August and September, they talked about the group's postcard progress and compiling a list of candidates for the quickly approaching election. They started their internal fundraiser for newspaper ads "to inform the voters of what we stand for and who the candidates are," and for 2,000 additional postcards to send to prospective voters in the county, reminding them of important races and dates. They also supported the local party's campaign to register voters by distributing voter registration door hangers.

By October, the members of CWG were anxious to see if all of their hard work had paid off. I spoke with several of the women that month and attended the October meeting—virtually, of course. Considering the women had been meeting over Zoom for several months by that point, I was surprised by how much difficulty there remained in navigating the technology. Cameras were on and off. Wi-Fi connections went in and out. Even though this is a group that had started over email and used a secret Facebook group to build its membership, it was still very much a group that thrived in person. At one point someone wanted to share a URL with the group, so she read it out loud while the others on the call physically wrote it down.

Along the road to the 2020 election, Texas had become competitive for the first time in decades. Pollsters and journalists speculated that the state was a toss-up, attributing the increase in Democratic support to its growing urban population and subsequent rise in youth engagement.[4] The Democratic Party had also channeled money into rural areas through a formalized coalition, in which CWG's county party had been involved. Michelle, the member of CWG who had become the member working most closely with the county party, told me about these efforts when I spoke with her at the beginning of October. "People at the higher levels were not paying any attention to rural voters at all," she told me, "we're not a lot of votes—we're the high-hanging fruit." She told me that the state party had helped connect rural counties so that they could teach one another about how to use technology to reach, inform, and mobilize Democratic voters in their area. Michelle was particularly involved in this side of their efforts.

> And just cause you're rural doesn't mean you can't use the computer, you can't use the phone. The urban people are so far ahead, they've developed all these tools. They use them. They're really good. We can use them too. . . It's basically, a lot of it is tech support, convincing them to use these tools that urban people don't think for a second about. They're just second nature. (Michelle, October 2020)

Beyond Michelle working to increase Democratic presence in other rural areas of the state, the women of CWG felt the state's growing competitiveness even in their own community. At their meeting in October, they talked about a pro-Biden billboard on a highway on the edge of town. No one knew who had put it up. They also mentioned that the county Republicans had scoped out billboard space to rent on their own behalf because they were so upset to see the Democrats' sign. As CWG had with the results of the 2018 election, they felt that the changes to their own political boldness had something to do with the political changes happening within the county.

For their part, the women seemed less worried about possible retaliation for these public displays than they had been in previous years. And if they were not less worried, they were at least less concerned. Virginia, for instance, told the group she found one of her Biden signs destroyed and stuffed in her mailbox. Nancy told the group she would need "a couple more signs if mine keep ending up in the ditch." Virginia echoed, "Me too." Signs were getting taken down, but the women were putting them back up.

Still, while CWG was not backing down, there was plenty of evidence to suggest that they *should* be worried that these public displays might provoke retaliation. A couple of days after the meeting, I got a letter from Deborah in the mail at my home in Illinois. She had mailed me a clipping from the local newspaper with a note that read, "I thought you might be interested in what's going on in 'our parts.'" The clipped article was about a weekly Trump parade that had allegedly turned hostile toward objecting bystanders.

Nancy told me that her and her partner were stockpiling ammunition in the event that there was "some sort of outbreak of anger, no matter which way we go." She had been wary of putting out a sign again this election because of the sign-stealing and vandalism happening around town. "I finally put my Biden sign out just this evening as I was coming home. I've been in and out of town. And we had an incident in [her town] where someone came up into the yard and messed with the house and messed with the signs. Lots of sign stealing."

There were other stories of recent retaliation outside of the group. Virginia told me that her landscaper, who is originally from Mexico, had a fire started in his yard after he put out a Biden sign. "They wrote stuff all over the sign and started a fire on his property and put big tree limbs across his driveway, so he'd have to get out and drag it all away." She had also given him one of her bumper stickers that said, "Yes, it's true, I'm a rural Democrat." When one of his other employers saw it, he was outraged.

Compared to years prior, CWG felt different even amid the fervor of the tone surrounding them. They recognized their community's imperfections, even its illiberalism, without retreating. In fact, the group's approach, more than in previous years, felt like leaning into their community rather than pulling away from it. Of course, they did this under the auspices of the local party, which was becoming more and more synonymous with CWG itself.

I asked several of the women if and how the group would continue after the election. They assured me it would go on full steam ahead. Deborah, for instance, told me that the women would deserve a rest if Trump lost, but that it would be back to work in 2021.

E: What's next for y'all if he [Trump] loses and what's next for y'all if he wins?

D: Well, what's next for us if he wins is a huge celebration and a rest. I think we're all just exhausted. I've never worked this hard on an election. I really have devoted my life to this since about April. And, if he wins, there will be some grief, but it would be just like it was before. We'll grieve, and then we'll get busy." (Deborah, October 2020)

Nancy said that she would not allow herself to imagine a situation in which Trump won. She felt a simultaneous sense of "hopelessness" and of grit imagining another election in which her candidate lost.

I don't know what I'll do. I just can't imagine that [Trump winning]. I run it through my head because I'm like that's it, I totally drop out . . . I work really hard on this stuff. There's one side of me just goes, okay you're done. Then I'm like hell no. (Nancy, September 2020)

The women had been working hard for four years to revive themselves and their country from a devastating loss. The thought that it might happen again was sometimes too much to bear, but the thought of giving up was too. They had put too much into this to let it go.

CWG had first started when the trauma of Clinton's loss and Trump's victory in 2016 had become impossible to bear alone. The women had come together originally to mourn and then to act, but it was their utter surprise and disgust at the election outcome that had brought them together. As they prepared for another election, I wondered if they could feel any of those same feelings. When I spoke to a few of the women, I heard a number of ways that they found their experience from 2016 trickling into their anticipation of 2020. For Ann, it was her learned distrust towards the polls' ability to predict the winner that made her anxious about 2020's outcome.

I worry with respect to the polls in terms of we got it wrong in 2016. Hopefully they have adjusted for some things, but that is where, I don't know—certainly I'm not going to stop trying to do whatever I can do to make sure people vote for Joe Biden." (Ann, October 2020)

For others, it was the "lesson" they had learned of assuming the election outcome was in the bag that made them weary of declaring a victor on election night, even if it was just to themselves. Nancy told me when she went to bed in 2016, she was "sure [she] was going to wake up to Hillary Clinton as president." "I learned my lesson" she said, "I won't do that this time." This was especially true going into the 2020 election, when record number of mail-in ballots made it likely that the outcome would come days, if not weeks, after election night.

Others felt that while 2016 was shocking, 2020 was not comparable because the stakes simply felt higher. When I asked Deborah if the 2020 election felt different to her than 2016, she said they were markedly different. They now knew the extent of what Trump could and would do to democracy, which made the election feel more important.

E: Does this election feel different for you than 2016?

D: Very . . . very different. It's scary. I'm very, very worried and I think a lot of people are very worried. You've heard the expression, everybody's saying it: it's the election of a lifetime for people that wanna keep their democracy. I think it's that serious. . . . And I'm 76. The first election I was aware of was Kennedy vs.—lord, who did he run against? I don't even remember. And then, the first time I voted was Nixon. So, I've been through a lot of presidents, both liberal and conservative, and I never thought that in my lifetime I would be afraid of losing our democracy. And I love this country. I always have. I still do. (Deborah, October 2020)

There was another way the women dealt with their anxiety around the election: they channeled it into energy. In the gear-up to the election, the women were mailing postcards to "low-propensity" Democratic voters in the county. They were preparing a series of newspaper advertisements for the local paper that were not just geared toward a party, but toward morality, even changing their original wording that addressed "Democrats" to "Americans." They were also looking to sponsor a radio ad on several tri-county stations, stations that one member described as playing "Texas boy music." The ad, which was put together by the state Democratic Party, featured what the group described as an "authoritative manly voice" listing military leaders supporting Biden.

The group was so fired up about these newspaper and radio ads, all of which ran under the name of the county's Democratic Party, that at the meeting in October they decided to nearly drain the entire budget so they could scale up the advertisements before Election Day. When Deborah asked the group what "reserves" they should keep in their budget, Roberta replied, "I'm comfortable with taking it down to zero if it means fighting this man [Trump]." The group ultimately decided to keep $200 in their account and spent the remainder of their budget on newspaper and radio ads to run before November 3.

When they signed off at the October meeting, the last one before Election Day, it was with reluctance. They were excited, maybe not about their county, but about their country. They were hopeful that the thing that had brought them together four years earlier would soon be obsolete. As the meeting wound down and the women prepared to close their browsers and rematerialize fully into their homes, I saw them switch gears. Cathy sighed and shifted in her chair before saying, "I have to leave and go make dinner." Gloria fidgeted in her seat, "I have to leave and go take care of my husband" she said.

Election Results

"Really, you just shoulda been there!"

On November 7, Deborah sent an email to CWG at 4:17 p.m. It came several days after election night and several hours after the major news networks had projected Joe Biden the winner of the 2020 presidential election[5]. The election had been called after Pennsylvania's 20 electoral votes tipped Biden's lead over the edge. Deborah's email to the group read as follows:

> We worked hard and hoped for more, but our labors were not in vain. We have a new President who will return dignity to the Whitehouse [sic], appoint competent staff members and knowledgeable leaders to government departments.
>
> For me, the best part is that we supported each other through the last very difficult 4 years. Thanks to ALL OF YOU. Especially a big thank you to whoever the first woman was at our very first gathering who said: "We have to do more than sit here and cry." That statement set us in motion.
>
> Our next meeting will be Nov. 9 and I will be in touch.
>
> Deborah

To say that the days between election night and when Joe Biden was finally declared the victor were tense would be an understatement. Watching major news networks during this limbo was like watching a football game at half-speed. Unfamiliar with how to format such prolonged counts, networks used titles for their programs like, "Election Night, Continued." That the extended time frame for counting was unfamiliar was also evident in how broadcast journalists fumbled with their language. As votes were being counted, journalists would refer to them as "coming in," as if voters had just at that very moment cast a ballot at the poll. And, as mail-in ballots were counted, journalists sometimes referenced them as "late," not to imply that they were submitted past the deadline, but that they came in later than those cast on election day or during early voting. It was not just the public that anxiously awaited a resolution, but those attempting to keep an entire nation calm and collected.

At the same time, to say that there was a feeling of resolution after Biden was projected the victor on November 7 would be inaccurate. The way in which election returns came in, slowly and not randomly, gave a feeling of uneasiness among those already on high alert to look for inaccuracies or oddities in the results. In turn, the amount of disinformation and denial following the election was remarkable, including claims that poll watchers were blocked from entering voting sites or that illegal ballots stuffed in suitcases were counted by poll workers. Some of these claims were even included in a Supreme Court brief submitted by Texas Attorney General Ken Paxton, which urged the court to review election results from several key states. The Court dismissed it.

CWG held their "meeting" on November 9, although its form resembled much more of a party than a meeting. The minutes from that day mentioned that a "small but jubilant group met for the November meeting to celebrate the Biden/Harris win and tend to a few items of business." Before their meeting had begun, they had their usual social hour, during which "Deborah waved a huge flag and blew a horn, while we welcomed guests—Cindy Champagne, Cheryl Chardonnay and Greta Gilbey." The only business they attended to seemed to be a discussion of how the Republicans were feeling amid their loss. They even failed to choose a date and time for their annual Christmas party. "By 7:25, the guests I mentioned in the first paragraph seemed to have taken over the meeting," the minutes read, "so we were unable to decide on a Christmas party. . . . However, we enjoyed a version of 'YMCA' danced by 3 of our members. Really, you just shoulda been there!"

The women were in good spirits. They were excited that the majority of the country had sided against Trump. Despite the number of Democratic votes in their county remaining largely unchanged, they were hopeful that with the tremendous gains made in Georgia, they could learn how to affect similar change in their community and in communities across Texas. "We must keep hope alive and continue our efforts," the minutes read. CWG and the local Democratic Party had "planted the seeds and they will eventually sprout."

It was not just CWG's county that had underperformed hopes of a Democratic surge. For its part, the entire state of Texas had underdelivered on the expectation of a close race. Overall, the state did see an increase in the Democratic share of the vote, but also an increase in the total number of Republican votes. And while urban strongholds in Texas saw gains in the number of Democratic voters, several border counties that were in play for both parties, like Brewster and Zapata, saw major gains for Republicans.

Following the 2020 election, the Texas Democratic Party would have its own shake-up after Democratic success in November was much smaller than originally anticipated. Party executive committee members blamed senior officials within the party for being unwilling to make substantive changes to their infrastructure and mobilization efforts,[6] although it is likely they were also outrun by a Republican Party that had poured money into its survival.[7] In the meantime, a group of women who, over the last four years, had lost friends, business, yard signs, and peace of mind drank champagne and performed a rousing rendition of "YMCA" over Zoom.

The Future of CWG

"I am what I am, and I do what I do."

At their Christmas party in December 2020, as they had done at the three Christmas parties before, the women reviewed what the group had meant to them over the course of the year, many while seated next to their Christmas tree. "I was so thankful to know I was not alone," Melanie said. "It's built my confidence to know there are others who feel the same," Nancy said. "I appreciate each of you individually and together," Ann extolled, "you give me hope and as well courage to do things that I probably would not have done before in terms of taking action on things that are important to me, and I thank you all."

One of the newest members, Lori, had only been a part of the group since the beginning of the pandemic. She only knew the women virtually. "I was just so happy to find Democratic people being active in the county, I wasn't really sure whether there was anybody here," she told the rest of the women. "It's been sort of awkward getting to know you on Zoom," Lori admitted, "so I'm looking forward to, after this is over, to have normal interactions with you and getting to know you better."

Coupled with these reflections were ambitions for the coming year—what the women aimed to do personally and what they hoped the group could help them accomplish. "Driving around [CWG's county] and seeing all the Trump signs made me feel really good that there was a group out there who don't have Trump signs in their yard," another member named Frances admitted. Frances said she was interested in having conversations with her "neighbors who had Trump signs in their yard." Her goal was to explore their "differences" through conversation.

At Frances's suggestion, Deborah advised that she wait until January to begin these conversations. "At the January meeting" Deborah responded, "Ann and Lori are going to talk about the 'Braver Angels' approach to talking to people." Braver Angels, a community organization that aims to "depolarize America" through empathetic and meaningful conversation,[8] it appeared, would be CWG's new strategy for having conversations with the other side.

Other members were hopeful that they could dissipate behavior from those on the right. Michelle said she planned to write letters to the editor claiming that it was illegal for Trump supporters to fly Trump flags along-side the American flag.[9] "I am in the mood to make a stink about it," she said. Frances replied, "I hate myself for thinking of Trump when I see an American flag," and all the women on the call nodded in agreement.[10] Other members were concerned with "the lies put out by right," and the need for "controlling" the distribution of misinformation.

All of these concerns told me that CWG was ready to continue. They had a vision for what was to come. They had not yet done enough. And although the women would walk away with a victory not within their community but within their country, their hope for progress was now set on the former rather than the latter.

That distinction, the one between local and national, is important. It is at the heart of CWG's story and will be at the heart of their future. CWG formed when they were both a national (partisan) minority and a local minority. They were driven by the desire to reclaim national government for the Democrats, but they were also looking to make a dent in their part of the state—to build a presence in their own community.

It is hard to predict what will happen as the differential between the majority in CWG's community and the majority in the country changes. There are a number of questions still to be answered. Will a national shift in partisanship affect the behavior and openness of Trump supporters in CWG's community? Will this shift cause them to retreat or double down? While some evidence suggests that a change in the national majority may decrease the "emboldening effect" that occurred after Trump's election by shrinking his platform,[11] this evidence can tell us only about how elite expression can affect citizens' expression. What remains to be seen is how people may feel emboldened *locally* by what is happening *nationally*. For their part, will the shift cause CWG's members to speak more openly because they feel emboldened by their party at the national level?

Beyond the distinction between national and local is the question of how the pandemic and the growing alignment between partisanship and health will affect those like the women of CWG. What happens when, as the women found out this year, one's choice in party also reflects one's practices in health? As politics becomes increasingly tied to both morality and health, does political secrecy and networked silence become paramount to one's safety, let alone one's survival?

As the group said goodbye before the new year, Jane told the women to "be safe." "We have lots to do," she said, "and we don't want to be missing any of this group." Illuminated by her Christmas tree, Roberta asked to share a (slightly paraphrased) quote from the writer and critic Dorothy Parker to close out the meeting. "I am what I am, and I do what I do," she recited, "and if you do not like it then to hell, my love, with you."[12]

8

Democracy Through Darkness

On October 31, 2020, a mere three days before Election Day, a video sur-
faced showing a group of trucks with pro-Trump flags surrounding and tail-
gating a Biden/Harris bus on Interstate 35. The bus was on its way from San
Antonio to Austin for a few remaining campaign events. Another video from
the scene showed one of the trucks trying to run a nearby car off of the road,
all while, according to other sources, the occupants of the truck yelled curse
words and threats at the driver. The caravan had allegedly organized using a
private Facebook group.[1]

A few months later, on January 6, 2021, much of the country watched
in horror as Trump supporters led an insurrection on the U.S. Capitol as
Congress worked to certify electoral votes. Stoked by months of Trump's
claims that the election was fraudulent and stolen, a mob broke into the capitol, vandalizing offices and firing weapons in the chamber as members of
Congress sheltered in place. They brandished American and Confederate
flags as they smashed windows. Outside of the Capitol building, they strung
a noose. Like the caravan months before, the insurrectionists had organized
using digital media, including open as well as closed groups on Facebook.

By the time you are reading this, there is sure to be more information about
how and why these events played out the way they did. My aim in telling these
stories is not to offer my own interpretation of what happened, but only to
point out that they *did* happen, and to point out *how* they happened: through
many of the same means that CWG came to exist.

Secrecy is not typically a good thing. It is associated with trauma, shame,
and subversive behavior.[2] It is not a thing we think of when imagining a
thriving, healthy democracy. Likewise, seeking out or creating groups of like-
minded people can also be a bad thing. In addition to the insurrectionists
who use closed Facebook groups to organize violent crimes against the
country, there are a number of other examples of how secrecy can hurt progress and democracy. For instance, neo-Nazi organizations rely on many of
the same features and processes of CWG: private backchannels for communication, confidentiality, insulated friendships, and support systems.[3] The

Democracy Lives in Darkness. Emily Van Duyn, Oxford University Press. © Oxford University Press 2022.
DOI: 10.1093/oso/9780197557013.003.0008

anti-vaccine community has also banded together with like-minded others through online communities to discredit scientific evidence that vaccines safely prevent disease—first spreading misinformation and beliefs within private online communities, and then outside of them.[4]

The people and groups discussed above are members of the public who are, at this point, an extreme. But as polarization has intensified, the stakes of public expression and the people who are afraid of it have, too. The story of 136 women in rural Texas, women who pledge allegiance to a flag behind closed doors, tells us this is true. The prevalence of political secrecy across the United States and Texas also tells us this is true.

My argument in this book is not that secrecy is good, but that sometimes secrecy is necessary. That growing hostility and prejudice between partisans have made political identity a risky one. In turn, managing the publicness of that identity has become more important not just to those on the fringe, but those in the mainstream as well.

But it is also true that when people use secrecy to come together it can give them support, courage, and a channel forward. The value of secrecy, then, is what people use it for: whether they use it as a peaceful tool for protection and progress, or as a tool for indignation and violence.

As I watched the events of January 6, 2021, unfold, I thought of CWG. I was sure the women knew people with the same sentiments as those ransacking our nation's Capitol. It reminded me of the threats they had experienced in their own community. It reminded me why they had formed in the first place.

It is tempting to fall into despair in light of these events. Not because of who the insurrectionists supported, but because of how they chose to display that support—through intimidation and violence. Although these individuals are not representative of all of Trump's supporters, or of those that cast their vote for him in 2016 or 2020, they do represent the illiberalism that has continued to creep into a liberal democracy. They also represent the same fears that I heard a couple of years before when I interviewed members of CWG.

While this book adds to that darkness, it also shows us light: that even if there is partisan intimidation, prejudice, and secrecy, democracy lives on. I see one example of optimism in a group of women who put out yard signs even when they were afraid. A group of women who found safety in numbers to enact political change, not violence.

The story of insurrectionists is not the only story of democracy in the United States, although it is a potent one. Our fear of one another is not the only measure of the state of our democracy, although it is an important one. There is also the story of the people who continue on, those who continue to engage despite being afraid. Perhaps another measure of the state of our democracy is how much we do or do not let our fear keep us from participating.

The subtitle of this book is "how and why people keep their politics a secret." I chose this subtitle because the lesson we should take from this book is not about CWG or the representative sample in the survey data, it is about people writ large. It is about the messy and complex people who make up our democracy—both the people whose stories are in this book and the people whose stories are not. The people who face conditions that increasingly make public partisanship a privilege. And whether that privilege means these people create a secret organization as CWG did, or simply hide their beliefs from certain coworkers on their Facebook page, they are both *strategically* hiding their politics in response to the conditions around them.

This book is about that negotiation: how people manage fear and conviction, identity and visibility. The story of CWG is evidence that the United States is facing increasing illiberalism, and it is evidence that political secrecy—whether it is the secrecy of political insurgents or the secrecy of progressive grandmothers—is on the rise. But it is my hope that while this book can speak to the darkness of democracy, it can also speak to its resilience.

How People Keep Their Politics a Secret

In my quest to explain how people keep their politics a secret, I pose a phenomenon I call "networked silence." Networked silence is about how people traverse multiple contexts—communities or networks of people—and strategically express or withhold their political beliefs in some of those contexts and not in others. I came to this idea after getting to know the experiences of a group of women in rural Texas whom I call CWG. I came to understand the scope of this idea after surveying Americans and Texans in 2018.

The term "networked silence" is a joining of two, to this point, separate theories of people and politics. The first is spiral of silence theory[5] from public opinion research, which says that people are less likely to express their political opinions when they perceive that they are in the minority. The second is networked individualism[6] from social network research, which posits that globalization and technology have given individuals more choice in the communities of which they are a part. Separate, these two ideas suggest that a person's choice of community is unrelated to their choice to express their political beliefs. In tandem, these two ideas suggest that people can and do express their beliefs in one part of their network while hiding them in another part.

Networked silence depends on the changing structure of networks and the role of digital technology in facilitating that change. Digital media has not only enabled people to engage in or create like-minded communities and groups, it has also given them more control over the publicness of that engagement. People can use the backchannel of digital media—creating private groups on Facebook, Google Groups, email listservs, WhatsApp groups—to talk about politics strategically with some and not with others.

As evident in Chapter 3, CWG relied on a secret Facebook group and private email listserv to form and function. The group used private email that was discreetly forwarded to other like-minded women in order to bring everyone together. As the group progressed into an actual organization, and as their numbers grew, it became more difficult and more chaotic for the women to discuss and share information solely over email. For example, individual members did not have access to others' email addresses through the listserv, which made it harder to interact with each other directly. As a result, the women came to rely on a secret Facebook group to post individual calls to action, links to articles, and express their thoughts and concerns. This allowed them to interact with one another in secret.

Both tools, the private listserv and the secret Facebook group, offered unique protections for the women. For one, it took the audience from invisible[7] to known. The women could, at any point, look at the membership list to see who had joined. They knew, within reason, who could see the things they posted on their group page or sent through the listserv. But it also took the audience from uncertain to confidential. The women knew that each member had agreed to the same confidentiality they had, which created a shared sense of privacy.

The role of digital media in facilitating networked silence is also evident in the survey data. Nine percent of both the U.S. and Texas samples reported having joined a private group in person or online to secretly discuss politics. Around 5% of both samples said they had joined a private Facebook group or other social media group to secretly discuss politics. Other research tells us that there are around 10 million Facebook groups in total,[8] but because Facebook will not disclose the number of private groups that exist on its platform,[9] let alone the topics of each, it is impossible to know the extent to which these groups facilitate secret political expression. What we do know is that these ways of engaging with others in secret are being used as a means for political expression, not just by a few people but by many.

Beyond what tools CWG used to engage in networked silence, they also managed their beliefs over time. Chapters 5 and 6 showed that the process of hiding your beliefs is often marked by negotiation and change. Chapter 5 showcased the *external* negotiations the women had with one another about whether or not to maintain their confidentiality. Chapter 6 explored the *internal* negotiations the women faced—if and how they would make their partisanship public. While people may choose to withhold their beliefs, they may not choose to do so in perpetuity.

How people keep their politics a secret is complicated by two increasingly blurry things. The first is the distinction between public and private. As scholars have documented, the digital world has transformed what is considered public communication and what is considered private communication.[10] In an age when content can be scraped, shared, or screen-captured, the question that bears asking is what speech is technically public and what speech is technically private? Does it take a confidentiality agreement, as in the case of CWG, to denote clearly private speech, or does privacy extend to those conversations where a third party was unexpected? Although this distinction may seem like a semantic one, what is public or private has real ramifications for individuals facing the choice to express their political beliefs. The women of CWG are evidence of this. It is one thing for a researcher to make a post-hoc distinction between public and private in an analysis of user comments, but how do people make these distinctions on their own when deciding to communicate or not? This is something we cannot know from scraping data. We can only learn about these calculations by questioning or observing people directly.

The second distinction is the one between online and offline. CWG's communication was not exclusive to the confines of their computers—they used these tools so that they could more easily connect locally, in person.[11] The transition from online to offline has been at the heart of Internet research since its dawn and is a concept both hard to anticipate and hard to trace.[12] This book echoes that complication. Building community online can lead to community offline, and vice versa, but they can also coexist. We do not live in a world where the two are as separate as they once were—where an online community might replace an offline community—but where online and offline spaces complement or supplant one another in meaningful ways.

My argument, and the idea of networked silence, is that people navigate these blurry boundaries by choosing the context in which they express themselves, and, alternatively, choosing contexts where they do *not* express themselves. But the other half of my argument is that people also have incentives to do this—to strategically hide beliefs in one context and not in another—and that these incentives have reached a different population than they ever have before.

Why People Keep Their Politics a Secret

While one part of this book is concerned with how people keep their politics a secret, the second part is concerned with why they do this. As with the first part, the lens through which I look at this question is my experience with CWG.

I am by no means the first to ask this question. There is a litany of research to say that people do not disclose their political beliefs for a number of social or individual reasons. For instance, they may withhold their beliefs because they are afraid of being isolated or ostracized from social groups,[13] or because they are generally avoidant of conflict.[14] The evidence from both CWG and the survey data in this book affirms these reasons, but also says that people are not just single-minded seekers of social connection. The choice to keep one's politics a secret—at least in some contexts, as networked silence suggests—is not a mere social calculation.

Certainly, the women of CWG were worried that they would be socially isolated from friend groups, family, and neighbors in their community. They told stories about getting kicked out of a knitting club for going against the group's prevailing political grain. They expressed worries about voting in Texas's open primary system and publicly declaring their party of choice. But the women of CWG also told stories that expressed fears of economic retribution and physical retaliation. The women are business owners worried about loss to their livelihood in the small community on which they relied. In fact, several had experienced economic loss—loss of a job, loss of a client—because of their political differences with the majority of their community.

The women also feared physical retaliation for their beliefs. One had experienced having her animal shot in her own yard and another received death threats over the phone for supporting an environmental policy. Some had yard signs stolen or vandalized, while others were worried their signs would be shot at or their car run off the road because of a political bumper sticker. These were fears I had not expected to hear—fears that are fundamentally different from worries of social disapproval that are so common in how we think about withholding one's political beliefs.

Chapter 6 also laid bare the reasons why people may hide their beliefs by showing what it will take for them to make them public. The women of CWG may have joined the group because they wanted their politics to be a secret, but not all of them remained this way. Many went on to join the local Democratic Party or make public declarations of their beliefs. Some ran for local office. They attributed this transition to the "courage" CWG had given them. Knowing that there were others in their community who shared their beliefs gave them confidence to express them to others. It was also because CWG allowed the women to practice talking about politics in a space that was supportive, giving them an opportunity to rehearse political conversations and learn *how* they should talk about politics in addition to *if* they should talk about politics.

As I stated in Chapter 1, the more novel argument of this book is less about political secrecy and more about who engages in it. The women of CWG—and ostensibly the Americans and Texans represented in the survey data—are average citizens and average partisans. They are not political extremists or members of a subaltern or antisocial movement. They are Democrats, Republicans, and Independents who fall within the general mainstream.

Even though the women of CWG's presidential candidate of choice won the general election in 2020, they remain a small minority of their community. Even though their nearest urban center went strongly for Biden, they remain in a rural community that went strongly for Trump. The point is that why people keep their politics a secret will depend very much on the social context of which they are a part. And as that social context becomes more and more homogenous—Democrats in some places and groups and Republicans in others—the more that mainstream beliefs can become marginalized.

At the beginning of this book, I mentioned my revelation that studying "silence" reveals only half the story. It is the basketball being passed as a gorilla comes into frame. Knowing that people do not express their beliefs is important. Knowing how and why they keep them a *secret* is another thing. That difference—between silence and secrecy—depends on if you find them. That is why as networked silence becomes both more possible and more likely, finding people's politics will require a different way of looking.

How to Look at Networked Silence

My ethnography of CWG is able to tell us about a select group of people without being limited by early assumptions. The representative survey data can reliably tell us about a wide range of people but is limited by the assumptions made at the beginning. Both of these methods answer different questions. The first addresses questions of complexity. The second addresses questions of scale. Both are important to understand a phenomenon. I would not have understood the complex experiences of CWG by surveying them alone, and I would not have understood the extent of political secrecy by only looking at CWG.

But there are also a number challenges to studying the phenomenon I describe in this book. As you might imagine, finding and studying something that is intended to be concealed, at least in some contexts, proves a very difficult task. I was able to do so because I had a point of access, my own personal attributes, time, and patience on my side. It is likely that those who are interested in politics and communication may not have these same features available to them.

There are still are other more systematic ways to make networked silence less elusive. For one, to uncover how and why people keep their politics a secret will require attention to the role of social and political power. Individuals choose to hide their political beliefs in some groups and not in others because they either believe they hold little power or are afraid they will lose the power they do hold. This means seeing not just the political majority in a group as important symbols of and pathways for politics, but the political minority as well.

Like previous scholars who focused on the role of social power in promoting or curtailing political discussion,[15] understanding networked silence, and why people keep their politics a secret in some cases and not in others, means looking at people's power *across* contexts rather than just in one. Only looking at the women of CWG in their community would uncover an apathetic citizen. Looking at the women within CWG uncovers an engaged citizen. The difference is where you look.

A focus on social and political power is especially important as they become increasingly intertwined and as partisanship becomes a line of social demarcation. The experience of power and powerlessness not only follows lines of historical and demographic privilege, but lines of majority privilege as well. Those in the political majority now hold the privilege to be publicly political, leaving those in the minority excluded from or intimidated from public discourse.

An interest in and study of people and their politics also requires a commitment to protection. People hide their political beliefs for a reason. To expose, intentionally or not, individuals alongside their beliefs would be to disrupt their lives and even potentially put them at risk of harm. In the case of CWG, I told no one where I went when I attended the group's meetings or events. I always conducted interviews in a private room. My emails with members were encrypted, all my field notes shredded, original interviews deleted, and actual names and identifying locations deleted from all interview transcripts. These guidelines helped me de-identify individuals with their statements and decontextualize the community and general area wherein the alternative community exists.

But studying networked silence and people's political secrets is made more complicated by the fact that digital media plays an important role in offering individuals a place to discuss and engage in politics in secret. For one thing, it is difficult to know how to ethically study secrecy online. The question of how to study online communities and social media has been around as long as each platform.[16] Yet these questions often overlook two important aspects of visibility: the public bias in data collection and the threat to people's *political* privacy.

Scraping content from social media platforms often results in data that is from public accounts. This data reflects only what individuals are willing to post publicly, not what they are intentionally keeping private. A reliance on public data will offer less and less valuable information about the public as people have growing incentives to manage the publicness of their partisanship.

Although the past decade has brought with it a global reckoning for data privacy,[17] this reckoning applies to political privacy as well. As channels for private communication become more widespread, people's use of and trust in digital platforms for privately discussing politics has expanded, too. And as is evident in the case of political insurgents and the 2021 election, these private spaces can be used for bad just as they can be used for good.

To their credit, platforms have taken some measures to protect the data (and communication) of their "users." For instance, not only is data scraping from secret Facebook groups not permitted without explicit access, but it is also in violation of Facebook's terms and agreements.[18] Scraping may also be in violation of group confidentiality agreements, which are common in closed groups, although there remain many ways around it. Even the storage of this data threatens political privacy because comments, messages, and posts, even those on private groups, are inherently associated with a personal and identifiable social media account. Platforms have also taken some steps to prohibit the use of private backchannels and groups to organize crime or engage in hate speech, but often these measures have been too little and come too late.

All of this is to say that the collection, management, and storage of private political communication is challenging. There are no comprehensive or consistent rules for how to handle this data across institutions or industries,[19] nor is there an ethical standard enforced across fields, although there should be. This means that, as of now, to explore political secrecy while doing so ethically will mean an approach that is perhaps not always quantifiable but is personal—an approach that looks a lot more like listening than scraping.

Why This Matters

While the goal of this book was to tell a story and build an understanding from that story, it is also my hope that this book will have practical implications for those who are reading it. In other words, I hope that this story can inform not only the study and understanding of networked silence and political secrecy, but also the way society and industry engages with it.

First, this book challenges parties and other typically public-facing political organizations to consider the ways in which the public nature of their organizations limits their membership. Although I was not expecting the relationship between CWG and its local party to be one of significance, their mutual influence was something that has and does hold the potential to change their community. This is because political parties and political organizations are essential tools for democratic decision-making[20] and channels for political action.[21]

But political parties typically rely on public political acts—participation in rallies and demonstrations, attending public meetings, making public donations to a campaign, and writing letters or emails to the editor of a newspaper are all considered typical measures of online and offline political participation.[22] Yet CWG's membership as originally distinct from the Democratic Party shows that this focus on public political action limits who actually joins. Reaching members who are a political minority in their community will require a hybridity for political parties, not just in terms of legacy and new media[23] or digital and in-person organizing,[24] but hybridity in terms of both public and private ways of organizing.

Based on the experiences of CWG, political parties might also consider how their infrastructure in noncompetitive districts matters more than they might think. When I first discovered CWG, the county's local Democratic Party was not particularly strong. The same few people had been running nearly empty meetings, begging the remaining local Democrats to stay in the party, and occasionally writing rebuttals to conservative letters to the editor since the 1990s. They were tired and discouraged. The statewide party had left records in their county, and in similar rural counties, untouched and out of date for years. Even Beto O'Rourke's 2018 Senate campaign, which was the first statewide Democratic campaign to visit their county in 20 years, had a presence in the community mostly because CWG and the local Democrats teamed up to promote him and the party in ways not done before.

The state and national Democratic Party's choice to give up on districts that do not seem viable also means giving up on any chance of breaking down the political stigma associated with their partisanship and any chance of rebuilding a presence in these areas at all. In fact, groups like CWG that offer protection *and* participation could be assets for parties looking to rebuild a stronghold in noncompetitive areas. That is because they offer protection for a different kind of member who would perhaps be wary of being publicly partisan, at least at first. Moreover, groups like CWG offer a chance for partisans to incubate and practice politics—to grow political and communication efficacy that can serve them in the truly public sphere and lead them to the party itself.

This means parties and their organizing strategies will also need to focus on the experiences of individual communities and consider the role of political stigma in how they recruit and engage activists in campaigns and in their attempts to persuade voters. Considering how and why people may keep their politics a secret can be strategic in the effort to make noncompetitive districts competitive once again. And this is good for democracy. It means representatives who are accountable to not just to those in their party, but those from the out-party as well.[25] It could also result in meaningful and consistent exposure to different perspectives within one's own community, which has the potential to help alleviate the social and political polarization currently facing communities across the world.[26]

In all fairness, parties are faced with difficult decisions to invest funds in viable elections over others. As a result, many party leaders choose to play the short game, investing in close races, rather than the long game, investing in less viable areas. But complete abandonment and even insufficient support will only put the short game in many areas of the country much further away.

Political parties are not the only organizations with a stake in evaluating the public and their opinions. Journalists and news media often assess, re-package, and purvey public opinion to the people. Given that this book says that members of the public can and do hide their opinions in places that are themselves not public, there are then a number of implications for how journalists choose to portray the "people" in their coverage.

One of the most common ways journalists convey public opinion is through conducting and covering public opinion polls. Polls can offer a reli-able picture of public attitudes by offering data on people's private attitudes,[27] although choices about which polls to cover or not cover often reflect a sys-tematic bias and distort actual public opinion.[28] Moreover, these "private" attitudes are only in response to the survey question and response options fabricated by the poll itself.[29] They offer little nuance to how the indi-vidual feels.

Polls are often depicted through the lens of a horse race in which the polls of interest are the ones in which majority and minority are close together, not when they are far apart. As a result, noncompetitive areas, like CWG's, be-come inconsequential and invisible in political coverage. This is made worse by the traditional tropes of a "winner takes all" red and blue map, which only enhances a focus on the majority while eliminating the minority altogether.

This kind of black and white (or red and blue) coverage has consequences for people, like the women of CWG, who live in communities where they are in the political minority. Just as the women of CWG took cues from their local paper, so too do people across the country take cues about their community's majority political preferences from news coverage.[30] Should the media portray public opinion as homogenous—focusing only on the red or blue majority—they further alienate those with minority, but important, beliefs, who feel outnumbered.

Polls are not the only way that journalists and news media convey public opinion. As the public shifts to online communication, journalists now in-creasingly rely on social media as a form of public opinion, displaying and using individuals' tweets, online comments, and social media posts to de-termine what is on the public's mind and how they feel about public issues.[31]

Yet the social data that is available to journalists comes either from what is accessible on their own social platforms or what is publicly available writ large. While it may feel like they have greater access to the public vis-à-vis social media, journalists really have access to a biased sample of opinions from people who are willing to publicly express them or to people they know.

This distinction is important. If journalists continue to rely on public social media posts, they will find a public that is either steadfast in their beliefs—the people they see—or disengaged from politics altogether—the people they do not. This dichotomy, like the dichotomies of a red and blue political map or of politically homogenous rural and urban communities, is both false and dangerous. Although a majority system may be how electors are decided, it is not how people live.

To be clear, I am not advocating for journalists to join as many closed Facebook groups as possible, or to engage in salacious political exposés. I am, however, advocating for a type of reporting that considers communities in context—a type of reporting that does not make assumptions about the political experiences of each community based solely on privately constrained survey questions or publicly available online content. This means listening to people in their communities, which is perhaps best done by the local journalists already in or familiar with them. This means considering the stigma that comes with a public declaration of partisanship and being sensitive to sources who seek to withhold their identities. It also means giving less attention to people's separation and more attention to their subtlety.

Journalists often rely on social media platforms because they are where much of the public exists. Digital platforms like Facebook and Twitter have been instrumental in creating private means of communication and organizing,[32] like the secret Facebook group in CWG, that allow individuals to engage with others in broader and more protected ways, for better or worse.

And this network of private channels is likely to grow over the coming years. For instance, in the spring of 2019, Facebook announced plans to unveil more tools for private and even encrypted communication on their various platforms, including on WhatsApp. As a result, the menu of available channels for private—and inaccessible—communication will grow. This means that those interested in assessing public opinion and behavior will need to engage in the kind of study I pose in this book: they will need to be embedded in people's communities, not just brief visitors to them.

But doubling down on private communication will also have implications for people who use these platforms and for the platforms themselves. For one thing, offering these types of tools may bring different people to the platform than those who were part of the platform before. For instance, it is possible that those seeking protected communication increasingly turn to the digital space, instead of interpersonal venues, to express themselves or engage in politics with others. In some cases, given the social, economic, and even physical ramifications of public political expression, technology platforms will need to protect and ensure that this content is in fact private, despite some existing evidence, like the Cambridge Analytica scandal in 2016, among others, that user privacy is not protected. In other cases, where private communication is dangerous, prejudicial, or aimed to incite violence, platforms will need to be astute moderators. Whether or not this should be up to the platforms themselves is a current argument at the heart of many institutions across the world, and not one that I attempt to answer conclusively here. What I can and will say in the context of this book is that this conversation should include a discussion not just of how anti-democratic citizens are prohibited from private spaces for communication, but how pro-democratic citizens are protected within them.

Technology platforms might also use the insights from this book as a useful lens through which to view the people who use their services. Private channels like direct messaging or closed groups are invaluable to people looking to engage in networked silence. How could platforms better tailor these services to the benefit of the people who use them? How can these spaces be designed or managed to encourage political expression and participation in ways that keep people protected?

Of course, this kind of thinking will require that the people behind decisions are in touch with the kind of social scientific work I review in this book. That they not only employ but listen to people who are trained to see and analyze the social and democratic world, not just the technological or financial one. Yet tech firms and social media platforms have been inconsistently and inadequately engaged with social scientific work in their product development and rollout.[33] Given that social scientists have been dedicated to and diligent in addressing changes in technology, democracy, and the intersection of the two, this is a missed opportunity for technology platforms and firms. As the evidence in this book shows, technology companies do and will play a large role in facilitating places for networked silence to occur. It will then be important for these companies to recognize and protect that role with members of the public and to engage the scientific community in understanding the democratic implications of their design and their choices.

Seeds, Not Sediment

A lot has changed since I went to the Women's March in 2017. The United States, the world, and all of us have endured a lot: social and political upheaval, economic crises, a global pandemic, and a national insurrection, to name a few. The Women's March, which ushered in a new administration and a new era of political turmoil, would only be the beginning of a long four years for both political sides.

In many ways, I see partisan politics in the United States continuing along a cataclysmic trajectory, something that many scholars have waxed eloquently about over the past few years.[34] What hangs in the balance is not a partisan issue, it is democracy. It is not owned by Democrats or Republicans. In fact, it requires that the two are fair, reliable, and representative tools for public opinion. The goal of this book is not to point fingers at either side, it is to remind us what is at stake.

I do not have a prediction for if or how things will change. There are many Democrats and Republicans, across many industries and ideologies, who are working to make sure that they do. What I do know is that there are seeds out there who are still waiting to sprout if we just give them some time and some help.

The hopefulness of my argument depends on whether you consider the women of CWG and those that engage in networked silence as seeds or as sediment—are they buried to sprout, or are they buried to settle? Are they buried to sink democracy, or are they buried to rebuild it? Many of the same tools that feed the darkest parts of society can also be tools to help repair it. This book gives at least some evidence that even amid attempts to be suppressed, democracy has the capacity to rise above intimidation.

The democracy on display in this book is not ideal. It offers a warning of the growing dangers and repercussions of partisan polarization and hostility. But it also offers us an example of how and why people persist in the face of opposition, how they move beyond threats to their identity and to their well-being. It tells us how people keep democracy alive *through* darkness. It is my hope that in writing this book we can see that our democracy may be dark, but it is not dead.

Interviewee Pseudonyms and Interview Dates

Pseudonym	2017 Interview	2018 Interview	2020 Interview
Paula	4/28/17	10/23/18	
Connie	5/1/17	10/18/18	
Linda	5/1/17	10/23/18	
Alice	5/4/17	–	
Joyce	5/8/17	7/2/18	
Melanie	7/17/17	9/14/18	
Gail	7/18/17	–	
Bonnie	7/20/17	8/16/18	
Roberta	7/23/17	–	
Jean	7/23/17	–	
Theresa	7/23/17	1/29/18 & 7/13/18	10/2/2020
Virginia	7/24/17	9/19/18	10/2/2020
Dawn	7/24/17	10/2/18	
Barbara	7/24/17	9/25/18	
Cynthia	7/24/17	8/13/18	
Kathleen	7/26/17	10/24/18	
Shirley	7/27/17	–	
Cathy	7/28/17	10/22/18	
Ann	8/1/17	9/17/18	10/5/2020
Nancy	8/4/17	8/13/18	9/30/2020
Deborah	8/8/17	7/29/18	10/5/2020
Audrey	8/8/17	–	
Sissy	–	10/18/18	
Michelle	–	–	9/30/2020

CWG Meetings

Month	Minutes or Observation
November 2016	Minutes
December 2016	Minutes
January 2017	Minutes
February 2017	Minutes
March 2017	Minutes
April 2017	Minutes
May 2017	Minutes
June 2017	Minutes
July 2017	Minutes
August 2017	Observation
September 2017	Minutes
October 2017	Minutes
November 2017	Observation
December 2017	Minutes
January 2018	Observation
February 2018	Observation
March 2018	Observation
April 2018	Minutes
May 2018	Observation
June 2018	Minutes
July 2018	Observation
August 2018	Observation
September 2018	Observation
October 2018	Minutes
November 2018	Observation
December 2018	Minutes
January 2019	Minutes
February 2019	Minutes
March 2019	Minutes
April 2019	Minutes
May 2019	Minutes
June 2019	Minutes
July 2019	Minutes
August 2019	Minutes
September 2019	Minutes
October 2019	Minutes
November 2019	Minutes
December 2019	Minutes
January 2020	Minutes

Month	Minutes or Observation
February 2020	Minutes
March 2020	Minutes
April 2020	No meeting
May 2020	No meeting
June 2020	Minutes
July 2020	Minutes
August 2020	Minutes
September 2020	Minutes
October 2020	Observation
November 2020	Minutes
December 2020	Observation

Survey Details

Survey data came from the Texas Media and Society Survey (TMASS), conducted by the Annette Strauss Institute for Civic Life at The University of Texas at Austin and fielded by the GfK Group (formerly Knowledge Networks) in June 2018. TMASS includes both a Texas-representative and a U.S.-representative sample and includes population weights (see Table C1 for a comparison of these samples with national and state demographics). GfK's probability-based sampling methodology has been supported by previous research (see Yeager et al., 2011) and is particularly useful for this book because it provides Internet access to respondents, allowing residents of rural communities, often underserved by Internet companies, to participate in Internet-based surveys.[1]

Hiding Political Beliefs

To measure whether one feels the need to hide one's opinions, I used the following survey question: "How often, if at all, do you try to make sure that others can't hear or see you when you talk about politics?" on a scale of 1 to 4 (1 = never, 2 = hardly ever, 3 = sometimes, 4 = often). Across the national sample, 22.3% of respondents said they tried, at least sometimes, "to make sure that others can't hear or see" when they talk about politics. On average, respondents said they hardly ever felt the need to hide their political conversations from others ($M = 1.71$, $SD = 0.91$). Across the Texas sample, a similar percentage (22.6%) said they tried, at least sometimes, to hide their political conversations from others ($M = 1.73$, $SD = 0.94$).

Offline/Online Secret Expression

I was interested in two main questions that measured secret expression either online or offline. The offline version asked respondents, "Which of the following have you done in the past two years . . . Met in private in person with a group of people to secretly discuss politics" while the online version asked respondents, "Which of the following have you done in the past two years . . . Joined a private Facebook group or other private social media group to discuss politics." Response options were dichotomous. Because of the low sample size on both questions, I combined responses to both into one composite variable, where answering yes to either question is coded as a 1 and answering no to both questions is coded as a 0.

In the U.S. sample, 9.4% had either "met in private in person with a group of people to secretly discuss politics" or "joined a private Facebook group or other private social media to discuss politics" in the last two years. When looking at the two separately, 4.5% of the sample had secretly discussed politics in person, while 5.4% had joined a private Facebook group or other social media to discuss politics.

Table C1 Participant Demographics, U.S. and Texas Samples

	U.S.		Texas	
	ACS 2016	TMASS 2018	ACS 2016	TMASS 2018
Gender				
Male	48.2%	48.3%	48.5%	47.8%
Female	51.8	51.7	51.5	52.2
Age				
18–29	20.6	20.4	22.9	21.1
30–44	25.4	25.4	28.3	28.8
45–59	26.3	26.3	25.4	25.9
60+	27.8	27.9	23.4	24.2
Education				
Less than high school	12.4	12.2	16.6	15.3
High school diploma	27.5	27.5	25.9	26.3
Some college/university	30.6	30.7	30.8	30.8
Bachelor's degree or more	29.5	29.6	26.8	27.6
Race				
White, non-Hispanic	64.3	64.5	46.4	46.4
Hispanic	15.8	15.5	35.6	35.9
African American/Black	11.7	11.7	11.5	11.7
Other, non-Hispanic	6.6	6.6	5.3	4.7
	CPS 2017	TMASS 2018	CPS 2017	TMASS 2018
Metro Status				
Non-metro	13.9	13.9	7.7	7.8
Metro	86.1	86.1	92.3	92.2

Note. U.S. Sample total N = 1,062; Texas Sample total N = 1,004. Gender, age, education, and race data is compared to data from the American Communities Survey (ACS) from 2016. Metro status is compared to the March 2017 supplement of the Current Population Survey CPS). Columns do not add up to exactly 100% due to rounding. There are some differences in the demographic question wordings between the ACS, CPS, and the TMASS survey. Both the U.S. and Texas frequencies are using weights for each sample.

In the Texas sample, the same percentage, 9.4% had either met in private in person to secretly discuss politics or joined a private Facebook group in the last two years. When looking at the two separately, 4.2% had met in person to secretly discuss politics and 5.6% reported joining a private Facebook group or other social media to discuss politics.

When comparing responses to both of these outcomes (likelihood of hiding political conversations and likelihood of secret expression online or offline), the two are related but not identical. In the U.S. sample, both outcomes were only modestly correlated ($r = .17, p < .01$), which was also true in the Texas sample ($r = .26, p < .01$).

Demographics

Across the U.S. sample (see Table C1), the average age was around 48 years old ($M = 47.52$, $SD = 17.34$), 51.7% of the sample was female, and 64.5% of the sample was white/non-Hispanic. Across the Texas sample, the average was only slightly younger ($M = 46.37$, $SD = 16.18$), slightly more female (52.2%), and less white/non-Hispanic (46.4%). In addition, respondents were asked what political party they most identified with, ranging from strongly Republican (1) to strongly Democrat (7). On average, respondents in the U.S. sample reported that they were undecided/Independent ($M = 4.19, SD = 2.09$), which was also true for the Texas sample ($M = 4.20, SD = 2.05$).

I looked at the relationship between gender, race/ethnicity, age, partisanship, and hiding your political beliefs (see Table C2).[2] While partisanship was not significant in the national sample, it was significant in the Texas sample. Democrats in Texas are more likely to hide their political beliefs than Republicans or true Independents in Texas. Whites were also more likely in the Texas sample to hide their political beliefs from their local community compared to those that are not White, but this was not true in the national sample. And while women were marginally more likely to hide their political beliefs in the national sample than were men, this was not true in the Texas sample.

When looking at how the same demographic variables relate to offline or online secret expression (see Table C3), there are again a number of significant relationships. In contrast to the relationships above, Whites were *less* likely to express themselves in secret than those that are not White in both the national and Texas samples. And while partisanship was not significant in the national sample above, it was significant in the national sample when it came to secret expression. The more a respondent associated with Democrats, the more likely they were to secretly express their beliefs in the national sample. This was not

Table C2 Likelihood of Hiding Political Beliefs, U.S. and Texas Samples

	Model 1: U.S. Sample		Model 2: Texas Sample	
	B	SE	B	SE
Constant	1.71***	(0.12)	1.38***	(0.13)
Female	0.10+	(0.06)	0.08	(0.06)
White	0.09	(0.06)	0.29***	(0.07)
Age	−0.00	(0.00)	0.00	(0.00)
Democrat	−0.01	(0.01)	0.04**	(0.02)
Adjusted R-square	0.00		0.02	
n	1,017		963	

Note. These analyses used OLS regression weighting for the U.S. and Texas samples separately.
*** $p < .001$, ** $p < .01$, * $p < .05$.

Table C3 Likelihood of Offline/Online Secret Expression, U.S. and Texas Samples

	Model 1:U.S. Sample		Model 2:Texas Sample	
	B	SE	B	SE
Constant	−2.03***	(0.45)	−1.39**	(0.47)
Female	0.10	(0.22)	−0.14	(0.22)
White	−0.57*	(0.23)	−0.73**	(0.27)
Age	−0.01+	(0.01)	−0.01	(0.01)
Democrat	0.12*	(0.06)	−0.02	(0.06)
Nagelkerke R-square	0.04		0.03	
n	1,049		984	

Note. These analyses used logistic regression weighting for the U.S. and Texas populations separately.
*** $p < .001$, ** $p < .01$, * $p < .05$.

true in Texas. Older individuals were also marginally more likely to secretly express their beliefs in the national sample, but not in the Texas sample.

Fear of Isolation

I drew from the original spiral of silence theory (Noelle-Neumann, 1974) and research on fear of social isolation as a state-based variable (Hayes et al., 2013) when measuring fear of social isolation in the survey. I considered fear of isolation as a state-based variable in that networked silence suggests fear of isolation can change across context. For instance, the women of CWG feared isolation from their knitting club, but not members of CWG. In contrast, considering fear of isolation as a trait-based variable suggests it is constant across contexts.

To capture fear of isolation as a state rather than a trait, I adapted Neuwirth et al.'s (2007) measure. The exact question wording was: "If your political opinions were to become widely known around your local community, how concerned would you be that people would avoid you or act differently toward you somehow?" Responses were on a scale from 1 (not concerned at all) to 5 (extremely concerned). On average, across the U.S. sample, respondents were not concerned at all that people in their local community would "avoid you or act differently toward you somehow" ($M = 1.66$, $SD = 1.06$). In the Texas sample, respondents were only slightly more concerned ($M = 1.72$, $SD = 1.12$).

Fear of isolation was consistently a significant predictor across both the national and Texas samples and across both outcomes. Those who have higher levels of fear of isolation from their local community are significantly more likely to hide their political beliefs than those with lower levels of fear of isolation, even when controlling for gender, age, race/ethnicity, and partisanship (see Table C4). This was also true for one's likelihood of secret expression. Those with higher levels of fear of isolation from their local community are more likely to engage in secret expression either offline or online than those with lower levels of fear of isolation (see Table C5). In both samples, the explained variance ranges from medium to large in size.

Table C4 Fear of Isolation and Likelihood of Hiding Political Beliefs, U.S. and Texas Samples

	Model 1:U.S. Sample		Model 2: Texas Sample	
	B	SE	B	SE
Constant	1.71***	(0.12)	0.81***	(0.13)
Fear of Isolation	0.27***	(0.03)	0.34***	(0.03)
Female	0.09⁺	(0.06)	0.13*	(0.06)
White	0.13*	(0.06)	0.25***	(0.07)
Age	0.00	(0.00)	0.00	(0.00)
Democrat	−0.01	(0.01)	0.02	(0.02)
Adjusted R-square	0.10		0.18	
n	1,011		956	

Note. These analyses used OLS regression weighting for the U.S. and Texas samples separately.
*** $p < .001$, ** $p < .01$, * $p < .05$.

Table C5 Fear of Isolation and Likelihood of Offline/Online Secret Expression, U.S. and Texas Samples

	Model 1: U.S. Sample		Model 2:Texas Sample	
	B	SE	B	SE
Constant	−2.91***	(0.50)	−2.15***	(0.50)
Fear of Isolation	0.44***	(0.09)	0.43	(0.08)
Female	0.08	(0.22)	−0.03	(0.23)
White	−0.52⁺	(0.23)	−0.80**	(0.27)
Age	−0.01	(0.01)	−0.01	(0.01)
Democrat	0.12⁺	(0.06)	−0.04	(0.06)
Nagelkerke R-square	0.10		0.09	
n	1,029		970	

Note. These analyses used logistic regression weighting for the U.S. and Texas populations separately.
*** $p < .001$, ** $p < .01$, * $p < .05$.

Semi-Structured Interview Guide 2017

Self-Description, Identity, and 2016 Election

How long have you lived in [name of town/county]?
Do you consider [name of town/county] home?
Do you have children? How old are they?
Did you attend any type of school after high school?
How old are you?
What is your race/ethnicity?
Would you consider yourself a Democrat? A Republican? An Independent?
Did you vote in the 2016 election? If so, who did you vote for?
How involved would you say you were in the 2016 election?
How did you feel and react after hearing the 2016 election results?

Opposition in the Community and in Relationships

Are you a member of a church or religious organization?
If so, how important is that church or religious organization to your life?
What does it feel like to be a member of your community?
Do you feel like you are a part of your community?
Are you married? Does your partner share the same political opinion(s) as you?
Does your partner know you are in the group?
How many people in your life and in your community know your political opinion(s)?
What risks are there in letting others in your life and in your community (outside of the group) know your political opinion(s)?
Where do you experience the most opposition to your political opinion(s)? What does that opposition look like?

Organization-Specific Questions

Why was this group started?
What is its purpose now?
How do you recruit members to your group? Who are you looking to recruit?
How would you describe the kind of people that are part of your group to outsiders like me?
Why are you a part of this group?
What does being a part of this group make you feel?
How do you think your group compares to the rest of the community?

Do you think it's important that the group is all women?

Do you think it's important to keep the group a secret? How do you keep the group a secret?

Does the group have rules? If so, what are the rules?

How does the group engage with politics?

How do you engage with politics now that you are a member of this group? Do you do anything you didn't do before being a part of the group?

Semi-Structured Interview Guide 2018

Self-Description, Identity, and 2018 Mid-Term Election

Would you now consider yourself a Democrat? A Republican? An Independent?
How have you been political engaged over the past year?
Did you vote in the 2018 mid-term primary? What was that experience like?
How do you think things are going to go in the mid-terms in your county?
What has been the community response to Beto O'Rourke running for office?
Do you think Beto O'Rourke has a chance to win in your county or in Texas?

Opposition in the Community and in Relationships

Has the political climate and hostility in the community changed over the past year?
Have feelings about Trump in the community changed over the past year?
How do you feel about being open about your political beliefs in your community now compared to how you felt a year ago?
Have you done anything to make your political beliefs public to your community over the past year? Do you have a specific example?

Organization-Specific Questions

What has been the group's focus lately?
Do you believe that focus is important?
How do you feel things are going in the group?
What do you think the group is doing successfully?
What do you think the group needs to do better?
What challenges is the group facing?
What has helped the group over the past year?
Where do you think the group is going? How will the group change?
Do you think it is important that the group remain secret?

Semi-Structured Interview Guide 2020

Self-Description, Identity, and Community

Has the political climate and hostility in the community changed over the past two years?
How do you feel about being open about your political beliefs in your community now compared to how you felt two years ago?
Have you done anything to make your political beliefs public to your community over the past two years? Do you have a specific example?
Have you been in active in the Democratic Party at all over the past two years?

Organization-Specific Questions

How do you feel things are going in the group?
What challenges is the group facing?
How has the group helped you over the past two years?
Where do you think the group is going? How will the group change?
Do you think it is important that the group remain secretive?
Do you think it is important that the group remain only women?

Reckoning with Racial Injustice

What was your reaction to the killings of George Floyd and other Black Americans at the hands of police this summer? What was the community's reaction?
Has the group discussed these events?
Does the group have a plan to address racial injustice?

2020 Election

Do you have any worries about the election outcome?
Are you worried that the 2020 election will be like or feel like 2016?
Will you vote in person or by mail?
Do you have a plan for watching the returns on election night?
Are you concerned that there will be any backlash in the community if Trump wins or if Biden wins?
What has the group done to prepare for the 2020 election? Is the group hopeful about the election's outcome?
Has the group discussed what it will do after the election?

COVID-19

What has been your experience with the COVID-19 pandemic?

How has the COVID-19 pandemic affected your community?

Is there a stigma associated with mask-wearing in the community? Do you feel that you can tell people's partisanship in the community based on if they wear a mask? Do you feel like you can tell people's politics based on if they wear a mask or not?

How has the group had to adapt to COVID-19.

Notes

Chapter 1

1. Stein (2017).
2. Kearney (2016).
3. CBS News (2017).
4. Tolentino (2017).
5. Chenoweth and Pressman (2017).
6. See Meyer and Tarrow's (2018) comprehensive collection of scholarship on the Women's March and the growing resistance movement in response to Trump's election.
7. A version of this same story appears in an op-ed I wrote for the San Antonio Express News (Van Duyn, 2018).
8. For instance, Eliasoph (1996) explains how *what* is public is evidence of *who* holds power. She suggests that the kinds of political conversations people are willing and able to have publicly are also evidence of who is given the power to construct the public itself.
9. Herbst (1994, p. 180) explores marginalized groups throughout history, considering how they build their own alternative communities embedded within a larger context.
10. Cramer's (2016, p. 14) work is particularly sensitive to how geographic place influences people's interpretation of politics and their relationship to elites. She argues that place has become especially important with a growing "rural consciousness" that pits the resources allocated to rural residents against those allocated to urbanites.
11. Patterson (2016).
12. Meyer (2015).
13. Lind (2016).
14. Rothkopf (2016).
15. Kurtzleben (2017).
16. See Gest (2016) and Hochschild (2016).
17. For instance, Sides et al. (2019) argue that Trump's victory is a reflection of the nativist and xenophobic attitudes of White Americans, providing evidence from survey data that support of Trump was correlated with prejudiced views of communities of color.
18. Like Sides et al. (2019), Mutz (2018) argues that support for Trump among White Americans was not due as much to economic anxiety as it was to social anxiety. To demonstrate this difference, Mutz draws on a concept from psychology called "perceived status threat," which says that when people feel that an out-group (e.g., someone from a different racial/ethnic group) threatens their overall status within a society, they are more likely to defend their own group and to place a "greater

emphasis on the importance of conformity to group norms, and increased outgroup negativity" (p. E4331). Comparing people's economic attitudes and their perceived status threat in 2012 and 2016, she finds that support for Trump was more highly correlated with perceived status threat than indicators of economic anxiety (e.g., job loss, a decline in income).

19. See Jamieson's (2018) comprehensive account of Russian interference in the 2016 presidential election, and Lukito's (2020) exploration of how Russia's Internet Research Agency (IRA) coordinated the spread of disinformation across multiple platforms.

20. Tong et al. (2020), for example, found that people define the phrase "fake news" in political terms—often using it to blame or attack those in the political out-group.

21. My colleague and I found that just being exposed to the term "fake news" led people to trust the media less than those who were not exposed to the phrase (Van Duyn & Collier, 2019).

22. Norris et al. (2020) find that misinformation helped contribute to a distrust in the election's outcome.

23. Jackson and Sparks (2017).

24. Enten (2016).

25. Iyengar and Westwood (2015); Lelkes and Westwood (2017).

26. For example, Levendusky and Malhotra (2016) find that Americans overestimate the amount of polarization between the political parties, while Yang et al. (2016) find that perceiving polarization between a country's political parties is especially likely among those who consume news online.

27. This is the idea of "networked individualism" (Rainie & Wellman, 2012), which says that mobile and digital media has enabled people to be free social agents, no longer existing only in a singular community but traversing multiple communities.

28. Hampton and Wellman (2001).

29. Mason (2018).

30. Mason and Wronski (2018).

31. Gillion et al. (2020).

32. Hersh and Ghitza (2018).

33. Desilver (2016).

34. Traister (2018) gives a narrative of how the 2016 election stoked anger among American women.

35. For instance, in Huddy's (2001) review of how social identity informs political identity, she argues that the salience of a social identity often influences the strength of that identity. In the case of the 2016 election, the focus on gender—both in Trump's behavior and language as well as the gender of his opponent—made gender identity both more salient and stronger.

36. United States Department of Agriculture (2018).

37. United Nations Department of Economic and Social Affairs (2018).

38. Texas Demographic Center (2018).

39. This is originally Bishop's (2009) argument, which, as evidence, compares the number of Democrats and Republicans living in a landslide county in 1976 (26.8%) and 2004

(48.3%). There have been a number of critiques to Bishop's approach. For instance, Abrams and Fiorina (2012) challenge his decision to look at vote choice at the county level. When looking at voter registration and party identification, they suggest that the prominence of landslide counties has declined over time. Since Bishop's publication, several academic studies have put forth evidence supporting the idea that people are geographically sorting. For instance, Lang and Pearson-Merkowitz (2015) find that evidence of political sorting at the county level has been evident since 1996 and happens most frequently in southern U.S. counties. Likewise, Tam Cho et al. (2013) track voter migration patterns using voter data and find that both Republicans and Democrats are likely to move to an area with a higher number of co-partisans. Johnston et al. (2016) also find evidence for geographic sorting across the regional, state, and county levels.

40. Kurtzleben (2016).
41. Evich (2016).
42. Grieco (2019).
43. Cramer (2016); Hochschild (2016); Wuthnow (2018).
44. Verzoni (2017).
45. Wuthnow (2013, 2018).
46. For instance, Mutz (2002, 2006) looks at "discussion networks," or those with whom people report talking about politics; Abrams and Fiorina (2012) look at the county level but do not consider differences in the types of county (rural vs. urban); while Enos (2017) looks at the city level entirely.
47. Rainie and Wellman (2012).
48. Noelle-Neumann (1974, 1993).
49. It is important to note here that this "control" can only speak to one's *intended* control over their communication. There are many reasons that digital media may also limit one's control. For instance, Marwick and boyd (2011) speak to the notion of an "imagined audience," in which individuals on social media imagine an audience for their message, when in reality the audience can be entirely different from what is expected. This "imagined" versus actual audience can vary because of the publicness of the individual's account, the scope of the platform, or the subsequent behavior of those interacting with their message (e.g., screenshotting). For example, Bazarova and Choi (2014) find that individuals adjust their self-disclosures and the goals of that disclosure depending on the perceived publicness of their communication. All of this to say that, in the case of networked silence, my argument is that individuals perceive that they have some control over their communication, whether the extent of that control is accurate or not.
50. Fraser (1990) discusses how marginalized social groups have used counterpublics to subvert the power dynamics that marginalized them in the first place. Herbst (1994) also considers the role of power in shaping what she calls "alternative communities" that emerge from the social marginalization of women, LGBTQ, and Black communities.
51. Simons and Chabris (1999) call the phenomenon they study "inattentional blindness."

52. Luker (2009) tells this same empirical story in her life-changing book on social science in an era of big data.
53. Cramer (2016); Eliasoph (1998); Fraser (1990); Herbst (1994).
54. See Appendix A.
55. See Appendix B.
56. See Appendix C.
57. See Appendix C.
58. See Appendix C, Table C2 and Table C3.

Chapter 2

1. Getting IRB approval for research of "closed" or protected groups, online or offline, will vary depending on the institution. In this case, the IRB at the University of Texas considered this study "Expedited" in that it dealt with sensitive subject matter and required identity protection. In the end, I was able to use the IRB's rules and protocol as a tool for ensuring to participants in the study that I was required by my institution to maintain their confidentiality, in addition to my own ethical code.
2. See Cramer (2016) and Eliasoph (1998).
3. Cramer (2016, p. 26) and Eliasoph (1998).
4. Fenno (1978) and Karpf (2012, p. 18)
5. This is an argument, as Cramer (2015) makes, against making transcripts publicly accessible, which can not only jeopardize the researcher's relationship with their subjects, but also undermines the value-add of the researcher's own interpretation of the data on its own.
6. For instance, the U.S. Department of Agriculture notes that the rural population in the United States has drastically declined since 2006—it declined by 21,000 between July 2015 and July 2016 (Cromartie, 2017).
7. Porter (2018).
8. Wuthnow (2013, 2018).
9. Hochschild (2016).
10. Wuthnow (2018).
11. Cramer (2016).
12. For example, Scott (2013) explores the experiences and formation of hidden organizations like Skull and Bones and the KKK. Wolfe and Blithe (2015) also document how legalized brothels in Nevada manage and operate with stigma from their community.
13. Moon and Holling (2020) offer a historical and contemporary accounting of how White feminism has left out other marginalized communities from its discourse. Traister (2018) also addresses how White women have consistently ignored and even perpetuated prejudice against women of color while advocating for the women's rights they hold exclusively to their own race.
14. McLeod et al. (1996).

15. Wuthnow (2018) poses this distinction among residents of small towns and rural communities where it is easy to know and see who is a local and who is not.
16. See Appendix C.
17. Luker (2009, p. 19).

Chapter 3

1. I am thinking here of work related to backstage communication and organizing within slave communities in the antebellum South (Scott, 1990), the Mattachine Society, a federalized secret organization for gay men (Meeker, 2001), as well as secret organizing within the suffrage movement in the United Kingdom (Crossley et al. 2012).
2. McVeigh et al. (2014).
3. Chadwick (2013) coins this term, which describes an interaction between old logics (legacy newspapers, interviews, press releases, rallies) and new media logics (tweeting on social media, sharing video content on YouTube).
4. See Karpf (2012), who documents the role of online political organizations in funneling political participation, and Wells (2015), who distinguishes between the types of actions encouraged by offline political organizations versus online political organizations.
5. This is precisely Baym's (2009) astute argument that "online and offline are not different entities to be contrasted. What happens via new technology is completely interwoven with what happens face-to-face and via other media" (p. 721).
6. These estimations range from 25 to 60. In general, people felt like there were a lot of others there, but with many arriving late, or leaving early, it was hard to get a clear number. That these numbers ranged so widely further conveys the kind of folklore attached to the story of the women's first informal meeting.
7. Ramsey (2018).
8. See Bishop's (2009) work on ideological/geographic sorting, and Gimpel's line of work on how one's physical context—neighborhood, density, and even geography—can shape political behavior offer evidence of this phenomenon.
9. As mentioned in Chapter 1, there remain skeptics to the idea that the American public is geographically sorting (Abrams & Fiorina, 2012).
10. Anoll (2018); Enos (2017); Huckfeldt et al. (1993).
11. Wuthnow (2013, 2018).
12. Cramer (2016).
13. See Skocpol's (2003) work on civic participation at the local level, and Zukin et al. (2006) on how political participation and engagement have become more or less tied to specific locations/districts over time.
14. For example, Karpf (2012) finds that online organizations like MoveOn.org often result in in-person "meetups" to connect members within specific areas.
15. See Benkler et al. (2015) on the "networked public sphere," which suggests that discourse across individual's networks creates broad and dynamic participation from

both citizens and organizations. See also Bennett and Segerberg's (2013) research on digital media's transformation of collective action to "connective action," where political movements are less hierarchical and more personalized.

16. Research on the secrecy-efficiency trade-off (Crossley et al., 2012) suggests that secret groups and organizations often have trouble recruiting members while also protecting their confidentiality.

17. For example, Gose and Skocpol's (2019) work shows the rise of resistance groups, largely led by previously disengaged suburban housewives, in reaction to Trump's presidency.

18. Skocpol (2003).

19. "Transaction costs" can be considered the "amount of resources needed to engage in a particular tactic (e.g. time, money, and skills)" (Van Laer & Van Aelst, 2010, p. 1151), which scholars consider significantly reduced in the digital space, but not necessarily producing ineffective action (see Karpf, 2010).

20. Wells (2015).

21. Karpf (2010).

22. Scott's (2013) book on "hidden organizations" offers a useful typology for classifying covert groups and organizations from transparent to shaded and from shadowed to completely dark. See also Simmel's (1906) foundational work on classifying secret societies.

23. Blee's (2012) book on the formation and transformation of activist groups in Pittsburgh shows how visibility is often negotiated among members as the nature of political activism takes participants from the planning stages of activism, which happen behind closed doors, to public-facing venues.

24. See Schulz's (2016) article on how the Underground Railroad has been retroactively glorified as the accomplishment of Whites, often omitting the role of and burden placed on runaway slaves themselves.

25. For instance, Scott's (1990) work documents the "hidden transcripts" (e.g., speeches, diary entries, other documents) that illustrate how subordinates spoke to those in power. He pulls many examples from the antebellum South, showcasing how slaves interacted with and spoke to slaveholders and their backstage interactions with one another.

26. Crossley et al. (2012).

27. For more explicit research on clandestine or "dark networks," like terrorist organizations or extremist hate groups (see Raab & Millward, 2003).

28. See Jackson et al. (2020) on how marginalized activists—including people of color, women, and trans communities—use Twitter to build counter-communities and counternarratives, as well as McKenna and Bargh's (1998) foundational work on how members of the LGBTQ community used the Internet to form support groups.

29. Pruchniewska (2019).

30. See Lei's (2018) book on the contentious public sphere in China, which showcases how Chinese citizens used the Internet to dissent against state authoritarianism.

31. See Downs (2016) and Lick et al. (2013) on the physical and psychological ramifications of this fear and trauma.

32. See Cho (2018) for a horrific example of how "outing" can even happen via an algorithm.
33. Chirrey (2003) offers a sociolinguistic analysis of the speech-act of "coming out" versus "outing" oneself.
34. Lindelauf et al. (2009).
35. See Marwick and Boyd (2011) on the "imagined audience," which highlights the myth that audiences are "discrete" (p. 115) and separate from one another, which is made even more nebulous by digital technology that can result in a near infinite audience.
36. Karpf (2012); Wells (2015).
37. For example, Huber and Malhotra (2017) find that online daters are more likely to be interested in and reach out to others online who share their political ideology. Likewise, Iyengar et al. (2018) show that compared to 50 years ago, people are now much more likely to be married to someone with whom they politically agree.
38. For instance, Hersch and Ghitza (2018) find that of all married couples in the United States in which both partners are registered voters, 29% are a "mixed partisan pair," or a partnership in which one partner is a Democrat/Republican/Independent while the other partner is of a different partisanship (e.g., D-R, R-D, D-I, R-I). Using 2014 mid-term election data, they also find that being married to someone of a different partisanship can decrease one's likelihood of voting, and that this is disproportionately so for Republicans married to Democrats.
39. For example, Scott (2013) documents the existence and structure of clandestine groups.
40. Dinas (2014); Valenzuela et al. (2019).
41. Gerber et al (2008); Haenschen (2016).
42. Downs (2016); Lick et al. (2013).
43. See Stroud (2011).
44. Hopkins (2018).
45. Mutz and Soss (1997) also find that the local newspaper affects how important members of a community think an issue is to others in their community—an idea called "agenda-setting," in which the media is known to affect what people think are the most important issues facing society.
46. See Hayes et al. (2013).
47. See Hart (2018) for a beautiful example of the value of letter writers.
48. For instance, see Darr et al. (2018) on the drastic consequences of newsroom closures and coverage decline on political participation.
49. Rojas (2010) defines corrective action as a "reactive" behavior taken to curtail or limit the effects of media on others. People are likely to engage in corrective actions because of what is known as "third-person perceptions" or the "hostile media phenomenon," in which people overestimate the impact that mass media has on others compared to themselves.

Chapter 4

1. Joiner (2017).
2. Wuthnow (2013, 2018).
3. In research on spiral of silence, scholars would refer to this fear as state-based rather than trait-based (Hayes et al. 2013). "State-based" refers to a fear of social isolation that is connected to a particular context, in this case the geographic community, while "trait-based" implies a fear of social isolation that is consistent across contexts.
4. Spiral of silence theory, as posed by Noelle-Neumann (1974, 1993), is the prevailing framework used to explain why people do not express their political beliefs. The theory suggests that people gauge the opinions of those around them to determine if their beliefs are in the minority or majority. When they believe they are in the minority, out of fear of being ostracized from those around them, they withhold their opinion.
5. See Appendix C.
6. See Berry and Sobieraj's (2013) book on how outrage rhetoric has formed around conversations of race and even stoked anxieties about having contentious conversations in every day political talk.
7. Wuthnow (2018).
8. In fact, there is a lot of resentment toward California and its residents among those from the conservative right, particularly in states that have been inundated by California residents moving to other parts of the country (see Thompson, 2020; Greenblatt, 2013).
9. For instance, Bäck et al.(2019) explore how young people withhold their political beliefs on social media because they fear being ostracized or rejected by peers, which can be conveyed even by the number of likes or comments associated with their post.
10. See Schudson (1998) for a historical review.
11. For instance, see Hayes et al. (2006) on "publicly observable political acts" and their rendering of nonparticipation as a form of self-censorship.
12. With the help of the county's Democratic Party, I used the Voter Activation Network (VAN) to access and analyze voter data from the county where CWG was formed. VAN scores partisanship using the Democratic Party's "party support score," which ranges from 0 to 100, where 0 indicates total support for the Republican Party and 100 indicates total support for the Democratic Party, with support determined by voting history. For the purpose of this analysis, I looked at only those who scored 60 or above, meaning they lean Democrat, compared to those who scored 40 or below, meaning they lean Republican. This excludes those who are seen as true Independents using this measure, which includes those who ranged between 41 and 59. Because this meant the party support score was no longer fully continuous, I divided the score into a dichotomous measure where "0" represents those with support for the Republican Party (ranging from 0 to 40) and "1" represents those with support for the Democratic Party (ranging from 60 to 100). To maintain the county's anonymity, I can specify that the average partisanship score fell around the lower quartile of Democratic Party

support. Meaning, across the county, residents heavily supported Republicans over Democrats.

13. For example, Kenski et al. (2020) analyze *perceptions* of incivility and find that women are more likely to perceive incivility and negativity in online comments than are men.

14. See research by Rheault et al. (2019) showing that female, highly visible politicians tend to receive more uncivil messages than do male politicians.

15. See Traister's (2018) book on the role of women's anger in past political and social movements, especially most recently in reaction to the 2016 election's role in reawakening dormant female political activists in suburban areas.

16. Hayes et al. (2006).

17. Traister (2018).

18. See Dahlberg's (2011) theoretical accounting of how counterpublics (used largely by marginalized groups—ideological or social) build shared narratives that challenge dominant belief systems, and Herbst's (1994) work on "alternative public spheres" through history, including Black newspapers in Chicago who produced counternarratives to mainstream publications.

19. For instance, research on the spiral of silence, which accounts for why people withhold political beliefs on a controversial topic, has focused on fear of social isolation, with no regard to how this interacts with an individual's economic calculations (Hayes et al., 2013).

20. This is the "spiral" part of the spiral of silence as posed by Noelle-Neumann (1974). Some research has looked at the longitudinal effects of majority and minority status on opinion expression. For instance, Thurre et al. (2020) explored the dynamics of right-wing populist expression over time across 15 European countries. In addition, researchers have looked at how the *future* opinion climate—that is, the direction to which people perceive public opinion is shifting—affects the willingness to express an opinion (Gearhart & Zhang, 2018).

21. Petrie (1894).

22. See Moy et al. (2001) on the differences between "reference groups" like one's family and friends compared to society at large. They find that individuals are less likely to express their opinions when they perceive that their family and friends disagree with them than when society at large disagrees with them.

23. Scholars define secrets as pieces of information that are "purposefully hidden or concealed" (Vangelisti & Caughlin, 1997, p. 680). By definition, they entail some element of shame or risk should they be uncovered. CWG is a secret, as are the politics of its members. The women intentionally hide the group and their beliefs because to express a dissenting political view in their community, however mainstream, is a reason for persecution.

24. Although these stories paint a consistent picture of women who are at once fearful of and sensitive to their community, there is no conclusive evidence that these stories actually happened. In other words, the women may have exaggerated these stories with time. There is, however, at least some reason to believe they are telling the truth. For one, the women were generally not eager to tell these stories. They would speak vaguely about their community until, 30 minutes into our conversation, they

divulged what specifically they had heard or experienced. The sheer repetition across narratives and the degree to which they held to these stories across time, a known indicator for reliability in qualitative research (see Lindlof & Taylor, 2017), suggests that if they were making these stories up, they did so with a good deal of finesse and consistency.

25. For instance, see Chávez (2011) on how migrant rights activists used protected enclaves to build connections, Downs (2016) on how LGBTQ individuals during the gay liberation movement were physically and psychologically harmed for being out, and Fraser (1990) for an historical and theoretical accounting of how certain social groups have been marginalized from the public sphere for decades.

26. See Toepfl and Piwoni (2015) and Wojcieszak (2009) for how far-right and far-left groups organize online and engage in discourse counter to the mainstream.

Chapter 5

1. See Rahat and Kenig's (2018) accounting of how people have increasingly turned away from traditional political parties and personalized their own political beliefs outside of party boundaries.

2. For instance, research on counterpublics has documented the creation and use of alternative spaces for discourse among the socially and historically marginalized, especially across lines of race/ethnicity and gender (Fraser, 1990; Herbst, 1994). While this self-sectioning can be attributed to choice, so that marginalized individuals define their interactions based on their marginalized identity, it is also potentially the product of constraints in the options available for social connection, or what sociologists would call propinquity, or the contextual availability of "similar alters" (Ruef et al. 2003).

3. Conover and Searing (2005), for instance, found that women in their focus groups are "socialized to avoid" political discussions. This avoidance of political conversation is also true online. Women are generally less likely to comment on national and state politics than are men (Van Duyn et al. 2021), yet women are more likely than men to comment on local news. The difference between women's likelihood to comment on national and state versus local topics may reflect the socialization of local community as an extension of the domestic sphere while state and national politics remain strictly political.

4. See research on communication accommodation theory (CAT), which details how and why people engage in different patterns of communication depending on with whom they are speaking. Giles and Ogay (2007) offer a helpful review on how CAT operates across gender and styles of communication (e.g., facilitative versus nonfacilitative).

5. Karpowitz and Mendelberg (2014), for instance, offer a smart and thorough review of instances where women are less likely to participate in political discussion and why.

6. See Enke's (2003) insightful take on how and why second wave feminists created separate "women's spaces" as a form of resistance.

7. For instance, Sunstein (2001) makes the case that expanding selectivity in media and social networks has caused greater opinion extremity. He attributes this to information "cascades," in which individuals are able to select and share information with like-minded others without anyone different to challenge it.

8. For example, Broockman and Kalla's (2016) research shows how contact with a trans individual that encourages perspective-taking (e.g., asking individuals to imagine a time they were judged for being "different") can reduce prejudice toward trans individuals. In addition, Wojcieszak and Kim (2016) find that presenting individuals with narratives about individuals from an out-group can increase message acceptance, particularly when participants were encouraged to engage in empathetic understanding.

9. Crossley et al. (2012); Lindelauf et al. (2009).

10. For example, Toepfl and Piwoni (2015) find that far-right individuals in Europe used comment sections connected to major newspapers in Germany to espouse counternarratives around the growth of the anti-Euro party Alternative für Deutschland (AfD.) In addition, a historical account from Herbst (1994) also showcases how, through their own newspaper publication, Black communities in Chicago created counternarratives to mainstream and largely White accountings of their neighborhoods.

11. This is precisely Sunstein's (2001) argument that without the other side present to challenge information or narratives, people become more extreme.

12. See Bennett and Segerberg's (2013) theorizing of how social movements have changed from "collective" action, which is typically structured hierarchically and driven by concrete acts, to "connective" action, which is looser and driven more by expression. In contrast to the "connective" movements and organizations often facilitated by digital media, CWG relied on the rules and rigidity of previous "collective" action movements to keep themselves secretive, but also on the flatter, less hierarchical structure of "connective" action movements to keep them open and expressive.

Chapter 6

1. See Appendix C, Tables C2 and C3.

2. Like this book, Traister (2018) also discusses how women reckoned with the complicity of staying silent but isolated, or giving into the growing urge to be furious, to make noise and be heard. She looks at this phenomenon not as much through the tension of public and private as through the compelling power of anger. She considers how anger can be a tool for connection: "[T]his is one of anger's most important roles: it is a mode of connection. . . If they are quiet, they will remain isolated. But if they howl in rage, someone else who shares their fury might hear them, might start howling along" (p. 230).

3. I discuss this idea of "communicative practice" in related work on secret online communities (Van Duyn, 2020).

4. External and internal political efficacy, which are long-standing concepts in political science, are independent but related to one another. Craig et al. (1990) were some of the first to explore and validate these dimensions as distinct concepts, and to link them and distinguish them from trust in government.

5. I use the term "communication efficacy" as it relates to politics, but the original theorizing came from research related to interpersonal communication and has been applied mostly to issues related to family secrets and health. The original concept was developed by Afifi and Weiner (2004), who define communication efficacy as "individuals' perception that they possess the skills to complete successfully the communication tasks involved in the information-management process," (p. 178).

6. Erving Goffman's (1959) notions of frontstage and backstage are useful when thinking about visibility and how people engage with or discuss politics in groups. What he calls "frontstage behavior" is truly performative, driven by norms and feedback from others. In the frontstage, individuals often hide parts of themselves, or communicate in ways that are in accordance with the beliefs, styles, or preferences of those around them. On the other hand, the "backstage" exists away from the view of others. Goffman posits that people may use the backstage to practice or rehearse frontstage activities precisely in an effort to be more accepted. Eliasoph (1998) extends Goffman's work to consider how backstage communication uniquely applies to politics. She details the experiences of informal citizen groups who discuss politics sparingly with others, but when in the backstage and away from the larger group, often express an interest in politics and a concern for their community.

7. This was also the promise of communicative practice that research on deliberative enclaves has long touted. For instance, Fraser's (1990) work on counterpublic spheres argues that counterpublics can serve as "bases and training grounds" insomuch as they allow "spaces of withdrawal and regroupment" (p. 68). Likewise, Karpowitz et al. (2009) find that engaging in deliberation about public issues with like-minded others can increase self-efficacy and knowledge about public issues, particularly for those they describe as "disempowered."

8. Scholars would call this "external political efficacy" (Craig et al., 1990) or the extent to which an individual feels they can influence the government. External political efficacy is usually considered in the context of government action, public policy, or the behavior of elected officials. But the feeling of external political efficacy felt within CWG was sometimes connected explicitly to the Democratic Party—the sense that the women could do little to influence the party itself.

9. In fact, parties have an incentive to be public in that in the political arena, exposure is often equated with success, an idea evident in most campaign communication research, particularly in the era of social media. For instance, Norris (2000) describes the transition from organizational party politics, where people received information about politics from party meetings, to mediated party politics, where they receive information from parties and party leaders communicated through mass media. From this transition, voters became synonymous with "consumers," where the goal

of party messaging was targeting and exposure rather than building loyalty (Gibson & Römmele, 2001). All of this to say that as parties have transitioned from localized networks to broader federalized networks that rely on mass media rather than interpersonal interaction, the value of publicness and exposure become key elements baked into their digital infrastructure (e.g., through social media metrics like shares, comments, likes) and at the heart of what they value.

10. Scholars who study politics and elections would note that this kind of participation is unprecedented when comparing midterm to general electoral participation. In general, midterm elections have trended 10–15 percentage points less in voter turnout rates than presidential election years (Desilver, 2014).

11. Kreiss (2012) details the rise of the VAN system within the Democratic Party where "the near universal buy-in across the Democratic Party network to the party's voter file and database and interface system provided by NGP VAN has resulted in a powerful and robust piece of infrastructure that the party's technology ecosystem convenes around" (p. 211). The role of data management came with the adoption of the VAN across the party, meaning that state (and even county level) parties who already had weak Democratic infrastructure were tasked with another role that some, like the state of Texas and CWG's county, were unable to or uninterested in addressing equally across the region.

12. Beto O'Rourke took between 18% and 25% of CWG's county, around 5% more than the Democratic candidate for Senate in 2014.

13. See Mutz (2002, 2006) and Lee et al. (2015) for work on how the composition of discussion networks or groups can encourage (or dampen) political conversation and/ or political action. This research poses two possibilities. One, that exposure to crosscutting or heterogeneous networks can make people more likely to discuss politics, but ultimately harm their overall political participation (Mutz, 2006). On the other hand, Lee et al. find that engaging in political conversation with like-minded others can lead to more conversation *and* encourage political participation when that interaction is with close connections or "strong ties." More recent research from An et al. (2019) suggests that the relationship between network composition and deliberation and participation is more intricate than *if* people engage but *how* they engage. In their analysis of subreddits for Clinton and Trump supporters, for example, they find that individuals become more open in homogenous discussion networks and change their communication styles when switching from a heterogeneous network to a homogenous one.

14. For example, see Levendusky (2009), who explores how parties have sorted with ideology at the national level; seminal work by Verba and Nie (1987) that considers how parties have historically mobilized and funneled political action; and research from Jones and Mainwaring (2003), which measures the rise of party nationalization across the Americas. Research on parties as organizations has mostly focused on messaging and candidate selection at the national level (Aldrich, 1995), and the few works dealing with local party politics are from several decades ago (e.g., Frendreis et al., 1990; Huckfeldt & Sprague, 1992).

15. The value of CWG's secrecy for the local party challenges party scholars and party leadership to consider not only the hybridity of organizing in person and online (Chadwick, 2013), but also ways of organizing that vary in their degree of publicness. That is, not only how parties use new and old forms of media to communicate with the public and promote their candidates and platforms, but also how they use public and private ways of organizing to meet their organizational goals.
16. Collins (2018).

Chapter 7

1. In a separate email before the June meeting, Deborah offered some additional advice for those unfamiliar with Zoom: "If you have never used Zoom, don't panic! It is really very easy to be a participant. I recommend going to YOUTUBE to watch a 'how-to' video. The one I recommend is Zoom for Dummies by Claudia. She is young, cute, and very clear. You will want her for a granddaughter."
2. In fact, according to the FCC's own study from 2018, "80 percent of the 24 million American households that do not have reliable, affordable high-speed internet are in rural areas" (https://www.usda.gov/broadband).
3. Milosh et al. (2020).
4. Albertson and Theriault (2020); Enten (2020); Weigel and Tierney (2020).
5. For instance, CNN was one of the first to project Biden the winner, at 10:29 ET.
6. Svitek (2020).
7. Montgomery (2020).
8. https://braverangels.org/.
9. It is possible that it is illegal to fly a Trump flag alongside the American flag, or to fly it once the election is over. This was the case in Phoenix, where a woman was told to take down her Trump flag because it violated a city ordinance prohibiting a flag flying beneath the American flag and prohibiting flying a political flag more than 30 days after the election had ended (Miller, 2020).
10. This is an ongoing feeling in the country, beautifully captured by Williams (2020).
11. I'm thinking here of work by Newman and colleagues, who found that when exposed to prejudiced elite speech, prejudiced citizens are more likely to express their beliefs (Newman et al., 2020).
12. For the full and verbatim quote, see Parker (2010).

Chapter 8

1. Politi (2020); Villareal (2020).
2. For instance, there is a long line of work in the interpersonal communication literature that addresses how secrecy can harm interpersonal relationships (see Vangelisti & Caughlin, 1997).

3. Caesar (2019).

4. See Koltai and Fleischmann's (2017) study, which interviews anti-vax community members, and Smith and Graham's (2019) study, which uses network analysis to trace the development of the anti-vax community and groups online.

5. Noelle-Neumann (1974, 1993).

6. Rainie and Wellman (2012).

7. See Marwick and boyd's (2011) work on "invisible audiences," which addresses people's inability to know exactly who can see or interact with their expression online, complicated by the fact that online expression can exist long after it is originally posted.

8. I took this figure from a report put out by Facebook on Generation Z, although the data they reference encompasses all users rather than just users from Gen Z ("Gen Z," 2019).

9. Abedi (2019).

10. This is a topic that Papacharissi (2010) discusses in her book. Among her arguments is that the public sphere has become increasingly personal. Individuals now connect their own desires and experiences with public issues and express these connections publicly.

11. Karpf (2012) addresses this in his work on "neo-federated" political organizations, which are organizations that use online connections to facilitate in person meet ups attached to specific places.

12. See Conroy et al. (2012) and Wojcieszak (2009) for smart ways to measure the transition from online to offline.

13. This is the essential argument of "social sanctions" in the spiral of silence theory (Noelle-Neumann, 1974).

14. For instance, Ulbig and Funk (1999) found that people who are more conflict-avoidant, as measured through a survey question, are less likely to participate in politics, including engaging in political discussion.

15. See Eliasoph (1998), Herbst (1994), and Noelle-Neumann (1974), who all discuss the role of social power in political discussion.

16. See Massanari (2018) and Zimmer (2010).

17. Although there have also been a number of efforts to make private data, which is owned by private companies like social media platforms, accessible to researchers while keeping data anonymous (see King & Persily, 2020).

18. https://www.facebook.com/apps/site_scraping_tos_terms.php.

19. Van Duyn (2020).

20. Schattschneider (1942); Verba and Nie (1987).

21. While these are foundational works addressing the role of political parties in mobilization and public organizing, there is not a lot known about the role and infrastructure and performance of political parties at the local level, let alone how parties operate in a contemporary era where people are both geographically and socially sorted.

22. Verba et al. (1995) review the traditional ways that political parties privilege public political acts, and Gil de Zúñiga et al. (2012) consider how these public acts have transitioned online.

23. See Chadwick's (2013) comprehensive theorizing of a "hybrid media system" that incorporates old and new media "logics," which change how issues are covered.

24. There are a number of studies that have focused on how political organizations or social movements use digital media to organize and how these approaches complement or stand apart from in person approaches (Bennett & Segerberg, 2013; Karpf, 2012).

25. In political science this is the idea that when representatives serve districts in which one party is an overwhelming majority, they are pulled to the political "middle" less frequently. Theriault's (2008) accounting of congressional polarization indicates that this issue has gotten worse amid geographic and social sorting among parties.

26. A line of research on the influence of "social contact" (see Broockman & Kalla, 2016; Wojcieszak & Kim, 2016) suggests that when people engage meaningfully with those holding different beliefs from their own, both their political attitudes and their social attitudes toward the other group can change.

27. See Herbst's (1993) book *Numbered Voices* on what polling data is good for and what it is not good for.

28. For instance, Searles et al. (2016) found that different television networks select different polls to cover depending on how close the polls are.

29. This idea relates to Zaller's (1992) RAS (receive-accept-sample) model, which surmises that polls force attitudes from individuals that would perhaps not exist without the prompt itself.

30. For instance, see Mutz and Soss's (1997) work on how people use local news to gauge public support for a local issue.

31. McGregor (2019) finds that journalists often use posts on social media as evidence of public opinion, using them as supplements for or sometimes in place of survey data. Similarly, McGregor and Molyneux (2020) found that journalists' use of Twitter can influence what they deem as newsworthy or not.

32. For instance, see Karpf's (2012) work on how political organizations have used Google Groups as a backchannel of communication, and Bennett and Segerberg (2013) on how entire social movements were created using Twitter.

33. For instance, see Tromble and McGregor's (2019) argument that platforms need social scientists to make proactive design decisions because the products they produce affect social (and democratic) outcomes.

34. For instance, Lilliana Mason has discussed the issues facing the United States not as a problem of just polarization, but of democracy itself (see Balz, 2020).

Appendix C

1. GfK's "Knowledge Panel" was used for this survey. Knowledge Panel uses Address Based Sampling (ABS), a probability-based sampling method that recruits both

English and Spanish speakers. Households that are recruited but do not have Internet access are provided with a "web-enabled device and free Internet service." As compensation for their participation, respondents are "entered into special sweepstakes with both cash rewards and other prizes to be won." GfK uses geodemographic benchmarks from the Current Population Survey (CPS) to weight the sample. The AAPOR RR3 for this survey, taking into account both recruitment into the panel and completion of this study, is 5.3%. For more information on GfK's sampling, recruitment, administration, and weighting, see their website.

2. It could be argued that this measure of hiding political beliefs is ordinal in nature rather than interval, and therefore should be analyzed using ordinal regression rather than OLS. When conducting these analyses using ordinal regression instead of OLS, the results are directionally the same and significance levels did not change.

References

Abedi, M. (2019, July 5). A look at "secret" Facebook groups — and how hateful content is monitored on them. Global News. https://globalnews.ca/news/5464645/facebook-secret-groups-rules/

Abrams, S. J., & Fiorina, M. P. (2012). "The big sort" that wasn't: A skeptical reexamination. PS: Political Science & Politics, 45(2), 203–210. https://doi.org/10.1017/s1049096512000017

Afifi, W. A., & Weiner, J. L. (2004). Toward a theory of motivated information management. Communication Theory, 14(2), 167–190. https://doi.org/10.1111/j.1468-2885.2004.tb00310.x

Albertson, B., & Theriault, S. (2020, October 30). It's time to pay attention to Texas. Brookings. https://www.brookings.edu/blog/fixgov/2020/10/30/its-time-to-pay-attention-to-texas/

Aldrich, J. H. (1995). Why parties?: The origin and transformation of political parties in America. University of Chicago Press.

An, J., Kwak, H., Posegga, O., & Jungherr, A. (2019, July). Political discussions in homogeneous and cross-cutting communication spaces. Proceedings of the International AAAI Conference on Web and Social Media 13, 68–79. https://doi.org/10.24251/hicss.2019.312

Anoll, A. P. (2018). What makes a good neighbor? Race, place, and norms of political participation. The American Political Science Review, 112(3), 494–508. https://doi.org/10.1017/s0003055418000175

Bäck, E. A., Bäck, H., Fredén, A., & Gustafsson, N. (2019). A social safety net? Rejection sensitivity and political opinion sharing among young people in social media. New Media & Society, 21(2), 298–316. https://doi.org/10.1177/1461444818795487

Balz, D. (2020, December 27). After a year of pandemic and protest, and a big election, America is as divided as ever. Washington Post. https://www.washingtonpost.com/graphics/2020/politics/elections-reckoning/

Baym, N. K. (2009). A call for grounding in the face of blurred boundaries. Journal of Computer-Mediated Communication, 14(3), 720–723. https://doi.org/10.1111/j.1083-6101.2009.01461.x

Bazarova, N. N., & Choi, Y. H. (2014). Self-disclosure in social media: Extending the functional approach to disclosure motivations and characteristics on social network sites. Journal of Communication, 64(4), 635–657. https://doi.org/10.1111/jcom.12106

Benkler, Y., Roberts, H., Faris, R., Solow-Niederman, A., & Etling, B. (2015). Social mobilization and the networked public sphere: Mapping the SOPA-PIPA debate. Political Communication, 32(4), 594–624. https://doi.org/10.1080/10584609.2014.986349

Bennett, W. L., & Segerberg, A. (2013). The logic of connective action: Digital media and the personalization of contentious politics. Cambridge University Press.

Berry, J. M., & Sobieraj, S. (2013). The outrage industry: Political opinion media and the new incivility. Oxford University Press.

Bishop, B. (2009). The big sort: Why the clustering of like-minded America is tearing us apart. Houghton Mifflin Harcourt.

Blee, K. M. (2012). Democracy in the making: How activist groups form. Oxford University Press.

Broockman, D., & Kalla, J. (2016). Durably reducing transphobia: A field experiment on door-to-door canvassing. Science, 352(6282), 220–224. https://doi.org/10.1126/science.aad9713

Caesar, E. (2019, May 20). The undercover fascist. The New Yorker. https://www.newyorker.com/magazine/2019/05/27/the-undercover-fascist

CBS News. (2017, January 22). What democracy looks like: Women's March on Washington. https://www.cbsnews.com/news/what-democracy-looks-like-womens-march-on-washington/

Chadwick, A. (2013). The hybrid media system: Politics and power. Oxford University Press.

Chávez, K. R. (2011). Counter-public enclaves and understanding the function of rhetoric in social movement coalition-building. Communication Quarterly, 59(1), 1–18. https://doi.org/10.1080/01463373.2010.541333

Chenoweth, E., & Pressman, J. (2017, February 7). This is what we learned by counting the women's marches. Washington Post. https://www.washingtonpost.com/news/monkey-cage/wp/2017/02/07/this-is-what-we-learned-by-counting-the-womens-marches/

Chirrey, D. A. (2003). "I hereby come out": What sort of speech act is coming out? Journal of Sociolinguistics, 7(1), 24–37. https://doi.org/10.1111/1467-9481.00209

Cho, A. (2018). Default publicness: Queer youth of color, social media, and being outed by the machine. New Media & Society, 20(9), 3183–3200. https://doi.org/10.1177/1461444817744784

Collins, C. (2018, November 8). Ted Cruz won because of rural Texas, but Beto made small gains for Democrats. Texas Observer. https://www.texasobserver.org/ted-cruz-won-because-of-rural-texas-but-beto-made-small-gains-for-democrats/

Conover, P. J., & Searing, D. D. (2005). Studying everyday political talk in the deliberative system. Acta Politica, 40, 269–283. doi:10.1057/palgrave.ap.5500113

Conroy, M., Feezell, J. T., & Guerrero, M. (2012). Facebook and political engagement: A study of online political group membership and offline political engagement. Computers in Human Behavior, 28(5), 1535–1546. https://doi.org/10.1016/j.chb.2012.03.012

Craig, S. C., Niemi, R. G., & Silver, G. E. (1990). Political efficacy and trust: A report on the NES pilot study items. Political Behavior, 12(3), 289–314. https://doi.org/10.1007/bf00992337

Cramer, K. (2015). Transparent explanations, yes. Public transcripts and fieldnotes, no: Ethnographic research on public opinion. Qualitative & Multi-Method Research, 13(1), 17–20. https://zenodo.org/record/893069#.YJluirVKiUk

Cramer, K. J. (2016). The politics of resentment: Rural consciousness in Wisconsin and the rise of Scott Walker. University of Chicago Press.

Cromartie, J. (2017, September 5). Rural areas show overall population decline and shifting regional patterns of population change. United States Department of Agriculture. https://www.ers.usda.gov/amber-waves/2017/september/rural-areas-show-overall-population-decline-and-shifting-regional-patterns-of-population-change/

Crossley, N., Edwards, G., Harries, E., & Stevenson, R. (2012). Covert social movement networks and the secrecy-efficiency trade off: The case of the UK suffragettes

(1906–1914). Social Networks, 34(4), 634–644. https://doi.org/10.1016/j.socnet.2012.07.004

Dahlberg, L. (2011). Re-constructing digital democracy: An outline of four "positions." New Media & Society, 13(6), 855–872. https://doi.org/10.1177/1461444810389569

Darr, J. P., Hitt, M. P., & Dunaway, J. L. (2018). Newspaper closures polarize voting behavior. Journal of Communication, 68(6), 1007–1028. https://doi.org/10.1093/joc/jqy051

Desilver, D. (2014, July 24). *Voter turnout always drops off for midterm elections, but why?* Pew Research Center. https://www.pewresearch.org/fact-tank/2014/07/24/voter-turnout-always-drops-off-for-midterm-elections-but-why/

Desilver, D. (2016, June 10). *Turnout was high in the 2016 primary season, but just short of 2008 record*. Pew Research Center. https://www.pewresearch.org/facttank/2016/06/10/turnout-was-high-in-the-2016-primary-season-but-just-short-of-2008-record/

Dinas, E. (2014). Does choice bring loyalty? Electoral participation and the development of party identification. American Journal of Political Science, 58(2), 449–465. https://doi.org/10.1111/ajps.12044

Downs, J. (2016). Stand by me: The forgotten history of gay liberation. Basic Books.

Eliasoph, N. (1996). Making a fragile public: A talk-centered study of citizenship and power. Sociological Theory, 14(3), 262–289. https://doi.org/10.2307/3045389

Eliasoph, N. (1998). Avoiding politics: How Americans produce apathy in everyday life. Cambridge University Press.

Enke, A. (2003). Smuggling sex through the gates: Race, sexuality, and the politics of space in second wave feminism. American Quarterly, 55(4), 635–667. https://doi.org/10.1353/aq.2003.0038

Enos, R. D. (2017). The space between us: Social geography and politics. Cambridge University Press.

Enten, H. (2016, November 10). *There were no purple states on Tuesday*. FiveThirtyEight. https://fivethirtyeight.com/features/there-were-no-purple-states-on-tuesday/

Enten, H. (2020, July 12). *Texas is a swing state in 2020, new polls reveal*. CNN. https://www.cnn.com/2020/07/12/politics/texas-swing-state-2020-election-polls/index.html

Evich, H. B. (2016, November 13). *Revenge of the rural voter*. Politico. https://www.politico.com/story/2016/11/hillary-clinton-rural-voters-trump-231266

Fenno, R. F. (1978). *Home style: Representatives in their districts*. Little, Brown.

Fraser, N. (1990). Rethinking the public sphere: A contribution to the critique of actually existing democracy. Social Text, 25/26, 56–80. https://doi.org/10.2307/466240

Frendreis, J. P., Gibson, J. L., & Vertz, L. L. (1990). The electoral relevance of local party organizations. American Political Science Review, 84(1), 225–235. https://doi.org/10.2307/1963639

Gearhart, S., & Zhang, W. (2018). Same spiral, different day? Testing the spiral of silence across issue types. Communication Research, 45(1), 34–54. https://doi.org/10.1177/0093650215616456

"Gen Z: Getting to know the 'me is we' generation." (2019, October 22). Facebook. https://www.facebook.com/business/news/insights/generation-z

Gerber, A. S., Green, D. P., & Larimer, C. W. (2008). Social pressure and voter turnout: Evidence from a large-scale field experiment. American Political Science Review, 102(1), 33–48. https://doi.org/10.1017/s000305540808009x

Gest, J. (2016). The new minority: White working class politics in an age of immigration and inequality. Oxford University Press.

Gibson, R., & Römmele, A. (2001). Changing campaign communications: A party-centered theory of professionalized campaigning. Harvard International Journal of Press/Politics, 6(4), 31–43. https://doi.org/10.1177/108118001129172323

Gil de Zúñiga, H., Jung, N., & Valenzuela, S. (2012). Social media use for news and individuals' social capital, civic engagement and political participation. Journal of Computer- Mediated Communication, 17(3), 319–336. https://doi.org/10.1111/j.1083-6101.2012.01574.x

Giles, H., & Ogay, T. (2007). Communication Accommodation Theory. In B. B. Whaley & W. Samster (Eds.), Explaining communication: Contemporary theories and exemplars (pp. 293–310). Lawrence Erlbaum.

Gillion, D. Q., Ladd, J. M., & Meredith, M. (2020). Party polarization, ideological sorting and the emergence of the US partisan gender gap. British Journal of Political Science, 50(4), 1217–1243. https://doi.org/10.1017/s0007123418000285

Goffman, E. (1959). The presentation of self in everyday life. Doubleday.

Gose, L. E., & Skocpol, T. (2019). Resist, persist, and transform: The emergence and impact of grassroots resistance groups opposing the Trump presidency. Mobilization: An International Quarterly, 24(3), 293–317. https://doi.org/10.17813/1086-671x-24-3-293

Greenblatt, A. (2013, August 29). How California is turning the rest of the west blue. NPR. https://www.npr.org/sections/itsallpolitics/2013/08/29/216150644/how-california-is-turning-the-rest-of-the-west-blue

Grieco, E. (2019, April 12). For many rural residents in U.S., local news media mostly don't cover the area where they live. Pew Research Center. https://www.pewresearch.org/fact-tank/2019/04/12/for-many-rural-residents-in-u-s-local-news-media-mostly-dont-cover-the-area-where-they-live/

Haenschen, K. (2016). Social pressure on social media: Using Facebook status updates to increase voter turnout. Journal of Communication, 66(4), 542–563. https://doi.org/10.1111/jcom.12236

Hampton, K., & Wellman, B. (2001). Long distance community in the network society: Contact and support beyond Netville. American Behavioral Scientist, 45(3), 476–495. https://doi.org/10.1177/00027640121957303

Hart, R. P. (2018). Civic hope: How ordinary Americans keep democracy alive. Cambridge University Press.

Hayes, A. F., Matthes, J., & Eveland, W. P., Jr. (2013). Stimulating the quasi-statistical organ: Fear of social isolation motivates the quest for knowledge of the opinion climate. Communication Research, 40(4), 439–462. https://doi.org/10.1177/0093650211428608

Hayes, A. F., Scheufele, D. A., & Huge, M. E. (2006). Nonparticipation as self-censorship: Publicly observable political activity in a polarized opinion climate. Political Behavior, 28(3), 259–283. https://doi.org/10.1007/s11109-006-9008-3

Herbst, S. (1993). Numbered voices: How opinion polling has shaped American politics. University of Chicago Press.

Herbst, S. (1994). Politics at the margin: Historical studies of public expression outside the mainstream. Cambridge University Press.

Hersh, E., & Ghitza, Y. (2018). Mixed partisan households and electoral participation in the United States. PloS ONE, 13(10), e0203997. https://doi.org/10.1371/journal.pone.0203997

Hochschild, A. R. (2016). Strangers in their own land. The New Press.

Hopkins, D. J. (2018). The increasingly United States: How and why American political behavior nationalized. University of Chicago Press.

Huber, G. A., & Malhotra, N. (2017). Political homophily in social relationships: Evidence from online dating behavior. The Journal of Politics, 79(1), 269–283. https://doi.org/10.1086/687533

Huckfeldt, R., Plutzer, E., & Sprague, J. (1993). Alternative contexts of political behavior: Churches, neighborhoods, and individuals. The Journal of Politics, 55(2), 365–381. https://doi.org/10.2307/2132270

Huckfeldt, R., & Sprague, J. (1992). Political parties and electoral mobilization: Political structure, social structure, and the party canvass. American Political Science Review, 86(1), 70–86. https://doi.org/10.2307/1964016

Huddy, L. (2001). From social to political identity: A critical examination of social identity theory. Political Psychology, 22(1), 127–156. https://doi.org/10.1111/0162-895x.00230

Iyengar, S., Konitzer, T., & Tedin, K. (2018). The home as a political fortress: Family agreement in an era of polarization. The Journal of Politics, 80(4), 1326–1338. https://doi.org/10.1086/698929

Iyengar, S., & Westwood, S. J. (2015). Fear and loathing across party lines: New evidence on group polarization. American Journal of Political Science, 59(3), 690–707. https://doi.org/10.1111/ajps.12152

Jackson, N., & Sparks, G. (2017, March 31). A poll finds most Americans don't trust public opinion polls. HuffPost. https://www.huffpost.com/entry/most-americans-dont-trust-public-opinion-polls_n_58de94ece4b0ba359594a708

Jackson, S. J., Bailey, M., & Welles, B. F. (2020). #HashtagActivism: Networks of race and gender justice. MIT Press.

Jamieson, K. H. (2018). Cyberwar: How Russian hackers and trolls helped elect a president: What we don't, can't, and do know. Oxford University Press.

Johnston, R., Manley, D., & Jones, K. (2016). Spatial polarization of presidential voting in the United States, 1992–2012: The "big sort" revisited. Annals of the American Association of Geographers, 106(5), 1047–1062. https://doi.org/10.1080/24694452.2016.1191991

Joiner, G. (2017, June 14). Texas land trends tracks a changing state. Texas Farm Bureau. https://texasfarmbureau.org/texas-land-trends-tracks-changing-state/

Jones, M. P., & Mainwaring, S. (2003). The nationalization of parties and party systems: An empirical measure and an application to the Americas. Party Politics, 9(2), 139–166. https://doi.org/10.1177/13540688030092002

Karpf, D. (2010). Online political mobilization from the advocacy group's perspective: Looking beyond clicktivism. Policy & Internet, 2(4), 7–41. https://doi.org/10.2202/1944-2866.1098

Karpf, D. (2012). The MoveOn effect: The unexpected transformation of American political advocacy. Oxford University Press.

Karpowitz, C. F., & Mendelberg, T. (2014). The silent sex: Gender, deliberation, and institutions. Princeton University Press.

Karpowitz, C. F., Raphael, C., & Hammond, A. S., IV. (2009). Deliberative democracy and inequality: Two cheers for enclave deliberation among the disempowered. Politics & Society, 37(4), 576–615. https://doi.org/10.1177/0032329209349226

Kearney, L. (2016, December 5). Hawaii grandma's plea launches women's march in Washington. Reuters. https://www.reuters.com/article/us-usa-trump-women/hawaii-grandmas-plea-launches-womens-march-in-washington-idUSKBN13U0GW

Kenski, K., Coe, K., & Rains, S. A. (2020). Perceptions of uncivil discourse online: An examination of types and predictors. Communication Research, 47(6), 795–814. https://doi.org/10.1177/0093650217699933

King, G., & Persily, N. (2020). A new model for industry-academic partnerships. PS: Political Science & Politics, 53(4), 703–709. https://doi.org/10.1017/s1049096519001021

Koltai, K. S., & Fleischmann, K. R. (2017). Questioning science with science: The evolution of the vaccine safety movement. Proceedings of the Association for Information Science and Technology, 54(1), 232–240. https://doi.org/10.1002/pra2.2017.14505401026

Kreiss, D. (2012). Taking our country back: The crafting of networked politics from Howard Dean to Barack Obama. Oxford University Press.

Kurtzleben, D. (2016, November 16). Rural voters played a big part in helping Trump defeat Clinton. NPR. https://www.npr.org/2016/11/14/501737150/rural-voters-played-a-big-part-in-helping-trump-defeat-clinton

Kurtzleben, D. (2017, August 24). Here's how many Bernie Sanders supporters ultimately voted for Trump. NPR. https://www.npr.org/2017/08/24/545812242/1-in-10-sanders-primary-voters-ended-up-supporting-trump-survey-finds

Lang, C., & Pearson-Merkowitz, S. (2015). Partisan sorting in the United States, 1972–2012: New evidence from a dynamic analysis. Political Geography, 48, 119–129. https://doi.org/10.1016/j.polgeo.2014.09.015

Lee, H., Kwak, N., & Campbell, S. W. (2015). Hearing the other side revisited: The joint workings of cross-cutting discussion and strong tie homogeneity in facilitating deliberative and participatory democracy. Communication Research, 42(4), 569–596. https://doi.org/10.1177/0093650213483824

Lei, Y. W. (2018). The contentious public sphere: Law, media, and authoritarian rule in China. Princeton University Press.

Lelkes, Y., & Westwood, S. J. (2017). The limits of partisan prejudice. The Journal of Politics, 79(2), 485–501. https://doi.org/10.1086/688223

Levendusky, M. (2009). The partisan sort: How liberals became Democrats and conservatives became Republicans. University of Chicago Press.

Levendusky, M. S., & Malhotra, N. (2016). (Mis)perceptions of partisan polarization in the American public. Public Opinion Quarterly, 80(S1), 378–391. https://doi.org/10.1093/poq/nfv045

Lick, D. J., Durso, L. E., & Johnson, K. L. (2013). Minority stress and physical health among sexual minorities. Perspectives on Psychological Science, 8(5), 521–548. https://doi.org/10.1177/1745691613497965

Lind, D. (2016, February 5). The "Bernie Bro" debate in the 2016 primary, explained. Vox. https://www.vox.com/2016/2/4/10918710/berniebro-bernie-bro

Lindelauf, R., Borm, P., & Hamers, H. (2009). The influence of secrecy on the communication structure of covert networks. Social Networks, 31(2), 126–137. https://doi.org/10.1016/j.socnet.2008.12.003

Lindlof, T. R., & Taylor, B. C. (2011). Qualitative communication research methods (3rd ed). SAGE.

Lopez, G. (2020, August 13). Donald Trump's long history of racism, from the 1970s to 2020. Vox. https://www.vox.com/2016/7/25/12270880/donald-trump-racist-racism-history

Luker, K. (2009). Salsa dancing into the social sciences. Harvard University Press.

Lukito, J. (2020). Coordinating a multi-platform disinformation campaign: Internet Research Agency activity on three US social media platforms, 2015 to 2017. Political Communication, 37(2), 238–255. https://doi.org/10.1080/10584609.2019.1661889

Marwick, A. E., & boyd, D. (2011). I tweet honestly, I tweet passionately: Twitter users, context collapse, and the imagined audience. New Media & Society, 13(1), 114–133. https://doi.org/10.1177/1461444810365313

Mason, L. (2018). Uncivil agreement: How politics became our identity. University of Chicago Press.

Mason, L., & Wronski, J. (2018). One tribe to bind them all: How our social group attachments strengthen partisanship. Political Psychology, 39, 257–277. https://doi.org/10.1111/pops.12485

Massanari, A. L. (2018). Rethinking research ethics, power, and the risk of visibility in the era of the "alt-right" gaze. Social Media+ Society, 4(2), 1–9. https://doi.org/10.1177/2056305118768302

McGregor, S. C. (2019). Social media as public opinion: How journalists use social media to represent public opinion. Journalism, 20(8), 1070–1086. https://doi.org/10.1177/1464884919845458

McGregor, S. C., & Molyneux, L. (2020). Twitter's influence on news judgment: An experiment among journalists. Journalism, 21(5), 597–613. https://doi.org/10.1177/1464884918802975

McLeod, J. M., Daily, K., Guo, Z., Eveland, W. P., Jr., Bayer, J., Yang, S., & Wang, H. (1996). Community integration, local media use, and democratic processes. Communication Research, 23(2), 179–209. https://doi.org/10.1177/009365096023002002

McKenna, K. Y., & Bargh, J. A. (1998). Coming out in the age of the Internet: Identity "demarginalization" through virtual group participation. Journal of Personality and Social Psychology, 75(3), 681–694. https://doi.org/10.1037/0022-3514.75.3.681

McVeigh, R., Cunningham, D., & Farrell, J. (2014). Political polarization as a social movement outcome: 1960s Klan activism and its enduring impact on political realignment in southern counties, 1960 to 2000. American Sociological Review, 79(6), 1144–1171. https://doi.org/10.1177/0003122414555885

Meeker, M. (2001). Behind the mask of respectability: Reconsidering the Mattachine Society and male homophile practice, 1950s and 1960s. Journal of the History of Sexuality, 10(1), 78–116. https://doi.org/10.1353/sex.2001.0015

Meyer, D. S., & Tarrow, S. (2018). The resistance: The dawn of the anti-Trump opposition movement. Oxford University Press.

Meyer, R. (2015, October 17). Here comes the Berniebro. The Atlantic. https://www.theatlantic.com/politics/archive/2015/10/here-comes-the-berniebro-bernie-sanders/411070/

Miller, D. (2020, January 1). "Trump 2020" flag sparks debate over resident's rights to fly political flags any time of the year. Fox 10 Phoenix. https://www.fox10phoenix.com/news/trump-2020-flag-sparks-debate-over-residents-rights-to-fly-political-flags-any-time-of-the-year

Milosh, M., Painter, M., Sonin, K., Van Dijcke, D., & Wright, A. L. (2020, November 9). Unmasking partisanship: Polarization undermines public response to collective risk. University of Chicago, Becker Friedman Institute for Economics. http://dx.doi.org/10.2139/ssrn.3664779

Montgomery, D. (2020, November 19). Texas Democratic losses reflect broader statehouse trend. Pew. https://www.pewtrusts.org/en/research-and-analysis/blogs/stateline/2020/11/19/texas-democratic-losses-reflect-broader-statehouse-trend

Moon, D. G., & Holling, M. A. (2020). "White supremacy in heels": (white) feminism, white supremacy, and discursive violence. Communication and Critical/Cultural Studies, 17(2), 253–260. https://doi.org/10.1080/14791420.2020.1770819

Moy, P., Domke, D., & Stamm, K. (2001). The spiral of silence and public opinion on affirmative action. Journalism & Mass Communication Quarterly, 78(1), 7–25. https://doi.org/10.1177/107769900107800102

Mutz, D. C. (2002). The consequences of cross-cutting networks for political participation. American Journal of Political Science, 46(4), 838–855. https://doi.org/10.2307/3088437

Mutz, D. C. (2006). Hearing the other side: Deliberative versus participatory democracy. Cambridge University Press.

Mutz, D. C. (2018). Status threat, not economic hardship, explains the 2016 presidential vote. Proceedings of the National Academy of Sciences, 115(19), E4330–E4339. https://doi.org/10.1073/pnas.1718155115

Mutz, D. C., & Soss, J. (1997). Reading public opinion: The influence of news coverage on perceptions of public sentiment. Public Opinion Quarterly, 61(3), 431–451. https://doi.org/10.1086/297807

Neuwirth, K., Frederick, E., & Mayo, C. (2007). The spiral of silence and fear of isolation. Journal of Communication, 57, 450–468.

Newman, B., Merolla, J. L., Shah, S., Lemi, D. C., Collingwood, L., & Ramakrishnan, S. K. (2020, February 17). The Trump effect: An experimental investigation of the emboldening effect of racially inflammatory elite communication. British Journal of Political Science. Advance online publication. https://doi.org/10.1017/s0007123419000590

Noelle-Neumann, E. (1974). The spiral of silence: A theory of public opinion. Journal of Communication, 24(2), 43–51. https://doi.org/10.1111/j.1460-2466.1974.tb00367.x

Noelle-Neumann, E. (1993). The spiral of silence: Public opinion—Our social skin. University of Chicago Press.

Norris, P. (2000). A virtuous circle: Political communications in postindustrial societies. Cambridge University Press.

Norris, P., Garnett, H. A., & Grömping, M. (2020). The paranoid style of American elections: Explaining perceptions of electoral integrity in an age of populism. Journal of Elections, Public Opinion and Parties, 30(1), 105–125. https://doi.org/10.1080/17457289.2019.1593181

Papacharissi, Z. (2010). A private sphere: Democracy in a digital age. Cambridge, UK: Polity.

Parker, D. (2010). Complete Poems. Penguin.

Patterson, T. E. (2016, June 13). Pre-primary news coverage of the 2016 presidential race: Trump's rise, Sanders' emergence, Clinton's struggle. Shorenstein Center. https://shorensteincenter.org/pre-primary-news-coverage-2016-trump-clinton-   sanders/#_ftnref22

Petrie, H. W. (1894). I don't want to play in your yard. National Music Co. Retrieved from the Library of Congress. https://www.loc.gov/item/ihas.100002843/

Politi, D. (2020,November 1). Trump cheers caravan of trucks that swarmed Biden bus in Texas. Slate. https://slate.com/news-and-politics/2020/11/trump-cheers-caravan-trucks-swarmed-biden-bus-texas.html

Porter, E. (2018, December 14). The hard truths of trying to "save" the rural economy. The New York Times. https://www.nytimes.com/interactive/2018/12/14/opinion/rural-america-trump-decline.html

Pruchniewska, U. (2019). "A group that's just women for women": Feminist affordances of private Facebook groups for professionals. New Media & Society, 21(6), 1362–1379. https://doi.org/10.1177/1461444818822490

Raab, J., & Milward, H. B. (2003). Dark networks as problems. Journal of Public Administration Research and Theory, 13(4), 413–439. https://doi.org/10.1093/jopart/mug029

Rahat, G., & Kenig, O. (2018). From party politics to personalized politics?: Party change and political personalization in democracies. Oxford University Press.

Rainie, L., & Wellman, B. (2012). Networked: The new social operating system. MIT Press.

Ramsey, R. (2018, November 16). Analysis: The neglected Texans responsible for 2018's GOP wins. Texas Tribune. https://www.texastribune.org/2018/11/16/rural-texas-can-claim-credit-for-gop-statewide-wins/

Rheault, L., Rayment, E., & Musulan, A. (2019). Politicians in the line of fire: Incivility and the treatment of women on social media. Research & Politics, 6(1), 1–7. https://doi.org/10.1177/2053168018816228

Rojas, H. (2010). "Corrective" actions in the public sphere: How perceptions of media and media effects shape political behaviors. International Journal of Public Opinion Research, 22(3), 343–363. https://doi.org/10.1093/ijpor/edq018

Rothkopf, J. (2016, January 29). Bernie Sanders' campaign is concerned about the "Berniebro," as they maybe should be. Jezebel. https://theslot.jezebel.com/ernie-sanders-campaign-is-concerned-about-the-berniebr-1755911898

Ruef, M., Aldrich, H. E., & Carter, N. M. (2003). The structure of founding teams: Homophily, strong ties, and isolation among US entrepreneurs. American Sociological Review, 68(2), 195–222. https://doi.org/10.2307/1519766

Schattschneider, E. E. (1942). Party government. Rinehart.

Schudson, M. (1998). The good citizen: A history of American civic life. Free Press.

Schulz, K. (2016, August 22). The perilous lure of the Underground Railroad. The New Yorker. https://www.newyorker.com/magazine/2016/08/22/the-perilous-lure-of-the-underground-railroad

Scott, J. C. (1990). Domination and the arts of resistance: Hidden transcripts. Yale University Press.

Scott, C. (2013). Anonymous agencies, backstreet businesses, and covert collectives: Rethinking organizations in the 21st century. Stanford University Press.

Searles, K., Ginn, M. H., & Nickens, J. (2016). For whom the poll airs: Comparing poll results to television poll coverage. Public Opinion Quarterly, 80(4), 943–963. https://doi.org/10.1093/poq/nfw031

Skocpol, T. (2003). Diminished democracy: From membership to management in American civic life. University of Oklahoma Press.

Sides, J., Tesler, M., & Vavreck, L. (2019). Identity crisis: The 2016 presidential campaign and the battle for the meaning of America. Princeton University Press.

Signal, J. (2016, June 7). The New York Times' Hillary Clinton campaign correspondent says she's being threatened by Bernie Sanders supporters. NYMag.com. https://nymag.com/intelligencer/2016/06/nyt-clinton-reporter-is-getting-death-threats.html

Simmel, G. (1906). The sociology of secrecy and of secret societies. American Journal of Sociology, 11(4), 441–498. https://doi.org/10.1086/211418

Simons, D. J., & Chabris, C. F. (1999). Gorillas in our midst: Sustained inattentional blindness for dynamic events. Perception, 28(9), 1059–1074. https://doi.org/10.1068/p2952

Smith, N., & Graham, T. (2019). Mapping the anti-vaccination movement on Facebook. Information, Communication & Society, 22(9), 1310–1327. https://doi.org/10.1080/1369118x.2017.1418406

Stein, P. (2017, January 31). The woman who started the Women's March with a Facebook post reflects: "It was mind-boggling." *Washington Post.* https://www.washingtonpost.com/news/local/wp/2017/01/31/the-woman-who-started-the-womens-march-with-a-facebook-post-reflects-it-was-mind-boggling/

Stroud, N. J. (2011). Niche news: The politics of news choice. Oxford University Press.

Sunstein, C. (2001). Republic.com. Princeton University Press.

Svitek, P. (2020, December 8). What went wrong with Texas Democrats' 2020 plans? State party leaders intend to find out. Texas Tribune. https://www.texastribune.org/2020/12/08/texas-democratic-party-complaints-results-2020/

Tam Cho, W. K., Gimpel, J. G., & Hui, I. S. (2013). Voter migration and the geographic sorting of the American electorate. Annals of the Association of American Geographers, 103(4), 856–870. https://doi.org/10.1080/00045608.2012.720229

Texas Demographic Center. (2018). *2018 estimated population of Texas, its counties, and places.* https://demographics.texas.gov/Resources/publications/2019/20191205_PopEstimatesBrief.pdf

Theriault, S. M. (2008). Party polarization in Congress. Cambridge University Press.

Thompson, D. (2020, January 31). Why Texans don't want any more Californians. The Atlantic. https://www.theatlantic.com/ideas/archive/2020/01/the-truth-about-the-california-exodus/605833/

Thurre, F. O., Gale, J., & Staerklé, C. (2020). Speaking up or silencing out in the face of rising right-wing populism: A dynamic test of the spiral of silence across 15 European countries. International Journal of Public Opinion Research, 32(3), 547–568. https://doi.org/10.1093/ijpor/edz034

Toepfl, F., & Piwoni, E. (2015). Public spheres in interaction: Comment sections of news websites as counterpublic spaces. Journal of Communication, 65(3), 465–488. https://doi.org/10.1111/jcom.12156

Tolentino, J. (2017, January 18). The somehow controversial Women's March on Washington. The New Yorker. https://www.newyorker.com/culture/jia-tolentino/the-somehow-controversial-womens-march-on-washington

Tong, C., Gill, H., Li, J., Valenzuela, S., & Rojas, H. (2020). "Fake news is anything they say!"—Conceptualization and weaponization of fake news among the American public. Mass Communication and Society, 23(5), 755–778. https://doi.org/10.1080/15205436.2020.1789661

Traister, R. (2018). Good and mad: The revolutionary power of women's anger. Simon & Schuster.

Tromble, R., & McGregor, S. C. (2019). You break it, you buy it: The naiveté of social engineering in tech—And how to fix it. Political Communication, 36(2), 324–332. https://doi.org/10.1080/10584609.2019.1609860

Ulbig, S. G., & Funk, C. L. (1999). Conflict avoidance and political participation. Political Behavior, 21(3), 265–282. https://doi.org/10.1023/a:1022087617514

United Nations Department of Economic and Social Affairs. (2018). *2018 revision of world urbanization prospects.* https://www.un.org/development/desa/publications/2018-revision-of-world-urbanization-prospects.html

United States Department of Agriculture. (2018). *Rural America at a glance: 2018 edition.* https://www.ers.usda.gov/webdocs/publications/90556/eib-200.pdf?v=2307.8

Valenzuela, S., Bachmann, I., & Aguilar, M. (2019). Socialized for news media use: How family communication, information-processing needs, and gratifications determine adolescents' exposure to news. Communication Research, 46(8), 1095–1118. https://doi.org/10.1177/0093650215623833

Van Duyn, E. (2018). There exists in Texas and elsewhere a hidden democracy. *San Antonio Express News.* https://www.mysanantonio.com/opinion/commentary/article/There-exists-in-Texas-and-elsewhere-a-hidden-13340213.php

Van Duyn, E. (2020). Mainstream marginalization: Secret political organizing through social media. Social Media + Society, 6(4). https://doi.org/10.1177/2056305120981044

Van Duyn, E., & Collier, J. (2019). Priming and fake news: The effects of elite discourse on evaluations of news media. Mass Communication and Society, 22(1), 29–48. https://doi.org/10.1080/15205436.2018.1511807

Van Duyn, E., Peacock, C., & Stroud, N. J. (2021). The gender gap in online news comment sections. Social Science Computer Review, 39(2), 181–196. https://doi.org/10.1177/0894439319864876

Vangelisti, A. L., & Caughlin, J. P. (1997). Revealing family secrets: The influence of topic, function, and relationships. Journal of Social and Personal Relationships, 14(5), 679–705. https://doi.org/10.1177/0265407597145006

Van Laer, J., & Van Aelst, P. (2010). Internet and social movement action repertoires: Opportunities and limitations. Information, Communication & Society, 13(8), 1146–1171. https://doi.org/10.1080/13691181003628307

Verba, S., & Nie, N. H. (1987). Participation in America: Political democracy and social equality. University of Chicago Press.

Verba, S., Schlozman, K. L., & Brady, H. E. (1995). Voice and equality: Civic voluntarism in American politics. Harvard University Press.

Verzoni, A. (2017, July 1). Shrinking resources, growing concern. NFPA Journal. https://www.nfpa.org/News-and-Research/Publications-and-media/NFPA-Journal/2017/July-August-2017/Features/Rural

Villareal, A. (2020, November 2). FBI investigating Trump supporters who swarmed Texas campaign bus. The Guardian. https://www.theguardian.com/us-news/2020/nov/01/biden-harris-bus-highway-texas-trump-train

Weigel, D., & Tierney, L. (2020, October 4). The seven political states of Texas. *The Washington Post.* https://www.washingtonpost.com/graphics/2020/politics/texas-political-geography/

Wells, C. (2015). The civic organization and the digital citizen: Communicating engagement in a networked age. Oxford University Press.

Williams, P. (2020, October 14). The changing meaning of the American flag under Trump. The New Yorker. https://www.newyorker.com/news/us-journal/the-changing-meaning-of-the-american-flag-under-trump

Wolfe, A. W., & Blithe, S. J. (2015). Managing image in a core-stigmatized organization: Concealment and revelation in Nevada's legal brothels. Management Communication Quarterly, 29(4), 539–563. https://doi.org/10.1177/0893318915596204

Wojcieszak, M. (2009). "Carrying online participation offline"—Mobilization by radical online groups and politically dissimilar offline ties. Journal of Communication, 59(3), 564–586. https://doi.org/10.1111/j.1460-2466.2009.01436.x

Wojcieszak, M., & Kim, N. (2016). How to improve attitudes toward disliked groups: The effects of narrative versus numerical evidence on political persuasion. Communication Research, 43(6), 785–809. https://doi.org/10.1177/0093650215618480

Wuthnow, R. (2013). Small-town America: Finding community, shaping the future. Princeton University Press.

Wuthnow, R. (2018). The left behind: Decline and rage in rural America. Princeton University Press.

Yang, J., Rojas, H., Wojcieszak, M., Aalberg, T., Coen, S., Curran, J., Hayashi, K., Iyengar, S., Jones, P. K., Mazzoleni, G., Papathanassopoulos, S., Rhee, J. W., Rowe, D., Soroka, S., & Tiffen, R. (2016). Why are "others" so polarized? Perceived political polarization and media use in 10 countries. *Journal of Computer-Mediated Communication, 21*(5), 349–367. https://doi.org/10.1111/jcc4.12166

Zaller, J. (1992). The nature and origins of mass opinion. Cambridge University Press.

Zimmer, M. (2010). "But the data is already public": On the ethics of research in Facebook. Ethics and Information Technology, 12(4), 313–325. https://doi.org/10.1007/s10676-010-9227-5

Zukin, C., Keeter, S., Andolina, M., Jenkins, K., & Carpini, M. X. D. (2006). A new engagement?: Political participation, civic life, and the changing American citizen. Oxford University Press.

Index

For the benefit of digital users, indexed terms that span two pages (e.g., 52–53) may, on occasion, appear on only one of those pages.

Figures and boxes are indicated by *f* and *b* following the page number

Printed in the USA/Agawam, MA
October 11, 2021

782267.023